# The Elliotts of Birtley

**Pete Wood**

Published by David Herron Publishing, Wellington Road,
Todmorden, Yorkshire OL14 5DY

This paperback first edition published 2008


ISBN 978-095406-823-3

Designed and typeset by Bryan Ledgard www.bryanledgard.com
Printed in Great Britain by Henry Ling Limited, The Dorset Press,
Dorchester DT1 1HD

# Preface by Peggy Seeger

Strange – I don't remember the first time I met the Elliott family but I remember practically every other time I met them. Doreen and I have agreed on spring of 1961 as the time when Ewan and I first entered No. 7 Browns Buildings. The meeting was set up by the singers who ran the Newcastle-upon-Tyne folk club at a period when many such clubs were combing their own environs for local folksongs. They had stumbled upon the Elliotts of Birtley and members of the Elliott clan were already singing at their club. Ewan and I were in the middle of recording actuality for *The Big Hewer* Radio Ballad so we went initially to collect miner's stories from Jack – but that meeting was so wonderful that later we visited them whenever we could, sometimes taking jobs in local clubs purely so that we could get our Elliottfix.

Coming from a large, middle-class, fairly quiet family home in the

United States, a tribe of six in this (to me) tiny terrace house (two- up, two-down) was a new and powerful experience. Ewan, having been brought up in a similar dwelling and neighourhood, was on home ground. I was content to watch, to drink the tea and eat the food, to run the tape machine and to glory in it all. I'm so glad this book has been written – I can live it all again.

Whenever we came, we were welcomed into the family room. Em would put the kettle on immediately. A petite woman, the real hub of the Elliott wheel, she would bring out more food than it seemed the little kitchen would hold. Jack would sit at the table with his back to the window, his majestic bulk nearly filling the room up. Their children all lived locally and the room would soon be bursting with them: elder-brother Pete, extrovert John, burly Len and Doreen, lively and cheerful, who has taken over Em's role as the Elliott wheel rolls into the new generations. All grown by the time we came, their relationship to their parents was deferential but equal. A totally functional family, they truly enjoyed one another's company. Everyone had something to contribute, and contribute they did, spurring each other on in a continuous flow of conversation, banter, wisecracks, jokes and memories. The songs and stories peppered, salted and spiced the get-togethers in a way that made us feel warm and included. Sometimes we'd swap songs. Sometimes it was just family talk. One evening Jack spoke for hours about the mine he'd worked in and the miners he'd worked with. I remember one of the sessions was devoted to how pronunciations of words differed depending on whether you came from Washington, Chester-le-Street, Birtley, Great Lumley, Houghton-le-Spring, Sunderland – it should be noted that these communities were within just a few miles of one another.

Over the years various members of the family came to visit us down in Kent and to sing at the Singers' Club in London. Doreen and Bryan's children, Kay and Jon, came for a week. They must have found our London suburb very strange indeed. Jack and Em came at another time and we drove them down to the Kent coast on a very cold autumn day. I was a keen swimmer and would jump into lakes, ponds, seas, pools, mountain streams wherever I found them. This day that is exactly what I did. Jack was visibly concerned – horrified if the truth be told – for the waves were quite high. While Ewan and Em conversed and walked amiably, Jack (apparently a strong swimmer) paced back and forth on the shoreline, ready and waiting for my possible call for help.

Some of the Elliotts contributed to the folk music revival and to their wider community during the ensuing decades. They visited folk clubs and sang and told stories, bringing the same home atmosphere that Ewan and I enjoyed into the public arena. Shortly after our initial meeting, they formed a unique folk club in Birtley, an inclusive and sharing singaround club, where many singers found their feet, their voice and their confidence. It's still running, after forty years, -recently under the direction of Doreen and Bryan. All-involved themselves in folk events all over the northeast singing, telling stories, bringing the Elliott saga forward, for a saga it truly is and it's not just about the Elliotts. Springing from, and completely integrated with, the rich social fabric of the mining communities of County Durham, and Birtley in particular, this saga redefines 'ordinary' people and the lives'they' live as extraordinary and complex.

The Elliotts, those still with us and those who have passed on, have done an invaluable job. They've been more than 'informants', more than cultural 'resources', more than 'field singers' (all terms sometimes thoughtlessly used in folk academia). They have shared themselves and the rich tradition that came down to them. In passing it on, they have forged themselves into a strong link in the vertical time-chain between the past and the future and the horizontal topography-chain that stretches from Browns Buildings to Birtley to Chester-le-Street to Newcastle to London to Wherever, reminding us that this is really what we should all be doing with our lives.

And all of this while having a helluva good time. What more could you ask?

**Peggy Seeger, November 2006**
(Speaking for herself and Ewan MacColl)

# Introduction

I first came across British folk music in late 1961, when I was a student in Sheffield. Up till then, it had been Woody Guthrie, Rambling Jack Elliott, and Pete Seeger. Like a lot of other people, I thought 'folk songs' were what cowpokes did on the plains. Songs like 'The Foggy Dew', 'The Twa Corbies', and 'Bobby Shaftoe' were things I'd had to do at school, and against some of this powerful stuff from the States seemed a touch naff. So I started to listen to a lot of songs and singers, and started writing the words of songs in a book in 1962. The first entry is 'Billy to Bob', an Elliotts' classic. I still don't know where I heard the song, but we did it as a group song at the folk club we'd just started. We didn't understand all the pitmatic, but it was a big hit, and thrilling to perform. Clearly the Elliotts were already being influential in the fast-accelerating Folk Revival.

I spent the next 12 years between Sheffield and the South East, growing with the Revival. I listened to, and met North East performers like Bob Davenport, the Marsden Rattlers, Lou Killen, and the High Level Ranters. I never saw Jack Elliott live, but heard lots of recordings, and delighted with everybody else as he mounted the Festival Hall platform in 1965, a sick but brave man. The family didn't then travel round the country as much as they did later, so they became a bit legendary for somebody who had hardly been to the North East.

But in 1974, I moved to the area for a job, continuing to sing and play as a hobby and securing occasional gigs. The Birtley folk club, then at the Three Tuns, was everything I expected, quite different from other clubs, with a gritty realism, and an authenticity. I was fascinated by the personalities of the family, and the other regulars. There was 'Chairman Pete', as I was tempted to call him, with his political attitudes oozing from every pore (and never so strongly as when he was inveighing against yet another folk promoter or budding artiste talking megabucks at him). And there was 'Uncle Reece', still going strong in his eighties, who I couldn't remember having heard sing on record. He was a different character and singer from Jack, but just as fine a singer and so interesting to listen to. I was interested as well to realise that the family did not spend all their time doing bitter political songs about the grimness of the pit. These people also sang funny songs, kids' songs, love songs, and some things they'd learnt during the Revival just like I had. I preferred going on residents' nights, because the regulars, and particularly the Elliotts, always had something different to offer. That was why I went to Birtley.

The idea of a book about the family came to me about 2001, which was spectacularly bad timing, as Pete Elliott, likely to be my most important source, had passed away the year before. Never mind, says I, I'll talk to Pat a lot, and she'll give me lots of information. So I talked to her and Doreen about the book, and they were very keen on the idea. Unfortunately I was slow getting going, and by 2003 Pat was seriously ill, and after a few months she too died, in January 2004. It seemed like the most prominent of the Elliotts would not be able to see this book, and more importantly would not be able to contribute. However, conversations with the irrepressible Doreen Henderson and husband Bryan convinced me otherwise, and I started the research in Autumn 2005.

I was a bit surprised that nobody was already writing a book, but any doubts I had about the value of the family's story were quickly dispelled as I found out more and more about them. The absence of Pete and Pat was offset considerably by two things. Pete had written a 'family book' of which six copies were printed, one for each of his kids, not for viewing by others. Fortunately for me, his youngest son Pete allowed me to look at this very revealing document and to use a considerable amount of Pete's views as expressed therein. The other thing was that Pete and sister Laura have given me some wonderful memories of their Mam and Dad.

Make no mistake, this is a formidable group of people, all the way down from the foundling ancestor of the 1830s to the younger Elliotts of the 21st century. I have learnt a tremendous amount from this project, not just in terms of music, politics, and history, but also about human beings.

**Pete Wood, July 2008**

# Acknowledgements

The two people who have given me not only the most information and strong opinion throughout, but also the most support, are Doreen and Bryan Henderson, she of course being an Elliott by birth and him being one by marriage. Quotes, especially from Doreen, are taken from at least eight formal interviews and innumerable other communications. Secondly, I wish to thank Dave Eckersley, not only for instantly agreeing to publish this book, but for unflagging enthusiasm and support and a great deal of much needed editorial suggestions. It would be a significantly poorer book without his input. People who have kindly allowed me to record interviews are: Pete and Laura Elliott, Bill Elliott, John Elliott, Johnny Handle, Louis Killen, Ed Pickford, Fra Fraser, Graeme Miles, Terri and Eric Freeman, Benny Graham, Don and Sheila Stokoe, Jim Irving, Paul Younger, Joyce and Danny McLeod, Ingrid and Barrie Temple, Dave Douglass, the Doonans and Stu Luckley, Ray Fisher and Colin Ross, Tom Gilfellon, and Doc Rowe and Jill Pidd.

Amongst many others who have helped with ideas, information, stories, and opinion and are mentioned in the text, I would like to thank especially the following: Jim Bainbridge, Bob Davenport, Bert Draycott, Roy Harris, George Henderson, Ted and Ivy Poole, Gavin Purdon, Dave Sutherland, and Mike Waterson.

Thanks also to Joyce Dickinson, Louis Killen, Johnny Handle, and Vic Gammon for reading various parts of the book and making helpful suggestions; Peggy Seeger for writing the preface; Doc Rowe for transcriptions of Pete and Pat's recordings and other materials; Ruskin College Library Oxford for access to the MacColl Seeger archive, Birmingham City Library for access to the Charles Parker Archive, and the University of Leeds Brotherton Library for access to two undergraduate theses, and all the Elliotts for all the materials they have provided. Thanks also to the team at Herron Publishing, Ali Crann, and Erica Hawthorne and to Bryan Ledgard for design, layout and a fabulous cover.

Thanks to the following for kind permission to use specific materials:

Durham County Record Office for reproduction of the photograph on the front cover of the two miners in front of Brown's Buildings and the photograph of Billy Green's Orchestra.

D.B.C. Pierre for material from the article he wrote on the Durham Gala in the Guardian 2004

Verso for permission to quote Seumas Milne, *The Enemy Within*, London, 1994

Johnny Handle and Ed Pickford for songs from their respective songbooks.

Gavin Purdon for photographs and quotes from his book on Cotia pit

The author and Herron Publishing would like to thank the following organizations for their support in this project.

The Durham Miners' Association

The Northumberland area of the National Union of Mineworkers.

Newcastle Branch of UNISON

The GMB Union

# Prologue

Early in 1832, the landlady of the Cross Keys public house in Wrekenton, a pit village in north Durham, opened the front door, and was a bit surprised to find, there on the step, a newly-born baby boy. Another young mother presumably had found it all a bit too much, whatever her circumstances, and had taken a desperate, but understandable approach to the problem. The landlady, whose name was Grace Taylor, immediately noticed two things. Firstly, the clothes swaddling the infant were of very high quality, and secondly there was a tag around the baby's neck bearing the name Francis Elliott. Whatever her thoughts at the time, she decided to adopt him, and brought him up as Frank Taylor.

Like all local boys, when he got to the age of eight he started work at the nearby Mount coal pit. Then one day, when he was about sixteen, he emerged from the pit, and "still in his dirt" was met by a horse and carriage and mysteriously whisked off. He returned after about a year, saying that he had been to London, and had been taught to read and write. This fact was of such rarity that it was apparently reported in the local newspaper. However, he continued to work as a pitman, and by the time he was nineteen, he had married a local girl called Margaret Ridley, was starting a family, and had moved to the nearby Harraton colliery, always known as 'Cotia pit.

One more unusual thing should be said about this foundling pitman. When he died, in 1903, he left several thousand pounds, a truly astounding amount for a working man (a deputy's annual salary was about £50 at that time). It's small wonder that his descendants have speculated vigorously about the man's true father. Was it the Earl of Durham, who owned the pits the lad was working in, and all of the land thereabouts, or perhaps Sir George Elliott, an equally wealthy coalowner at the time? The rumour is that Frank was sworn to secrecy as to the identity of his mysterious benefactor, and carried the secret to his grave. His descendants, an unusual family descended from an unusual man, have continued to speculate enthusiastically for over a hundred years about the foundling who was their founder. For example, recent research has shown that Sir George, a national figure and MP in the late 19th Century, and owner of the firm that made the first transatlantic cable, was seventeen years old and working as a pit boy in nearby Penshaw colliery at the time, something which seems to discount him. The family's reaction to this was the speculation that perhaps Grace Taylor was the mother and when George Elliott became rich, he then did the 'decent thing'. Whatever the truth, young Frank and his descendants would continue to bring coal out of 'Cotia pit for another 120 odd years.

We know all this because Frank Taylor found out about his birth when he got married, and changed his name back to Elliott. He was the grandfather of Jack Elliott, the central figure in the story about to be unfolded.

On 7th May 1962, a dozen or so people gathered in the Community Hall of a mining town on the A1 just south of the Tyneside conurbation. Although still being called a 'mining town', it was already clear that this would not be so for very long. British Oxygen and other heavy industries had largely replaced the fields and farms along the main road, and the National Coal Board would soon be forced to close many of the pits. But most of those twelve gathered that night belonged to a family with coal running through its veins.

This group was the Elliotts and their friends and this was the first night of Birtley Folk Club. At that time, the Folk Revival was just getting under way, with folk clubs springing up all over the country, and soon every town of Birtley's size would have at least one. Jack and Pete Elliott, regulars at the Folksong and Ballad Club in Newcastle, were surprised that it closed for the summer. They couldn't see the reason for this, and so they decided they would start one of their own.

Their club was a bit different though. The Elliotts were somewhat older than other club organizers, who were generally students or other young people for whom folk songs were new and exciting, an antidote to the saccharine outpourings of pop music. It was something they could call their own. Jack Elliott, fifty four years old and head of this family, had worked at 'Cotia pit all his life, as had his father, grandfather and three brothers. He lived in a pit house just down the road from the club at Brown's Buildings, Barley Mow, the place where Frank Elliott had moved to in 1850. Unlike most other club organisers, they'd been singing all their lives, Jack with his brother Reece at the pub, and the family in the kitchen at home. Jack played many instruments, and had a wide taste in music, including jazz, American folk songs, and opera. At home, they sang a great number of kids' street sings and game songs, but they also had pit songs, Child ballads, music hall songs, local folk songs, and national folk songs.

The singaround format they set up at the club was unusual, and many of the songs sung that night were 'home brewed' in the sense that they came from the local community, and were often to do with the mining work many of the singers were involved in. There were very few guitars in evidence. The family had joined the burgeoning Folk Revival, a phenomenon which they would embrace wholeheartedly, to the great benefit of both parties.

And so an institution was born, with singers and songs of such character and determination that it is still running at the time of writing, forty-six years on. Renowned as atheists with strong left-wing political views, all of them were also strong characters, with a robust way of expressing their views, an earthy humour, and a great zest for life. This is the family then that became known as the Elliotts of Birtley, who became known to the world of folk music throughout the UK and the rest of the world for their singing. This book celebrates this achievement, but also seeks to explain what the family have to offer us, perhaps something harder to define, about traditional human values in the 21st Century.

*The Greens' 'Orchestra', with great uncle Bill Green on double bass*

# Chapter 1
# Before the War

*"If it's got two T's, it's us"*

## Victorian Elliotts

On his death Frank Elliott left what for a pitman was a small fortune. Also a will was read out, an almost unheard of event amongst working-class folk at that time. His great-grandson Pete Elliott relates, "My Dad had a tale to tell about the reading of that will. Peter and Lance, two of his sons, were, if not the black sheep of the family, certainly a darker shade of pale, and they went to his house on the day of the reading. Great-Uncle Peter, (or the Grey Gallowa, to give him his nickname), said to my Granda Lance (Lanter), 'Thoo sit and pray beside the coffin Lanter while Aa gan an' hear what we get.' Granda sat with bowed head until Peter came through the door shaking his head. 'They's nowt for either of us,' says the Grey Gallowa. 'Nowt?' says Lanter. 'Bugger all,' came back. 'Wey y' greedy owld bastard,' says Granda, his pious thoughts forgotten." We're left to guess why they didn't get the money, but we do know that his other two sons, John and young Frank, got it.

Frank not only had this mystery surrounding his origins and the money, but kept what the family call 'the diary', an heirloom highly valued by the family, but rarely seen by most of them, having been passed down from oldest to youngest sons alternately, and now in the possession of the great-great-grandson 'young Pete Elliott'. From this family record and the stories, it's possible to trace the family from Frank Elliott, through his sons Peter (Grey Gallowa), Young Frank, and Lance (Lanter), who was the father of Reece and his brother Jack. Jack's family Pete, Doreen, John and Len are at the centre of this book.

The diary is actually titled 'Old Notes', but for the purposes of this book, we'll call it 'Frank's book'. This valuable piece of social history is a handwritten series of news items culled from local newspapers, plus a few rare personal entries. He started it in 1861, but it has entries from 1767, well before he was born, the last entry being 1887. Where he got the entries from before he was born is another mystery. Some years have no entry, whilst others extend over several pages. The events he was most interested in were pit disasters and public executions, mostly local, but some of the more notable ones from elsewhere in the country, including the last public execution at Newburn in 1868. The later part is full of reports of sporting events, such as pigeon shooting, rowing matches on the Tyne and the Thames, and local bowling matches, particularly on the Town Moor in Newcastle and the Black Fell, near to the place where he was found on the doorstep. The book is also peppered with other international events, such as the French Revolution (1848) and the Battle of Inkerman (1854). The winner of the St Leger at Doncaster is recorded for every year of the book covered. Here's a very tiny sample from 1838:

**Dec 19th Explosion at Wallsend. 11 lost.**
**June 25th Beeswing won the Silver Waggon. It was on a Monday.**
**June 28th Victoria crowned.**

Again, in 1848:

**Aug 20th The first train went over the High Level Bridge with 10 coaches at her.**
**Aug 15th Explosion at Morton Colliery. 15 lost.**
**Surplice won the Leger.**
**February 24th French Revolution.**
**Nov 21st William Nicholson of Stockton born, the great Boat Rower.**

Apart from the date of the wedding of the eldest son Lance, there are few family references apart from this one, which relates to the amputation of his son's leg and its wooden replacement.

**May 16th Frank Elliott went to Newcastle Infirmary. (1878)**
**April 1st Frank Elliott got his leg amputated at N.Castle Infirmary by Dr Hume. (1879)**
**August 1st F. Elliott got his wood leg from R. Clarke's, 31 Mosley St. Newcastle upon Tyne. (1880)**

This is a reference to his third son, who was injured down the pit. Young Frank was one of the two sons who inherited the foundling's money, and had in fact been set up in business by his dad following his accident and loss of his leg. Later, Old Frank had a house built for young Frank on land owned by Lord Ravensworth. The building is still standing, and still known as 'Frank's Place'. It was here that the infamous will was read.

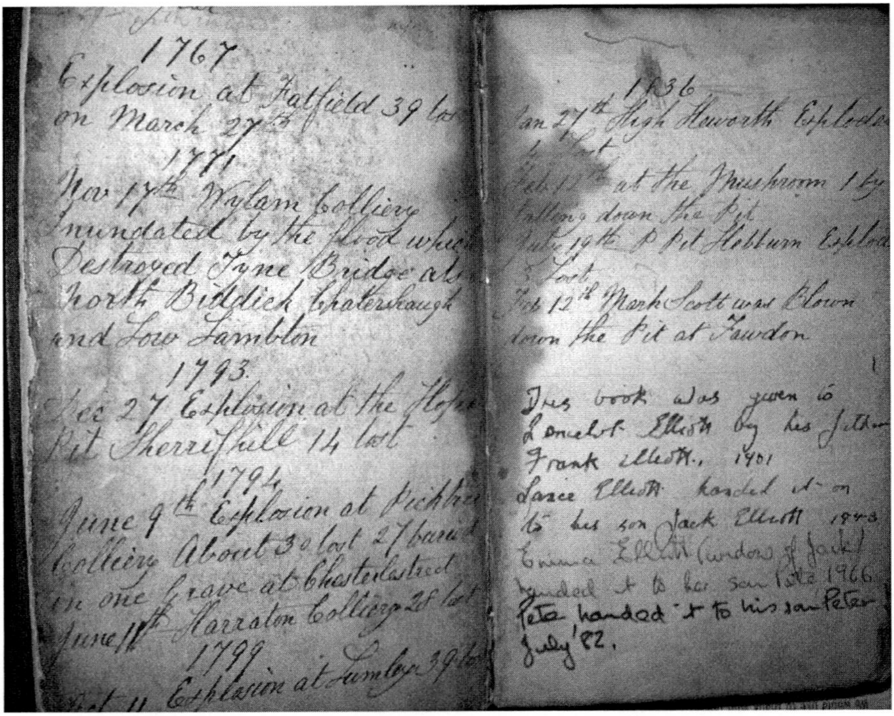

1767
Explosion at Fatfield 39 lost
on March 27th
1771
Nov 17th Wylam Colliery
Inundated by the flood which
Destroyed Tyne Bridge also
North Biddick Chatershaugh
and Low Lambton
1793
Dec 27 Explosion at the Hope
Pit Sherriffhill 14 lost
1794
June 9th Explosion at Picktree
Colliery About 30 lost 27 buried
in one Grave at Chesterlestreet
June 11th Harraton Colliery 28 lost
1799
Explosion at Lumley 39 lost

1836
Jan 27th High Haworth Exploded
Feb 12 at the Mushroom 1 by
falling down the Pit
July 19th Pit Hebburn Exploded
Feb 12th Mark Scott was blown
down the Pit at Fawdon

This book was given to
Lancelot Elliott by his father
Frank Elliott. 1901
Lance Elliott handed it on
to his son Jack Elliott 1948
Emma Elliott (widow of Jack)
handed it to her son Pete 1966
Pete handed it to his son Peter
July '82.

*The first pages of Frank's book. The keepers are shown at bottom right'*

Frank's grandson Reece remembers old Frank as "a short man with beard, brown coat velvet collar. He was kind to me. He had been bound aged eight. Where he got the education I could never understand. No lights, 10 hour shifts. He started at Black Fell, a pit at nearby Wrekenton, a small village now in the outskirts of Gateshead, and finished at Harraton, which was the proper name of 'Cotia pit. All his sons went down the pit, and all his daughters married pitmen except the eldest, who married an undertaker at Hexham. He was a 'Maister shifter'." The master shifter was in charge of a gang who went in between shifts to do whatever support work was needed with roof props, rails, or clearing stone, and generally make the area ready for the next shift. Looking at Reece you realised that here was a man who had been in the trenches, had learnt songs as a child from singers who had been young during the Crimean War and been born when Victoria celebrated her coronation. History draped his shoulders.

Frank's youngest son Lance, the father of Jack and Reece, was a deputy at 'Cotia, and with a family of seven, he tried improving his income by becoming a 'Maister Shifter' like his father when he was twenty-five. His son Reece, who was born in 1894, quotes him. "19 hours pit work's too much for any man. Aa'm going back to deputy work." Reece comments that "it was the beer that done it", a theme taken up by Lance's grandson Pete Elliott.

> "Granda played the melodeon, especially when he was in his cups, which brings to mind a fact about his character over which his offspring all agreed. During the week he was a stern but loving parent who would carve wooden cricket balls, cut hats out of planks and stitch split footballs for his kids. Come the weekend, when he went on the beer, everyone in the house went in fear and trembling. On a good night he would be full of the joys, handing out coppers and playing his melodeon with such gusto that he would bust the bellows. On a bad night, and there were many, he would enter the silent house with a scowl on his face and woe betide anyone who offended him, male or female. A bloody good hammering would result. He would also take 'the horrors', pitmatic for delirium tremens or the DTs, and would scream and rave with his eyes standing out, on stalks. On one famous occasion he stuffed mats and furniture onto the fire until he fell down in a stupor. On another occasion, he and a fellow drinker, who was also a helluva big man called 'Pluck' Ferguson, went on the booze up Waldridge way one winter's night, fell down drunk and woke up literally frozen to the ground.
>
> It remained however his proud boast that he never lost a shift through drink in his life. He was forced to retire when he was sixty through coal dust giving him pneumoconiosis, which the Lambton, Hetton and Joicey Coal Company insisted was asthma. Asthma my arse! He died aged seventy-five, when I was eighteen, and I missed him greatly. I had only known him as a kindly old man, his big drinking days long behind him. We as kids had always experienced some difficulty in understanding him when telling his tales, for in addition to speaking pitmatic he also had the Northern burr, that is he rolled his r's, almost unheard nowadays, even in Northumberland where it lasted longest."

*I dreamt I had died and to heaven did go,*
*"Where do you come from?" they wanted to know.*
*"I come from Brown's Buildings."*
*My how they did stare.*
*"Come right inside, you're the first one from there."*
*Alley-O, alley O,*
*For we kill all the bobbies that come down our way.*

# Jack

When Jack Elliott was born in 1907, to Lance and Jessie, Britain was at the height of its economic prosperity, and although little of the nation's riches reached down to the working man, there were jobs to be had, and life was as good as it had ever been. His father was a deputy, and all his older brothers were working in the pit. So, for Jack (or John Joseph, as he was christened), childhood was a great time, as his son Pete describes.

> "Away from school Jack would be developing his skills in the pursuits of the children of his day. Some were still well-known activities like football, although the ball would probably be a pig's bladder, obtained from his father perhaps at pig killing time, or some neighbour. Later on he took up the position of goalkeeper and played for the local team, The Barley Mow Swifts. His cricket, at the appropriate season of the year, would be played with both bat and ball made from wood, either the off cuts from pit props, or wood obtained from the many plantations in the area, with the added spice that they belonged to the Earl of Durham; and were patrolled by 'gameys', as gamekeepers were commonly termed. Blackberrying, conkers and Bonfire Night of course had their appropriate times of the year, and again could have the thrill of trespassing added into the collecting of the necessities.
>
> Other games which also had their seasons, but have long since vanished from the realm of children's pastimes included tip cat, where the object of the game was to knock a square sectioned, pointy-ended wood block a prescribed distance; quoits, either grass or clay ended, (still played by men in those days, and where considerable sums of money could change hands), proper marbles, where the marble was impelled by the action of flicking it between thumb and forefinger and terms such as 'nee fullocking' could be heard, i.e., the person shooting the marble shouldn't inch forward with his marble. 'Jack Shine the Maggy', (light), and 'Give a Holler' were involved forms of 'Hide and Seek'. These are just a fraction of the pastimes and games that kids used to amuse themselves in those pre-wireless and television days."

Jack was born in Brown's Buildings in Barley Mow, three rows of pit houses alongside the Great North Road. His grandfather Frank had moved there in 1872, and Jack, apart from a short spell after he married, lived there, at Number 7, for the rest of his life. It's difficult to imagine now, but Barley Mow was a hamlet between Birtley and Chester-le-Street, surrounded by fields and farms. Like many other Durham villages and hamlets, it only existed because of the pit. The pub, the chapel, the community hall, and the houses the pitmen lived in, were all owned by the Earl of Durham.

It has been the home of the Elliotts for about one hundred and thirty-six years, including Jack's second son John, who had a house there in the '60s, and daughter Doreen, who still lives with her husband Bryan in a smart modern house built on the site of one of the three rows, the other two being still there. Pit houses were built by the owners, and were only available to miners with families. Though basic, they were often very substantial, as their continued existence after a century and a half of the rumble and roar of Great North Road traffic testifies. But as Doreen says, they were never allowed to forget who allowed them to live there. The oven, the toilet, the cistern, all were stamped 'ED' for the Earl of Durham. And, if a pitman's sons did not also go down the pit, he was out.

It was just after the First World War when Jack left school and needed a job. It seems to have always been the case that parents tried to dissuade their sons from pit work, and certainly Jack's father advised against it. He tried to get him to join the police, and the story of Jack's reaction is best left to his son Pete.

> "For Jack, having a choice of career at all represented a marked improvement in pit family circumstances, for there was no such choice for his three brothers. His father was forced to send them to the pit, on pain of him losing his job and he and the family being evicted from their pit-provided palace, (if you'll pardon an untruthful bit of alliteration). Jack thought about it, but then decided that a life segregated from the rest of the populace by virtue of spying and shopping your neighbours was not for him and he chose the pit where he would be amongst his marras (workmates) from the Barley Mow. It points up the fact that even at that young age he was fun-loving and gregarious."

So, at the age of fourteen, Jack started at 'Cotia as a pony driver, handling the 'gallowas' as the pit ponies were known, and doing other lad's work.

Jack was always musical, singing and playing a range of instruments. His father, Lance, had played portable organ, mouth organ, and "home melodeon" so enthusiastically that he regularly burst the "bellas" (bellows), and had to patch them up with tape. Jack's first instrument was the Jew's harp, which he learnt from the woman next door. He tried the fiddle, but didn't enjoy proper lessons, and took to other instruments like the mandolin, ukulele, banjo, and mouth organ because he could pick them up by ear. Jack's father had a cylinder gramophone and Jack a wind-up one, and they had a wide range of musical tastes. Jack was good with his hands, repairing watches and clocks, and mending shoes, which helped supplement his wages. He was very sociable, and a formidable darts player, being reputed to be able to knock a cigarette out of somebody's mouth with a dart, and once was runner-up in the News of the World darts final. Doreen recalls her father as a young man and his musical inheritance.

> "From all accounts he was a good looking, happy extrovert, who always had money in his pocket. He was a good dancer and really had an easy life compared to his brothers. A happy go lucky lad. The musical inclination also came from the Greens, Jack's mother Jessie's side of the family. They were of gypsy stock, and had the name of Lee-Ramn. Three of Jessie's brothers formed a trio, with fiddle, bass fiddle and viola. They were all self-taught, and their youngest brother (also called Jack) lived with Jack's family and played the fiddle. Jack Green was always known as 'Gunner', due to having been a good barefist scrapper in his youth, and the champion at that time was known as Gunner. He lived with his sister Jessie, Jack Elliott's mother, following a severe accident at the pit, which left him with horrific head injuries. He got no compensation, but was offered 'a job for life'by the coal owner. Talk about slavery! Bill Green was known as 'Aa doubt it' on account of using this phrase when the band played to prisoners at Durham jail.
>
> In fact I should have said that the trio were really good and played for the prisoners in Durham jail. They always finished off with a hymn, which had the refrain 'We'll all go to heaven when we die' and Bill always said 'Aa doubt it' as he played on his bass fiddle. The music played a great part at weddings, funerals, and special birthdays. I remember when the youngest daughter of Lance and Jessie got married. They had moved to a two-roomed house, and wedding receptions were always held in the homes. There was Uncle Jack with his fiddle, Maggie's son Joss on his accordion, both sitting on top of the chest of drawers playing non stop, excepting for the beer which came in a grey hen (a stone bottle for keeping beer and other drinks). Granda would be on his home melodeon, mats rolled up. Great nights!"

# Reece

*Reece Elliott*

One of Jack's older pitmen brothers was 'Uncle Reece', as he was known to the family and later on the folk world. Reece was a tall man, who had a broken nose and when he hadn't shaved, which was every day that he was going to work, he looked a fearsome sight. He was a great singer and had a rich store of kids' rhymes and other short 'homely' songs. He had a great memory for "the aad days" and kept his interest in the songs until his death in 1981 at the age of eighty-seven. According to his nephew Pete, "He was a gut-feeling socialist, serving for many years on Fatfield Parish Council, and was also a very strong 'clubman', being the founder secretary of the Barley Mow CIU club."

Like his brother, he had a gift for words, and was always fascinating to listen to. He remembered the German street bands of the early 1900s, and his grandfather's non-stop singing of 'Twas in Trafalgar Bay', one of the many broadsides about Nelson's epic death and victory. Doreen tells us,

> "Reece's nickname was 'Dooky'. He was a big man, bigger than me dad, and houses then were all low and he had to dook to get in, and that's how he got the name. Uncle Lance was 'Skin' because he was a cheat. He used to skin folks at the marbles, and that. An me granddad was 'Lanter'. Why I don't know. My dad's name was 'Bunty', though nobody seems to know why. Len, that's Uncle Len, wouldn't tolerate a nickname, he was an officer in the army during the First World War. Uncle Lance and Uncle Reece were both in the Grenadier Guards, you know, they were six foot, so they were in the Guards. At Catterick barracks one day they met Uncle Len and 'Ah Hi, how are ye getting on?' 'Back,' he says, 'and salute me.' Howway-ye knaa. Brothers! Wow! But, he was a clever man."

Apparently Len was terrified of being accused of favouritism. At fourteen, he had not wanted to go down the pit, and started at the local sawmill when he left school. However, Harraton Colliery knew the birthdays of all the boys living in the pit houses, and soon demanded that he go down the pit or else the family would be thrown out. (This effectively was a form of the old 'binding' of young men to the pit.) He was a very determined man, rising from the ranks during the First World War to become a second lieutenant by 1918. On his return to the pits, he studied to get his undermanager's ticket for the mines. However, he was also a militant trades unionist, and eventually got blacklisted from several pits in the area. Having got an ordinary job at the 'Rec' (recreation ground) in

Birtley, he characteristically started evening classes in horticulture, becoming an FRHS in 1934. In addition to this, he was a local councillor, and still kept his interest in the pits, visiting Germany and Russia in the '40s and '50s to study mine working. (Doreen says he should have got Robens' job! Alfred Robens was the Chairman of the National Coal Board, later to achieve notoriety for his handling of the Aberfan mining disaster. )

Here's what Reece had to say about his return from the War.

> "Naturally ah come back in 1919. Ah could o' stopped on. The' were wantin' volunteers to gan to White Russia, and all owwer, but ah says, 'Ah's gannen yem.' So anyway you had to gan up and see the colliery manager, but ah says to me father, 'Ah'm ganna have me month's leave before ah see any colliery manager', and me father says, 'Please theesell', and ah did."
> (quoted from Gavin Purdon's book *'Cotia Pit* (1)).

Jack had started work just after the First World War, about 1921, and after the usual apprenticeship of pony lad and putter, he was ready for facework, starting on the cutters when he was seventeen. So impressive was this young man that his thirty-year-old brother Reece, who had started down the pit at the time Jack was born, started 'working marras' with him. Jack was working the machine, i.e. hewing the coal, and Reece 'back filling', that's to say keeping the machine free of coals and dust so that it kept on running. In those days, marras were paid as a pair, and it was up to them how they split the money.

This was also handy when it came to hiding the 'keepy backs' from their wives. "Where's your pay note?" Em would ask. "Reece has it," says Jack, while the same exchange would be happening at Reece's house. Doreen tells of how every payday Jack would go to the toilet as soon as he came in. The reason for this was revealed one day after Em had been cleaning in there. When she went in, there were two footprints on the toilet seat. Jack had been hiding his 'stash' in a hole in the wall above the toilet. Em pocketed the money, and not a word was said, until the next day, when Doreen found them laughing about it. No bitterness, no recriminations, no muttering behind the back. This was a solid marriage with a solid family, whatever the difficulties. Although Jack had the more demanding role in the partnership with Reece, which lasted for twenty odd years, the pay was always split equally until Jack's injuries put an end to his facework days. The two brothers were also famous as singers in the bar of the Barley Mow, the Wheatsheaf, and other pubs in the area.

*Headgear at 'Cotia pit*

# 'Cotia Pit

Harraton Colliery, or 'Cotia Pit, operated from 1594 to 1965, and was extremely productive. Before the railways, the pits nearest the river were the most productive, and on the nearby River Wear, keelboats used to ship the coal from Washington Staithes down the river to Sunderland. As early as 1638, 10,000 tons of coal were being shipped each year, and by 1787, there were 15 separate wagon-ways running coal from the colliery to the Wear, over a two-mile stretch of land which had no less than 23 other pits. Three hundred keelmen were kept busy taking the coals to the ships.

Gavin Purdon, the son of songwriter Jock Purdon who was a deputy at 'Cotia, has written a book about the colliery, and has this to say. 'Harraton Colliery worked several coal seams: the Five Quarter, Main Coal, Maudlin, Brass Thill, Low Main and the Hutton Seams. It was an old fashioned pit and many considered it to be little more than the product of a bygone era reluctantly drawn into the twentieth century. The old colliery was set in its ways, but they were proved by trial and error to be the right ways, and tradition dies hard down the pit, where unproven ways could cost a man his life. For centuries production at Harraton had been limited to what men and animals could endure and there had been no other way of working the colliery but by the time honoured method of pick and shovel. 'Cotia pit and its old style coal hewers were like body and soul, one could not be separated from the other. The steady "Pick Pick Pick" of the hand hewer at his toil was the very heartbeat of the colliery and when it ceased, the pit itself was dying. Many old 'Cotia men believed this and as it turned out, rightly so.'

According to Paul Younger, an environmental engineer and great friend of the family, whom we will meet later in Chapter 5, 'Cotia was "unusual in working such a large number of seams, most only having four or less, and was also unusual in straddling the Wear / Tyne watershed. Before the Wear trade really picked up in the 1700s, it likely supplied coals to the Tyne. As such it was never a narrow-minded place. Rather, as the name 'Nova Scotia' suggests, it was always a favoured destination for Scots miners coming south to avoid the even worse, near slavery conditions in Scottish pits. 'Elliott' is of course a Scots name; though now also a Durham one, forever. I feel there is a metaphor in the richness and outlook of the pit itself for the musical wealth and welcoming outlook of Jack, his family and his marras."

## Jack and Reece reminisce

Jack and Reece had good memories and a captivating manner of talking about their lives. This is best shown on a memorable recording by Charles Parker, in preparation for the radio ballad *The Big Hewer* in 1961. The contrast between the articulation of these two big, strong, dignified colliers, and the life they described makes the listener continually wonder why men like this did not have worthier work. When the two men were asked about the conditions in the pit, it's dust and water that they singled out as the worst aspects. The dust has always been the constant threat to a miner's health whether from the coal or the stone that you had to cut through to reach the seams.

Reece: "Terrible the dust. We chowed tobacco. They did try the management did try to keep it down. They had ... it was very primitive ... they had a feller going round at night time, walking the roadways with a barrel on top of a tub, with a hose underneath so he could spray it. For a certain time, but they couldn't keep it down."

Jack: "They now have this infusion of the dust, you know they put it in a hole and it like bleeds through coal. And it kind of keeps the dust down. But I didn't mind coal dust, it was the stone dust. I could, oh dear me, it used to burn your chest. You sometimes had to cut stone to get from a low part to a high part, and the dust used to get on your lungs. You could tell it burnt, it was hot, fiery, we used to put handkerchiefs over our eyes and nose, wet, to try and keep the dust away. Terrific. I could never stand the stone. Coal dust didn't bother me much, if I could chew baccy, but if I hadn't any baccy, well it was just too bad."

Reece: "Can you imagine, you get on to a face, 16 inches, and you see ... 40 yards away up these 16 inches, and you wanting a drink? Can you imagine yourself crawling all the way down to where your jacket was to get a drink then come crawling all the way back? We used to make the tobacco do the job. I've seen me, and he's seen me, oh, many's the time, reeching (retching) with the dust at the back of your throat. Eventually with reechin, you're sick, well if that happens you're all right."

(Doreen adds: "You bought the baccy by the length. It was called twist, and mi dad cut it into six pieces, for his week's use. I once entered a competition for a new name for the twist, and proposed 'marra'. What's a pitman without his marra? I thought it was neat, I was 14 at the time but it got nowhere!")

It's difficult in this day and age to understand the everyday reality of the two miners' statements until you make a comparison. They talk in terms of a 16" or 18" seam to work in whereas today we would talk of 16 or 18 inches to describe a TV screen. To get an idea, the diameter of the wheel on a small family saloon car is 22½" and the wheel arch is 25½". It's impossible to imagine crawling into that space, let alone working there wielding a pick! However, the thin seams had the best quality coking coal, fetching a high price, and that's why the men had to struggle with them.

The water used to keep the dust down brought its own hazards, especially with the introduction of electricity down the pit.

Jack: "Then you get too much water, water on the face, and I was never very happy with water on the face where there's cutters. I always had that fear with the trailing cable, 40 yards of trailing cable, 40 yards up, just needs a little leak and you've had it. Electric machines, aye. I started on compressed air."

Reece: "When we first got water on the face, I says to me brother I says I'm not satisfied, through my little bit of experience in the army, electricity, current, 'cos water is the best conductor for electricity. So I asked the head electrician about this I says, 'Could you guarantee we could go through water with this machine?' He says,

'I couldn't.' And I says, 'Well then, it's not worth me dying.' If we come to what in our opinion was too much water, we stopped the machine."

Jack: "I cannot describe the conditions. All your clothes were wet, everything you handle's wet, stuck all over with small coals, you cannot handle your tools. You cannot work down the pit with water. They issued us with capes, waterproof capes. Well, you couldn't work with them, you sweat inside, clammy sweat, not a natural sweat I may say. I'd sooner have bad roof, or dust, or anything as water. I think water's the worst thing in the pit."

When they were off work, miners certainly knew how to enjoy themselves. As well as the music, at home and in the pub, they were great sportsmen, and enjoyed both participating and spectating, or even gambling. It's noticeable that however poor people are, they do need some excitement, and gambling could fulfil that. As we see in the next extract, it could often amount to a sizeable amount of cash, and any losses would have to be explained to the wife. Bowls were a popular pastime, as was all kinds of racing, including pigeons and whippets, upon whom these big men would lavish all kinds of attention.

Reece: "25 ounces used to be the lowest. 25, 30, 35, and 40 was the largest. Ounces. These were the bowls men used to bowl across the Town Moor at Newcastle, or on the sands at Newbiggin, or the sands at Hartlepool, that's Seaton Carew now. Generally it was for side stakes. There was me and my brother could be matched, you know. Stakes could be … well … generally from about £20. You can imagine about fifteen fellers in this, maybes a pound each. Matchin', ties, we always called them handball. It was played in what you call an alley. Bar alleys we used to call 'em. There's only one as I remember now, in the county of Durham, and that's at Owston (Ouston) –that's about a half a mile from here. I think that's the last one in the county of Durham. It's still there, at the end of the old institute. And I remember, I think it was Jacky Molineux, I saw him play there, it was either Easter Monday or Whit Monday.

Pigeons were always raced in the North of England. The milers used to fly here, generally on a Saturday morning again. And again, it was for side stakes, one loft against the other. There'd be three, up to seven lofts. I remember them putting the stamp on, stampin' the feathers of its tail, before the bird was thrown. Then there'd be two judges at the far end, where the lofts were, all in the one square. With a stopwatch. Sometimes the handler would handle the hen pigeon. He'd shout, 'drop', and when the bird dropped, then they'd stop the watch.

We had whippets that used to run at rabbits, about half a mile away from here was what they called Half Acre's Ground. That was up on the Black Fell, where my Grandfather Frank came from. There was a field there, they reckoned that this used to happen. They would have a handicap on a Saturday. If there was any money left, well they'd have a day off on Monday, and they'd play another one on the Monday. And if there was not, well, they'd move on to the next Saturday."

There were also bigger celebrations on the holidays that broke up the monotony of work.

Reece: "What they use to do, at a colliery, say Harraton colliery, is have a gala day. Say on Easter Monday, where what they would do, the manager would rig up a roadway identical to what it was like in the pit. Only instead of a stone roadway it would be made of canvas. But the same rules, terms, and everything. They would fill up the tubs in the same way as they would do down the pit. With the ponies, the ponies were brought to bank for that day. I think the feller is still alive today, that I saw win the last one. It was held at Fatfield, I think it was Tommy Roseberry, and if I remember rightly, he's a bookmaker today. Still alive today. Big strong feller. The thing was, for to be a good putter you had to be strong, for the simple reason that if the tub came off the rails, this big strong feller would get a hold of it with his two hands, 'arse on', i.e. with his back to the tub and his backside just under it, and put it right again, whereas an ordinary feller would have to have some help. That was what they call The Big Putter. Twelve hundredweight a full tub, eight hundredweight, an empty tub's four hundredweight."

The pit dominated all aspects of life in these communities; the landscape, the regulation of family and social life all revolved around the pit. Pete Elliott gives a wonderful description of the pit when he was a lad.

"You first became aware of its existence by the sight of black-faced men in raggedy clothes trudging homewards down Vigo Lane. It became a matter of pride for us to recognise the rolling, sailor-like gait of Dad and Uncle Reece from as far as a half-mile away, before racing up to greet them. Later on, when buses were laid on, another sure sign that there was a pit in the area was the sight of men waiting to go to the pit. They would be all parked along the side of the Barley Mow pub, crouched down on their hunkers, like spuggies on a wall. How the hell their bodies got used to sitting in such a position was totally beyond me. A further means of becoming aware of the pit's existence before actually seeing it was the sound of the buzzer (siren), signaling the start and end of each shift. Even though the pit was over two miles away, we could still hear it clearly."

*"They would be all parked along the side of the Barley Mow pub, crouched down on their hunkers, like spuggies on a wall."*

In such a community a man depended on his 'marras' and better still if, like Reece, he was reputed to have good 'pitsense', as the underlying threat of accident or disaster was always there. The pit was always the measure of life and death.

Reece: "Incidental accidents, but never any major explosion or ... not in our time. But Easington, that wasn't many years back. Matty Nightingale was there. Explosion, oh it was terrible, Easington Colliery. You see it could be off a spark. You see, me and him have seen sparks coming off the cutter or the pick. Friction sparks. The question is: could these sparks cause an explosion? Only needs a pocket of gas, coal dust, and then there is an explosion. But we never used to think about an explosion. The only thing that worried me was falls of the roof. And generally, I was a good judge of the roof. I could tell when it was going to come. Pitsense."

Jack: "Even above the noise of the cutting machine, you could hear a prop crack, you could hear the rumbling."

Reece: "With modern chocks, you've got a chance. Until the face timber starts to break, there's no cause for any alarm. I've been in places where we've had to scatter, 'howay, off, time we were off', but generally we've backed a winner."

Jack: "Ten seconds, a hundred yards."

Reece: "I've never been barred in. I shouldn't like to be barred in."

(The Easington explosion on 29th May 1951 was the worst such incident in modern times, killing 81 men and two rescuers. Strong rescue men were put off such work after Easington, including Jock Purdon, whom we will meet later. The disaster led to compulsory changes to the ventilation systems of all pits, just as the Hartley disaster of 1862 produced legislation that all pits had to have a rescue shaft. Amazing that it takes such awful disasters before basic safety measures are taken.)

Events such as these made a strong impression on the young Pete and he recorded his memories for his children.

"An event which could cause a stirring of extreme fear through our hamlet was if the buzzer went at a time which was not a recognised shift time. This meant that someone had been killed. Both from respect for the victim and to give time for the death to be investigated, all the men would of course leave the pit, when the buzzer blew. The women and any men not working would gather in a crowd anxiously waiting to hear who the victim was. The women would be hoping against hope that it wasn't blind chance, and the need to earn a crust, that had led to the death of the main provider for the family."

Jack: "I was in a fall when I was sixteen. Fall of stone, big fall. I was lucky that time, I was on the changes. All of a sudden these props started to crack, and I made a dive to get out, but the whole lot came on top of us … I was fast by the legs. Yankee Jim (Roberts) pulled me out. Two minutes after they got me out it closed 'as tight as a box', and took them three days to shift that fall. I was lucky as two stones locked themselves over the top, like a V. There was one stone four foot, six inches round, two foot thick, lying beside of us. Tell you how lucky I was. I was off six weeks. When I did start down the pit again, I kept looking at the top, seeing if it was sound till I gradually got over it. It made me very very wary after that about the roof."

Reece: "You see, I've many a time said this. You remember during the war about the Bevin boys. (Bevin boys were young men drafted in to keep the pits working, often from other parts of the country with no experience of mining, and nicknamed after Ernest Bevin, the minister responsible for the scheme.) I always said that was a mistake from the start. The pitman is bred for the pit, and he gets his intelligence about the pit from his father. He's got what they call this pitsense such as setting timber, watching for faults in the roof and the like of that. You couldn't tell Bevin boys that, not in that short a time. It takes years. You grew up with it. I used to listen to me father, and his brothers.

My two sons are in the pit, and it seems as if they're going to stay. They're making good money, and like all young fellers they're wanting good money, and they're needin' it. But it's different altogether. The conditions are better. The pay conditions, the working conditions are different. But mind ye, they're not soft or owt like that, it's still the pit. The atmosphere when you get down there's just the same. And it's the pit. You're wondering if there's going to be a fall, or an explosion, or there's gas, or some water that nobody knows anything about through plans of old pits being lost, and the like of that."

Jack: "And then there's all the wrigglin', swimmin', we used to call it, because we were so deep in the small coals and dust. I reckon me and him have crawled all the way from Barley Mow to London in our time! I remember, we were crawlin' down this low face, about eighteen inches, I was in front of my marra, and my foot got fast, and I tried to shake it free. Then I looked round, and I had this chap's chin fastened up against the top. I'd got my foot underneath his chin, and he couldn't shout, to tell me what was the matter. Well, you had to laugh."

Had to laugh! That's not how Don Stokoe, also a miner's son, sees it. It's the sort of terrifying experience that pitmen forget when they "get to bank" (the surface, out of the pit). Instead, they resort to humour. Perhaps the most chilling story is the time when the two of them were in the cage when it plunged. They thought they were done, and as they raced downwards, stared at each other and gave the customary pit greeting, "Noo ..." followed by a curt nod of the head.

*"I reckon me and him have crawled all the way from Barley Mow to London in our time!"*

If a miner survived accidents and disaster, poor health was always a payment for a life working down the pit, and many miners paid full fare. Jack's comments about his father Lance were all too common a story.

"Me father, he had to stop work when he was sixty-two. The last shift he went up to that pit, he got halfway up and he crawled back on his hands and knees, he couldn't make the rest. He couldn't walk any more than ten yards, and he had to stop for breath. It was pitiful to watch him. Heave, sigh. Standing at the bus stop, after he'd walked his ten yards, the bus come, and he couldn't get on. Had to wait for the

> next one, 'cos he couldn't get his breath. That's what the pit did. No compensation, but it was pneumoconiosis. My father was a good worker. Only missed 5 shifts in 25 years, and that was a record. And he's been known to work 12 shifts a week when he was twenty-one."

### *"It's an awful job, and the sooner they're all closed the better."*

Reece was born 13 years before his brother and died about 13 years after him, and never had serious illness, whereas Jack died of lung cancer before he was sixty. Not only that, but Jack had a serious accident when he was young, and finally developed a back injury as a result of all the contortions of working in small spaces; the "swimmin'" referred to earlier. So not only did he get a raw deal when it came to the genes, which gave him his lung disease, but also he didn't have much luck with chance either.

> "I always remember when I had to go up to the hospital. I got pains in my back, surgeon examined me, X-rays, and he says, 'You must have a terrible hard job, laddie.' I says, 'No, I haven't,' I said, 'coal cuttin's not a HARD job.' He says, 'Do you do a lot of wriggling about?' I says, 'Yes, I'm afraid I do.' Well, I was thirty-three year old at the time. He says, 'Well, I'm going to have to tell you now, you've got the spine of a man seventy year old. Your vertebras all lipped with constant wriggling.' Thirty-three years old, and I had the spine of a man of seventy! That's from the RVI at Newcastle. I've had two discs taken off, and thought I was going to be in a wheelchair at the finish. I've been on light work, have been for 12 year now. That's what the pit did for me. I wish I'd taken my father's advice now. But there's none of my sons in the pit. You couldn't make pit work attractive if you whitewashed it from one end to the other. It's an awful job, and the sooner they're all closed the better. That's my honest opinion about the pits."

As a result of this, he was put on light surface work for the rest of his time at the pit, meaning low wages and harsher times again. Jack was just as eloquent when describing their home life and the effects of working the pit on the family.

> "Pitman's home? Tin bath in front of the fire. If you were in a hurry, you'd had it. You had to boil the water on the fire. A pan. We had a kip, like a cut down beer barrel. And if you were last on, well, you might as well sit in for the night. The second man might get bathed, you know,

pit muck. There might be a drop of hot water left. Or you might just wash your hands and face. I've seen mi father do that. On pay Friday, he'd lay down on the mat. That was generally what happened. See, while two of them were getting bathed, when it come round to his turn you couldn't get him up. 'Oh, to hell, I'm lyin' here.' He'd wash his face and gan to work in the morn. But it didn't often happen.

Growing Up? There were four lads five lasses, thirteen originally, but there were only nine left. As the family grew bigger, you got shifted into bigger and bigger houses. Eventually we had the biggest house in Brown's Buildings. That was a 5-roomed house. There were twenty-one children in the two biggest houses. That's when people would come round asking 'Does Dr Barnardo live here?' What used to happen was: me mother would say try and get a swap with so and so she'd at least only had to cook one dinner! The foreshift was 4 o'clock in the morning. That meant that if two or three of you were on, more than one were working wet. There were no pithead baths in them days. The stockings and shirts would have to be rubbed out in the same kip as what you'd bathed in. Sometimes five men came off shift at same time, all wanting a bath."

# Em

Jack was a skilful dancer, and Doreen tells us that it was when Jack was seventeen, and practising his considerable skills at a local dance in the Drill Hall in Birtley in 1925, that he met and fell in love with Em Wilkin.

Em, who hated her full name Emma, was then twenty-one, four years older than Jack. Her father was the town barber, which should have made them relatively prosperous, but he had a drink problem, and was often violent. Her mother had died when she was only eleven. So the young Em had to work as a skivvy for a family of six children. This wasn't unusual in those days but her response to this tough start in life was. As Doreen says, it was here where the seeds of her passionate socialism and empathy with the underdog took root. "She hated her job, where she didn't even have the dignity of being called by her first name, and she also worried constantly about the brothers and sisters she'd left with her drunken brutal father."

Jack and Em met and were two opposite characters; she was a five foot quiet shy girl, (though as Pete says, she was "ten feet tall in courage, determination and intelligence") and he a six foot two outward looking extrovert. But they fell in love and had a very passionate affair, which

*Jack and Em outside the Huts*

meant Em very quickly fell pregnant, and as Jack was only seventeen, below the age of consent at that time, there was a problem. Jack's mother withheld consent, despite having done the same thing herself. This situation is somewhat of a tradition in this family, and such private matters may have been common to other working-class families besides the Elliotts. However, as with the aristocrats, it was usually a private concern and not broadcast at large. Maybe it's only the middle classes that had problems with premarital sex.

However, she was persuaded to relent, and the couple were married on 6th June 1925, just a few weeks before Pete was born. Jack was a strong, well-liked character, who had met his match in Em, a woman of indomitable spirit well able to hold her own, run the household and start a family. Whilst Jack was an affable, easy-going character, Em was more of a 'terrier'. She also tended to see things as black or white, right or wrong, which gave her something of a tunnel vision about morality and rightness, and informed her political views. "Grey," as she would say, "was nee colour."

Like Jack, she too was an excellent singer and came from a musical family. Her great-aunt Olive, who married a violinist named Percy Swift, had formed a musical troupe with her two daughters, named Zilla's Gaiety Girls. (Zilla was a family name of the Wilkins.) They were very successful at one time, but no record of them has been found. "She was a beautiful singer," says Doreen of her mother. "You know, her family were musical, and my great-aunt Tid from Sunderland had a troupe of singers and dancers, and they wanted me mam to go, 'cos she did have a lovely voice, but granda wouldn't allow it." According to Doreen, she and the other kids were brought up with a mother and father who "always sang". So, it sounds like marriage to Jack had freed her from a form of bondage, and now she was ready for singing!

Doreen also comments that her mother, although an excellent cook and mother, would "as soon read a book as cook a meal. Do you know, one time when I was on the chapel anniversary (where everybody comes in their best new clothes), mi dad made me mi petticoat, because me mam had made me this dress and you could see through it. It was made out of pillowcase would you believe? He says, 'I know exactly what we'll do,' and he cut this petticoat out, and sewed it up. That was mi dad, the dressmaker!" Her mother no doubt had her nose in some political treatise in the other room. No ordinary family, this!

*I was gannin' inbye on the engine plane,*
*I could hear the putter "I'm off the way!"*
*Ah, wae! Give us a life, my arse is sair*
*If I had this tub put I would put nae mair"*

# The 1926 Strike and the '30s Depression

Jack and Em married in 1925, and baby Pete came soon after. It was tough enough in those times, starting a family as a pitman, but they were about to undergo some of the worst times of their lives. It is generally reckoned that Britain reached the height of its prosperity in 1913, and certainly mining was then at its height, with the number of pits, men, and coal output at their greatest level ever. The First World War had changed that, and the early '20s found the price of coal falling due to competition from the Continent, which was rapidly catching up with Britain.

Coal was always at the centre of the General Strike in 1926. By 1925 the mining industry was under strain. Heavy use of coal to fuel the war machine had depleted the rich seams, and the First World War had severely affected exports, allowing other countries like the United States to exploit the gap in the market. In contrast, productivity had fallen to an all-time low of 199 tons per man per year, a reflection of a workforce depleted by the human cost of service in the armed forces.

Part of the 1925 Dawes Plan to help rebuild Europe after the First World War allowed Germany to export 'free coal' to France and Italy as part of their reparations, causing a disastrous fall in prices for the British coal industry. In spite of all this the mine owners sought to reinstate their previous levels of profits, often at the expense of miners' wages. This, added to longer working hours, fuelled the miners' dispute, which was backed by the TUC. (2) The Samuels Commission, set up by the Government to investigate the industry's problems, reported in March 1926. It recommended that the industry should be reorganised and that miners' wages should be reduced to save profitability; it also recommended that the interim Government subsidy to the miners' wages be withdrawn.

Given this carte blanche, the mine owners delivered new contracts to the workforce including a reduction in wages, district wage agreements and an extension of the seven-hour working day. This was accompanied by the threat, "Accept the new terms or face a lock-out!" "Not a penny off the pay, not a second on the day" was the response of the Miners' Federation of Great Britain. (2) The battle lines were drawn, the coal owners insisting on a wage cut, the miners refusing. The Government sided with the owners, and the miners won the sympathy of working people across the land. So much so that in May of 1926, the TUC called a general strike, and chaos reigned, with very ugly scenes and bad feeling on both sides. By 4th May there were about one and a half million strikers throughout the country from John O' Groats to Land's End. (3) Even King George V took exception to accusations that the strikers were just revolutionaries. "Try living on their wages before you judge them." (4) Just as in the more recent 1984 Miners' Strike, the police were ordered to crack down hard.

The strike spread to affect all areas of daily life and in some cases disrupted public transport. Here are some examples from the North East, courtesy of local newspapers.

'The Home Office Situation Report read: "On 7 May, the Home Office

Situation Report noted that police can protect the unloading of ships, but the difficulty is to get the convoys through the district just outside the city boundary." The activities of the strikers caused bus services to be withdrawn, and "in the North West area, strong pickets have stopped private cars and refused them passage without a permit. Food transport was practically stopped at Consett last night but today the police organised convoys and got all traffic through successfully." The Chief Constable of Durham forecast more trouble with food supplies "next week" and intimated that another five hundred men would be useful.' (5)

On 8th May, both the *Northern Echo* and the *Newcastle Chronicle* were reporting the obstruction of traffic by strikers in the Stanley area of North West Durham, and on the Newcastle to Consett road all vehicles were being turned back by a large crowd of miners thought to come from Chopwell. Birtley and the immediate district were as involved as any area, and clashes between the strikers and police came to a head in May.

'In the early hours of 10th May, the *Newcastle Chronicle* reported an apparently organised attempt to stop road traffic on the main Newcastle–Durham road. Baton charges by the police dispersed the crowds. The police were informed that large crowds were assembling along the Great North Road at various points between Chester-le-Street and Low Fell. Consequently about a dozen policemen set out from Chester-le-Street in a lorry and were joined by other police at Birtley. Before Birtley was reached, however, a baton charge was made to scatter a crowd, which threw stones at the police. Just north of Birtley, at the Teams colliery, a further use of police truncheons was made. At this spot, pickets had attempted to block the road with railway sleepers. During a fight between the police and pickets, three policemen were injured.' (5)

A Special Constable drafted in to maintain order on the streets said, "It was not difficult to understand the strikers' attitude towards us. After a few days I found my sympathy with them rather than with the employers. For one thing I never knew the appalling poverty which existed. If I had been aware of the facts I would never have joined up."

The General Strike lasted just nine days, and when the TUC were told by the Government that they "had no power to compel employers to take back every man who had been on strike", they called the strike off and left the miners to fend for themselves. (2) In those days, each coalfield had its own separate union, and over the next few weeks the various areas went back to work one by one. Towards the end of November 1926, miners around the country, exhausted, betrayed, deserted, resumed work in all the major coalfields with the exceptions of South Wales, Yorkshire and Durham. Then, on 30th November, South Wales and Yorkshire returned to work, and the Durham Miners Association reluctantly had to instruct its men to return. The family thought the reasons for the return were not political, not because of the betrayal by the rest of the country, but for the old, old reasons why workers so often lost their fights with their bosses. They were starving. The Elliotts had had to get by on Co-op credit or whatever they could pawn or sell. Jack and Em described these times to Philip Donnellan for the film *Private Faces*, to be discussed in Chapter 2.

Jack: "We'd about £5 put by, but that sharp went, the coals went, went seeking coals, firewood, anything that would burn. I've walked as far as 8 mile with a barrow, couple of bags of coal from Waldridge, up on the fell, 'Cotia pit heap, digging the heap. Worked in places there we wouldn't dream of workin' in down the pit. We'd want danger money. Then things got progressively worse, and money ran out altogether, no more money left in the unions. We did get a bit of help from abroad, Russia and America, and we started with these vouchers, the co-operative store honoured these vouchers. We got 8 shillings a week for to keep the two of us and the little laddie, Peter. It was hard."

Em: "Peter was just a baby. The problem was of course trying to keep your morale going, on an empty belly. It was a very, very difficult thing, and I remember being so awfully hungry one time, we got these vouchers on Friday, and this was Thursday, and we'd had very, very little to eat, and I had made some rice pudding for Peter with the last of the dried milk that was allocated to us because we had a baby, and there was a man, a fish man came round, with herring, five a penny, and we were awfully hungry and we'd only one halfpenny in my purse at the time, and we hunted around, and hunted around, and found another halfpenny. We bought the five herring, and it was the most delicious meal that I've ever eaten in my life. We had to cook it in water because we hadn't any fat, but we were so desperately hungry."

Jack: "I could have taken another job, but I'd be as bad as a blackleg if I'd done that."

The lock-out had lasted for seven months, the greatest industrial conflict in British history. But the miners had lost, and when they did go back, they were at the mercy of the owners. The wages were cut, and thousands of pitmen were laid off in the North East alone. In County Durham, the strike and the depression that followed had meant the loss of 64,000 jobs in the pits between 1924 and 1931, about 40 per cent of the workforce. In certain areas, collieries had closed, which meant, quite simply, 100 per cent unemployment. Jack and Reece remember these times only too clearly.

Reece: "1921 the minimum wage strike, and shorter hours. Well, we got over that, and it come to 1926, the big strike. Now from 1926 almost to 1936 was terrible in this area."

Jack: "I was only man working in the whole street of 30 houses. You daren't answer the bosses back because you knew there were plenty men waiting for your job. We used to work 16 hours down pit, no extra pay, just got what I cut, and that's no lie. No overtime, just what you cut."

Reece: "The management after 1926 in this area and at Harraton colliery, they picked his men, who he was going to have, and it so happened that I was one that was picked. I divvent knaa what for. Well, I had three kiddies at the time, and I was thankful, like that I was working. The only thing else was the dole."

Jack: "If there was an accident at the pit, the first question I would ask that man was 'Was he in a hurry?' And nine times out of ten he was. Ninety per cent of the accidents could be avoided if you just took time to think."

Reece: "The coal owners had the piece rate screwed down to a fine art, that a man had to be all out to get a living wage in them days. We're talking about the days of the Depression. In the days of the Depression, I'd go to work in my pit suit. All I had left at home was a jacket a pair of trousers and a waistcoat. And the staple diet in them days was corned beef, ... potatoes, ... turnip, ...coarse bread, ... and margarine. No butter. No butter at all. Because that's all you could afford."

*Tell my ma when I get home,*
*Boys won't leave the girls alone*
*They pull my hair and break my comb,*
*Tell my ma when I get home.*

# The Bairns

So, the 1920s were not prosperous times in the coalfield, and the way young couples in the area got a house at that time was to move into 'The Huts'. These had been built to house Belgian refugees who were working in the munitions factory in Birtley, and by general agreement were much better houses than the miners were living in. As the Belgians gradually returned home during the early '20s, the thing to do for the locals, especially young couples, was to move in overnight and effect a squat. And that included Jack and Em. It was rough, and there was a general air of lawlessness about them, but it was a house. Jack had to erect a substantial fence round it to keep people at bay, and that's where they started their family.

Pete Elliott, Jack and Em's first child, came bawling into the world in 1925, and left it 74 years later still railing against the iniquities of the class system, through song, speech, and in everyday chat. He was born in 'The Huts', and spent his early childhood there. He describes one next door neighbour as "whinging and chapel-fyeced", and the others as "dirt poor squatters from Gateshead", dodging the rent man, foul-mouthed, whose kids had to go to school barefoot in the snow. Although there was a police fund to provide footwear for deprived kids, "that lot would have pawned the boots for beer money". The huts lasted well into the '30s, and became a bit of a talking point in the area, with lots of legends. One concerned the toff who, driving past in his Rolls Royce one day, remarked "How posh the people of Birtley must be, they even have curtains up in their hen sheds."

By the time the Strike had finished in 1927, Jack had done his apprenticeship, and was ready for the face. Although they were back at work, times were still hard, with everybody deep in debt, and with machinery coming in to replace the pick and shovel, there were fewer jobs. Anybody speaking out of turn, you were out. There were plenty of men hungry for your job, and it was to get worse with the Depression of the '30s. Still, the young, fit twenty-year old Jack Elliott with a wife and family to support was not too worried about these things, and he took to the new machine cutters with enthusiasm. He was an excellent pitman, working at the face for the next twenty years alongside his brother and marra, Reece.

A year after Pete came sister Doreen, who turned out to be his political soul-mate. Her arrival coincided with Jack's wages reaching three figures, £1 1s 1d, and he called her that, "One pound one shilling and a penny", for some time. Like her mother Em, she is a toughie, a match for any man. But both women were a product of their times, and in a tough man's business like mining, they knew when to bide their tongue and take a back seat. So when it came to folk clubs, it was Jack and Pete who went to the Bridge in Newcastle, while Em and Dot stayed home. When it came to recordings of the family in the '60s and '70s, they were dominated by the men. There are fewer stories about the women, mainly because they got out less.

A pity really, since both of them had great voices, and a way of handling a song that is of the tradition and which owes very little to commercial music. "Yes," says Doreen, "I sing similar to me mam. We used to sing 'Henry' together, a song I learnt as a child from Renee Pearson next door." The two of them were recorded singing this ballad for the family LP in 1961, as fine an example of uncomplicated, unpolished traditional singing by two women, mother and daughter, as you are likely to hear. 'Henry' is the family's version of 'Lord Randal', possibly the commonest traditional ballad in the English-speaking world apart from 'Barbara Allen'. Em and Doreen's style chimes well with recorded versions of traditional singers from all parts of the British Isles, America and Canada. Although they might have been less prominent in the singing, this was not so at home, where they were more than a match for the men, in every way, and quite unlike the other women in the pit community. Doreen was and is politically passionate, and in this regard misses Pete very keenly. She is also brimming with enthusiasm for the music and for life in general, and has been the main source of information in the writing of this book. In fact, without her, it would have been puny indeed.

Jack and Em's kids were born too late to recollect the really tough times their parents had lived through in the 1920s and early '30s, but Pete Elliott remembers well growing up around the pit and the area round about.

> "You entered the pit-yard, coming from the Barley Mow, at the point where Vigo Lane makes a curve towards the new Methodist chapel. The stables were on your right and the field just before you reached the stables had a secure building in the middle where the explosives for firing down the coal were stored. The fields on both the left and right of the approach road would have gallowas in them. These were the pit-ponies used for hauling tubs of coal from the faces underground. It was a favourite practice among we young lads to see how long we could stay on their backs, like in a rodeo. Since the gallowas, in their unaccustomed freedom, were full of piss and vinegar, the rides were never of long duration and you were liable for a kick that could put you in dock if you didn't get quickly out of the way once you were catapulted off.
>
> The new chapel is sited just about where the pit pond was, and this was certainly responsible for a degree of the smell that greeted you on your approach. It was a black, evil looking hole that the water from underground was pumped into. I'm sure that it drained away by seepage, for I never saw an exit from it.
>
> Behind the pond stood the building that housed the screens, which was responsible for a lot of the din that was always around. In it old men and boys picked off stones, slate and shale, (or 'splent' as it was

known), from the conveyor belts as they carried along the production of the pit.

Over all the many noises that could be heard was the steady whine of the fan, and that was one noise that no-one would wish to have stopped, for it was the men's lifeline. It was a huge rotary fan that drew air down one shaft, round the pit and up the other of the two shafts that were in the yard. Both of the shafts had names, but I can only remember the Billy; the other escapes me.

Towering over all the buildings was the pit-head, with the winding gear consisting of two great wheels over which ran the wire ropes from the winding house and from which the cages were suspended, to be raised and lowered to the various seams."

They would of course know bad times in the war and the late '40s, but their childhood in the '30s seems to have been a pretty happy affair. This account of Doreen's paints a picture of an idyllic childhood.

"On summer nights, we kids would play in the poppy fields across the road and play endless games, usually with lots of singing. Everybody sang. Sometimes Mrs Lynn would bring out the wind-up gramophone and play popular records like Gracie Fields. Or me dad's band would play for us and accompany us (him on the mouth organ of course, which he was very good at). They'd do jigs, or pop songs like 'I Wouldn't Leave my Little Wooden Hut'. Our mams would skip with the kids, and the men would sing the kids' game songs. Then we'd have the 'boody' concerts, which took place in somebody's garden with the dry midden outside netty as the changing room, and the songs were play-acted. 'Boody' was the name for the currency which the kids used, broken bits of china, with those bits with patterns on them being the most valuable. We used rhubarb leaves as plates, and the boody was used to decorate them. The concerts took place mostly in the school holidays. The song I remember most is 'Henry my Son', which came from Renee Pearson next door. Brother John was always getting wrong for singing rude songs."

John Elliott was the third bairn, and in later life has always seemed more relaxed about everything than his older brother and sister. However, in his day he was as articulate, passionate, and forthright as anybody else. In the film *Private Faces*, where he and younger brother Len struggled knee deep in water to fix a water pump, it is John who spells out what pit life is really like. Although initially taking Jack and Em's strong advice not to go down the pit, after nationalisation he and his younger brother Len felt confident enough about the future of the mines to transfer their engineering skills to the 'Cotia. John was, in the words of Bryan Henderson, Doreen's husband, "good with his hands". He took after his dad, whereas older brother Pete took after his mam. He was very good at the job, and eventually became a foreman fitter at 'Cotia, a promotion which led to him moving to Brown's Buildings. It seems that most of the family were destined to live there. John has always been particularly unassuming with his singing, and often gives other people more time by singing one of his many short songs, in his characteristic unselfish way, rather than do a long song.

*Map showing the shafts and wagonways round 'Cotia pit (from Gavin Purdon's book* 'Cotia Pit*)*

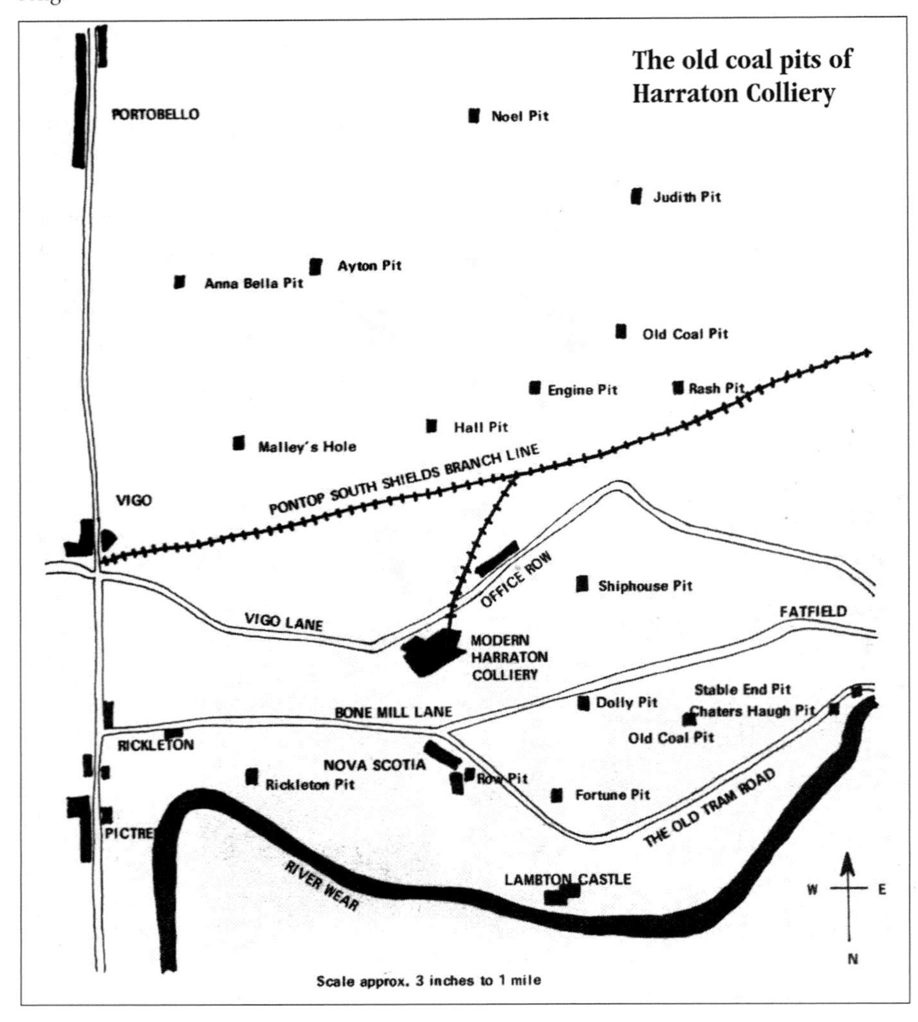

The youngest of the brood, Len is definitely an Elliott in terms of feistiness, but has never been quite as keen as the rest on the singing. He was a strong union man, and was at one time nominated as a Labour MEP. Anyway, Len is still in the area, and still turns up on the big occasions. I guess he likes the folk songs, and is a really fine singer, but it doesn't dominate his life as with the others. But he did his time in the pit as a fitter with John, and is the best raconteur in the family.

The first three bairns were born at the huts, but by the time Len came along, in 1933, they'd moved to Pelaw Grange, a set of cottages just down the road from Barley Mow. "It was a two-room flat on the first floor, reached by outside wooden steps, which froze in winter, and were a health hazard at all times," says Doreen. "The living room cum dining room cum washhouse cum kitchen was home to six of us and housed all possessions and furniture. The scrub table was in front of the window, where us kids spent many a happy hour watching the trains go by and the pitmen getting bathed in the pond. Men still in their pit muck diving in armed with soap and coming out as familiar faces. They splashed and yelled and swam like schoolkids on holiday. Incidentally, the best watercress was to be had from that pond, and dad and I loved it. The bedroom had three beds, a dirty linen box, a chest of drawers, and a wardrobe. Mam and Dad were in a double behind the door, Pete and John in a ¾ bed and me and Len in a single. The floor was bare excepting for the proverbial clippie mat. I loved that bedroom; no bad dreams, no nightmares. There just wasn't room!"

Yes, "one up" meant parents and four kids in one bedroom. This was not a good experience for the family, and Pete and Doreen have many things to say about it. Here's just a glimpse of this from Pete.

> "We had a midden type netty which we shared with the crusty old maid who lived below us with her bachelor brother. He was a canny old bloke who had been a good fiddle player in his younger days, giving lessons to the lads in the village. Since no-one in their right mind would venture down those stairs to the bog on a caad neet in winter, or a warm night in summer for that matter, we had a pisspot, (or po as it was politely called), under the bed; as did most families until the advent of the indoor toilet. On the bed would be any bloody thing that would keep you warm. Top-coats and even mats would be pressed into service in some houses as bed-clothes in winter. Bedrooms were as cowld as a polar-bear's arse and once you got out of bed you got dressed as quickly as possible in order to conserve heat."

They must have lived here for three years, until Pete was 11 years old. Eventually, the owners were persuaded that this was a large, growing family that needed something better. The tide had turned, things were generally getting better as the country emerged from the Depression. Jack and his family were bound for ... Brown's Buildings, Barley Mow.

References for Chapter 1

1. Gavin Purdon, *'Cotia Pit*, Instat, c 1971
2. Peter Mathias *The First Industrial Nation* Routledge 1986
3. *British Worker* 4th May 1926
4. David Sinclair *Two Georges: Making of the Modern Monarchy* Hodder & Stoughton 1988
5. Quoted in Anthony Mason, *The General Strike in the North East*, p. 66, University of Hull Publications, 1970

# Chapter 2 Depression, War and Revival

## Better times

The move to 'The Buildings' took place in 1936, coinciding with an upturn in the family's fortunes. The Depression, which had so ground everybody down following the General Strike, had come to an end. Demand for coal was improving, and wages were rising. The family was, in fact entering a 'golden period', which unfortunately in their case would be all too short-lived. The year 1937 brought the pithead baths, which meant not only that the men didn't need the tin bath, but also the kids could use them on Saturdays. And despite the netty still being outside, and the rest of the family still using the tin bath, Number 7 Brown's Buildings must have seemed like the proverbial palace. 'Cotia was one of the earlier pits to have baths, but it was their own welfare scheme that provided the money, not the owners, who only 'allowed' the men to put up the baths in the pit yard.

Number 7 was a two up two down old pit house, built in 1823, with walls of sandstone 15 inches thick. As Pete says, "This was no exaggeration, as the spuggies used to make their nests within the walls and waken us at sunrise with their chirping, which is a bloody early house in April or May." The new house was still crowded, no hot water and with everything done on the fire, but this was luxury compared with the previous one, and light years away from the huts where Pete, Doreen, and John had been born. Pete, the eldest, remembers these times very clearly.

> "This translated into the bike for me, and Doreen got a superior version of what was known as a fairy bike. Doreen couldn't believe that this piddlin' little bike was hers, as she was the second oldest. All thoughts of a benign Santa Claus left her for good! Another innovation that our improved finances brought was the wireless, or radio as it is now more commonly called. This enabled us not only to listen to more music, but it brought plays, comedy shows and talks into our house and our lives. The wireless was an Ecko, a black shiny gadget with a

semi-circular top and a gauze grid through which the sound emitted, typical of the period. It ran off lead-acid batteries that weighed a ton and were trickle-charged through the mains. It did sterling service because Pat and I were bloody glad of it when we were first married, many years later. For me the musical high spot of possessing the radio was sitting beside Dad on a Saturday and listening to Django Reinhardt and the Hot Club of France LIVE from Radio Paris, weekly. Even in those early days I was hooked on stringed instruments, particularly the guitar."

The music formed an important part of all the children's upbringing and Doreen remembers the radio, with Carson Robinson advertising Oxydol, the gramophone with its cowboy songs, and Saturday night outside the pub where the kids would stand outside listening to the men sing. "And you could tell it was nearly hoying out time as soon as Geordie Dalton got up to sing 'Sons of the Seas', and we said we'd better go home because we'll be in trouble." The men would sing anything, Uncle Reece was particularly good with nursery rhymes for example, but there was a pecking order. Even though Reece was 13 years older than his brother, he always gave precedence to him as character, singer, and general man's man. Although there had been a great improvement, miners were still the poor relatives to the rest of the community. But as Doreen says, she didn't know they were poor until she started at the secondary school in Chester-le-Street, where they met people from a different class.

The other improvement which took place at this time was the family's first holiday. It had taken years of Union battling to win the right to a whole week's holiday, which came in 1938. Miners were thrilled, even though the pay for that week was deducted piecemeal from their wages over the year! In the first year, they'd got no money, so, as Pete says, "Just to laze around for a whole seven days was great for the first year, but in '39 Pop resolved to have a proper holiday. After scrimping and saving the whole year, we were transported by lorry to Crimdon Dene campsite, near Hartlepool. We shared a hired tent with Uncle Ernie and his family and spent a whole week by the sea. It was a smidgin crushed inside the tent with ten bodies in it, but we thought we were figuratively farting on fine fabric. Crimdon could have been Cannes as far as we were concerned!"

1939 was also the start of the war that had been brewing in Europe. It didn't have much effect in the coalfields, especially during the 'phoney war', which lasted nearly all of the first year. Pitmen of course were exempted from the armed services, but teachers were not, so Pete found himself at the age of thirteen with a half-time education. This led to him tramping round the engineering firms and factories in the area looking for a job. He was absolutely determined not to go down the pit, although this was severely tested by some of his experiences. Two years into the war, Doreen also left school at fourteen and started at Walter Wilson's the grocers. Her job was to take the groceries, via a horse and cart, as was the custom in those days, to people who lived in outlying districts.

The war brought all kinds of uncertainty with it. In his family book, Pete says, "I once started to list all the jobs our young 'un has had in her life and gave up after fifteen. She would make the *Guinness Book of Records* if she could remember them all herself. From a humble delivery lass she progressed to Post Office clerk, fever hospital nurse, invoice clerk, factory nurse etc." Doreen confirms that the figure was 28 up to her marriage, and when pressed for the reasons for this, she admitted that as well as the social conditions of the time, she could sometimes be a bit of a stroppy employee, especially when it came to union rights and walkouts.

For many, the good times that came at the end of the '30s had come to an abrupt end. It had been a false dawn, the economy picking up only because of re-armament and the rush to war. Now there was rationing and air raids. The Elliotts, along with everybody else involved in Barley Mow, were poor, but times were particularly tough after Jack had been hospitalised during the war with irreversible damage to his spine. He was never able to work underground again, with the result that the family became the poorer for it, and were dependent on a ten-shilling voucher to be spent at the local Co-op. No biscuits, cakes, tinned fruit, sweeties, booze, or fags! Actually, they were all right for booze because Jack used to brew his own beer.

*On the mountain stands a lady,*
*Who she is I do not know,*
*She has lots of gold and silver,*
*All she wants is a nice young man.*
*So come in my Johnny, dear,*
*Johnny dear, Johnny dear,*
*So come in my Johnny, dear,*
*While I go out to play.*

# After the War

In 1945, when the war ended, the Elliott children were becoming adults, with Pete, now twenty, down to Len at twelve, all still living at home in Brown's Buildings. Still singing the family songs at home, whilst Dad and Uncle Reece sang at the pub.

Doreen again, "I remember we used to have family parties, if anybody got married, and me Uncle Jack, who was 'Gunner', (he was never anything else but 'Gunner'), he used to sit on top of the drawers, with a fiddle, and Joss Patterson, whose mother Aunty Maggie was an Elliott, he used to sit at the other end of the drawers, with a melodeon. He used to call it a home melodeon. Why, I do not know, we always said get your home melodeon out. And Granda 'Lanter' (Lance) had always played a home melodeon. You remember, the one who used to burst his bellas." (They might have had a model called the 'Home Melodeon' or it might have been a Hohner.)

They didn't sing many pit songs then, but preferred Frank Crumit songs, and the hit songs of the day. All the younger folk were into jazz in those days, and one of them was Bryan Henderson, a friend of Pete's and soon to be husband to Doreen. He tells of going down to London at the time of the Festival of Britain. "I remember going to London in the festival year, 1951, and going down this street, Tottenham Court Road I think it was. There was four or five of us. We got these eight records, all jazz, made at the Festival Hall. It was all big bands in those days. Being a cathedral city, Newcastle couldn't show films on Sunday night, so it was all live entertainment. You could fill the Odeon with the big bands."

Pete and his mate Bryan were part of a group who shared the growing interest in the jazz and blues coming out of America. Pete remembers,

> "Another activity we all did together was going to jazz concerts, traddy jazz being our favourite. By an arrangement with the Musicians' Union, British jazz outfits could bring over American bluesmen to share the bill with them. It was like having a dream come true, seeing and listening to those jazz legends I'd only been able to hear on record. By a quirk of English law at the time, live concerts could be put on in cinemas on a Sunday evening, but not films. As a result, large cinemas like the Odeon in Newcastle used to book big name British bands like Chris Barber and Humphrey Lyttleton."

The post-war period brought socialist policies to the country in abundance, including the nationalisation of the pits, water, electricity, gas and the railways, and also gave us the National Health Service. For the Elliotts, this should have been their Utopia, the promised land. These seismic shifts will be looked at in the next chapter, but meanwhile, on a local level, there were significant changes. This was a time when the Birtley League of Youth was started, and Pete Elliott gives a wonderful description of the way this, the music, and weekend holidays all melded into one. It was a great time for these young people.

> "Doreen, Len and I had helped form the South Birtley Labour Party League of Youth. Typical of political parties, you could be a 'youth' until twenty-seven years of age. In fact, I believe the Tories stretched it to thirty, but you'd expect those buggers to be slow developers. There were a real nice bunch of lads and lasses who joined with us, albeit from different backgrounds and standards of education. There were around ten of us in the L. of Y. and sometimes accompanied by courting partners and friends we had some great bank holidays together. I'm not sure of the chronological order of those holidays, but we went to Amble, Warkworth, Unthank, Whitburn, Allenheads and Crimdon Dene. I used to take my guitar along as we had no canned entertainment on holiday in those days, and many's the night of singing we had round the old sea-coal fire. One of our favourite songs was 'Just A-Wearying for You', and all the lasses, whether brought with us or acquired, would be misty-eyed and loving by the end.
>
> For the weekend at Warkworth we hired an old converted bus from Annie Lynn who lived up the street from us. It got pretty cold at night, (this was at Easter time), so we filled up the pot-bellied stove with coal to gently warm us through the night. Unfortunately the wind changed both direction and force, and a howling gale came belting under the door, into the stove and straight up the chimney. Lionel's brother Bryan (Henderson) and I, being the worrits in the party, woke up to a great roaring sound and a stove and three-quarters of the chimney bright red. We desperately tried to rouse the others, but they just snottered on while we lay wide awake all night, ready to drag them out if it took a-haad. The others were right of course, all that happened was that the bus got like a sauna.
>
> At Whitburn the lads were in a converted bus and the lasses in a converted ambulance. It was no mod-cons in those days, but we were young and daft and those weekends were a laugh a minute. We went camping at Crimdon and anticipated two modern fashions by more than fifteen years. We cultivated beards and wore long-peaked caps that we had to buy from a sports shop, sold as tennis caps. My Mam persuaded me that I looked like Bill Sykes and I shaved mine off, but

Bryan kept his full set right up to now and Len cultivated his into a Van Dyke. I was much later in growing mine."

Bryan, a mate of Pete's, was along for all the usual reasons, but most importantly for him and this story, it was on these jaunts that he met Doreen. He naturally started going round to the Elliotts' house in Brown's Buildings, and there he found a family that didn't just go to political meetings and the library, but were in a left-wing book club. Although Bryan came from a "posh house", with hot water and a tiled bathroom, he found the "damp, broken down hovel" that was Number 7 Brown's Buildings absolutely fascinating. It was always open house, the place where everybody dropped in, for crack, music, or whatever. And, of course, as well as Doreen and the politics, Bryan had a lot in common with Pete Elliott, particularly jazz. As he says, "They weren't run of the mill people. They were the centre of attention. Everybody sang, but they were more about personality and politics."

*"They weren't run of the mill people."*
**Bryan Henderson**

Not only that brought the youngsters together. They would go and hear the speakers in the town, standing and debating on all sorts of subjects.

"Before going to the concerts we used to go to the Bigg Market to hear the open-air speakers; political, religious, anti-religious, Lord's Day Observance Society, voting reformers etc. etc. One night a great hulk of a man who could he heard two streets away, (and there were no such things as outdoor mikes in those days), was ranting on about his holy-roller type of primitive religion. A little wee feller at the front kept heckling him about such points as whereabouts in your body was your soul, until the big bloke, crimson with rage, hollered at him, 'Listen brother, if Aa hadn't of been saved, Aa'd carry y' doon yon street and hoy y' strite ower the bridge inter the bloody Tyne.'"

They would also go to hear Jack Brighton speaking at the Sunday night Newcastle market, a bit like a Tyneside Speakers' Corner. Brighton, nicknamed 'The Atheist Bishop', was another denizen of Brown's Buildings, and for Pete was, "Apart from my parents, the main mentor of my youth. He had an exceptional intellect, and was an extremely skilled debater, who could demolish religious opponents with humour, caustic wit, and sheer force of logic. I often went to hear him debate, and was soon encouraged to ask questions, which meant that I learnt to overcome my shyness at speaking in public at an early age."

Doreen in particular found the whole atmosphere of the political occasions very exciting, especially the heckling. Jack's nickname derived from the fact that he had achieved great status with the atheists in the area, who were identified by their joining the Secular Society. Doreen reckons there were about 12 atheist families in Birtley at the time, not all of them pitmen. She also agrees that there was a strong link between atheism and communism. If there were bad times, the government did not help workers, not it seems did the church.

Their politics and character would have made the Elliotts something special in their own community, somewhat unorthodox, but it was the singing that really made them stand out. Singing was definitely in the blood and would burst out on every occasion in every location. For instance, on Sunday mornings the men would go to the Pelaw dog track, which had a bar little more than a hut. It opened at noon with the bar packed with pints partly pulled, ready and waiting. A big swill for two hours, just like the tales you've heard from Australia. Importantly for our story, if you sang, you got drink vouchers. So needless to say, Jack, Reece

*Jack, Em, Len and John outside Brown's Buildings*

and John were much in evidence. (Bryan found the sheer quantity of drink far too much, but is our faithful chronicler, and incidentally had his wedding reception there.)

Doreen tells of one occasion when her father and her cousin Joss went camping for the weekend on the beach at Frenchman's Creek at South Shields. Joss, still with us in his eighties, was a great patter man, very funny, just like Jack. He was a good pitman, a 'composite worker', one of those who were regarded as the best men, who could turn their hand to anything down the pit. When the pit closed, he took a job sweeping at a local factory, but he lasted no more than a week. "I'm not a wife, pushing a bloody brush around all day." Whilst away, they proceeded to go busking, with mouth organ, melodeon, and of course, voices. This was at a time when a busker was regarded as almost 'unclean', and Em was horrified. "Did anybody I know see you?"

## John, Nan, and Bill

By 1950, John Elliott had married Nan, the "bonny Gateshead lass" who brought songs from these foreign parts, and moved to the Ford area, where Gateshead Stadium is now located. At that time, John and Len were in engineering, and had not followed Jack and Reece down the pit. But, as John's son Bill recalls, his father had started at 'Cotia as a fitter, and had a colliery house at Fatfield. Bill's description of his childhood shows how little material things had changed for mining folk. He had been born in Em and Jack's sitting room at Number 7 Brown's Buildings and had grown up in an 18th Century stone cottage, which he says was "great for a kid, but a nightmare for me mam". There was the tin bath, the outside netty, the cobbled street, and their garden was by the River Wear, with the remains of the old staithes. The Sunderland keelmen had in the past stayed overnight if they'd had too much to drink, and the house had at one time been a brewery. The area is now part of Washington, with houses and staithes long gone, but in those days there were fields all around. John would walk to the pit at 'Cotia, with his dad walking the same distance from Barley Mow from the opposite direction. In common with the other Elliotts, John and Nan sang around the house, but the family sessions all happened at Jack and Em's.

Although Pete, John and Doreen had a dozen kids between them, the only one that has got involved with folk music, or even music in general, is John's son Bill Elliott. As the first grandbairn to Jack and Em, the family had lots of opinions as to his name. Jack suggested Jack, to which Em immediately retorted, "Why, every Tom, Dick and Harry is called Jack." As Pete said, the gaffe passed into family folklore.

As a lad in the 1950s, Bill would bike over to his granddad's on a Sunday afternoon, where the whole family would gather for tea. It would all happen in the kitchen cum living room where the instruments were kept. They would sings songs, and then the instruments might get the occasional strum, but they often listened to records, mainly by American folk singers such Jimmy Rodgers, Rambling Jack Elliott, the Carter family, and Cousin Emmy and the kinfolk. There were blues singers like Big Bill Broonzy and Sonny Terry and Brownie McGhee. Bill also remembers watching Newcastle play in the 1955 Cup Final on the black and white telly at his granddad's (they were the only ones to have a telly then). John's family later moved to Number 25 Brown's Buildings. Doreen and Bryan were living at Fatfield then, and eventually they also moved to Brown's Buildings. Fate was at work here; the family couldn't keep away from the place!

Although he was taken along to family gigs at other clubs, such as the Bridge in Newcastle and Shotley Bridge, it was not until after Jack's death that Bill was old enough to go to the family's club regularly. He particularly remembers the Christmas nights, which usually had the Sunderland mummers (Mike Elliott, Eric Maxwell, and others). He did some family songs, but also his own stuff, particularly Irish songs he'd heard from the Fury brothers. The Furys gave him a lifelong love of Irish music, but he learnt guitar from Pete, using his granddad's old instrument. Bill and his wife Roz are still active singers on Tyneside, with their own band.

*"Why, every Tom, Dick and Harry is called Jack"*

**Em, on the occasion of finding a name for her first grandson**

# The Others

The year 1953 was memorable for the Queen's coronation, the climbing of Everest, and the discovery of the structure of DNA. But more importantly for the Elliotts, the other three of Jack and Em's kids got married, all in the same year. Like many other working-class families the Elliotts saw the break-up of traditional communities with the explosion of urban growth in the '50s and '60s.

Pete moved to Newcastle, where his wife Pat came from, and continued to see his dad for a pint each week. They were moved from central Newcastle to the new town of Killingworth on the northern edge of the city as part of the new social housing and relocation programmes of the times. Built as an idyllic new town with futuristic walkways and open spaces, and car-free, 'Killi' rapidly became a byword for bad news. As Pete says, the design meant that the police couldn't get in to sort out the trouble-makers, and whereas when they moved in you had to have three references to get a house, within a few years you had to have a criminal record to get out! Lots of people in the know saw the 1996 TV series 'Our Friends in the North' as being based there. This play, set in the '60s and '70s, used the themes of corruption and the abuse of power against the background of cultural change in the North East. Still touring nationally as a stage play, 'Friends' remains a potent icon on Tyneside. The notorious tower blocks at Killingworth were a recognisable example of the urban blight of '60s inner city development, echoed in towns and cities throughout the country. As elsewhere, there were celebrations in Newcastle when they were blown up.

Like many working-class families they experienced the worst of these initiatives, and they met a lot of violence there. Bruce, the eldest son, was stabbed by a neighbour, who was then attacked by Pat with a frying pan. Pete had two nervous breakdowns, largely brought on by living there with such a big family on not much money, but it took them till 1977 before they managed to get a nice house in Washington, which was also, of course, back near the rest of the family, and near to the community they knew and recognised.

After a long courtship, Bryan Henderson whisked Doreen off to the registry office. This is Doreen's version.

> "We got married in November, 1953, we had our wedding feast in Em's sitting room, and yes we did have ham and pease pud. Then we all went to the dogs! Pelaw dog race track (scene of the big Sunday beer swill described earlier)."

However, the newlyweds had to catch the bus to go on their honeymoon to Allenheads.

> "A cottage on the moors, never been used since the summer, and it was now the end of November! The worst honeymoon we ever had, and not a bus until the Tuesday. I went to bed like Nanook of the North. My frilly nighty never saw the light of day."

The newlyweds moved into Number 7 Brown's Buildings along with Pete and Pat, who had married in the June, and taken the back bedroom.

(This was after Len had married in the March and had managed to get two rooms at Chester-le-Street.)

There were so many people living in Brown's Buildings around this time. It had been a palace when they moved in as kids 17 years before, but now they were grown up and bringing partners with them! Despite the crowding the crucial benefit of this was that the family continued to sing whenever they got together, and that was frequently. Eventually of course, they all found places, and had their own homes.

*Comes a little blue-bird through my window,*
*Comes a little blue-bird through my door,*
*Comes a little bluebird through my window*
*Hi diddle om pom day.*
*Take a little step and dance in the corner,*
*Take a little step and dance on the floor,*
*Take a little step and dance through the window,*
*Hi diddle om pom day.*

# '50s music and early folk clubs

It's hard for younger people to realise the straitjacket that was popular music in the 1950s. It was tenors and sopranos singing anodyne pop music and stuff from the shows, Alma Cogan and Edmund Hockeridge, *Oklahoma* and *South Pacific*. American Tin Pan Alley dominated, and English traditional music was at its lowest ebb. Thankfully, there were pockets where it still thrived, and the Birtley Elliotts were one of those pockets.

As we saw earlier, Jack and Pete had catholic tastes in music, enjoying and playing jazz and blues, as well as listening to opera and classical music. No style of music was excluded but only quality was included! However, the whole family were singing the 'home grown' songs, nothing to do with records and radio and films, and effectively keeping a bastion of English traditional song going through those dark days.

Then in 1956 came liberation, albeit still involving American music, with Rock 'n' Roll from America, and Skiffle from Lonnie Donegan. It is clear that Donegan had much more impact on some people than Elvis, and through him they were led into folk music a few years later. Martin Carthy and your author are two examples, and it looks like the Elliotts were the same. This interest was natural for a family that sang together so much. For the first time in living memory, pop music had songs that said something, some of them even political. For Pete, skiffle was a natural extension of his interest in jazz, especially Django Reinhardt's music, which he and Jack used to listen to on Radio Paris before the war. They started a skiffle group, a skiffle group led by a man of 48, hardly typical of the genre!

> "Our lugs clagged up against the set. I wish that I could boast that my skill was within a million miles of Django's, but it was good enough for the rhythm section of a skiffle group. With a couple of mates from work, one of whom was a helluva good jazz and swing piano player and could double on guitar, the other able to get by on washboard or tea-chest bass, myself on guitar and rhythm mouth organ, then sharing washboard and chest, and Dad on his array of instruments, we formed the Jack Elliott Skiffle Group. Our audiences were pensioners' associations all round the Birtley area and we played and sang for a cup of tea and a wad. I can say with all honesty that although we have performed all over the country, those nights doing folk, old-time popular songs and jazz music for appreciative pensioners were some of the best nights ever. And if Dad were here I'm sure he'd agree."

They were getting a bit of a reputation in Barley Mow, according to Doreen. Years after this period, Doreen remembers a neighbour, Bill Jeff, saying "It's about time you were discovered. We used to leave our doors and windows open on a Sunday when you were singing. And Daisy next door said exactly the same thing." But they must have wondered sometimes what was going on. Up to nine lads would come in with instruments, singing for corned beef sandwiches served up by the indefatigable Em. Other groups of people came round just to play darts, or maybe just for the crack. The first 'all-purpose drop-in facility'.

The early folk club scene had been developing for some time. Even before the magic year of 1956, there were folk clubs in London, Bradford, and Manchester at least. These were largely doing American songs, although Bert Lloyd and Ewan MacColl were pioneering British songs in London. Both these men were self-declared communists who saw folk music to some extent as an expression of the class struggle, and together they built upon the growing interest in folk music derived from the popularity of skiffle.

MacColl had been born to Scots parents and had graduated from radical theatre back to music where his socialist values emerged in political songs. Lloyd, a committed Communist since the 1930s, had worked around the world from whaling fleets to Australian sheep ranches and had returned to be active in the Workers' Educational Association (WEA). But both were collecting traditional songs, singing them, and starting to issue records, particularly through Topic Records, which had its roots in the Communist Party. This company was then the only record company issuing albums of traditional music, both American and British, and played a crucial role in the '60s Revival. Although it shed its political origins some time ago, it has continued to this day to be the foremost folk music label in the world.

In 1958 the first folk club started on Tyneside. To start with, it was a special night at the Jazz Club (much as skiffle had started as a special subset of British jazz bands like Chris Barber and Ken Collier). Louis Killen, a cabinetmaker by trade, had come into contact with Ewan MacColl while working down south, and was singing folk songs in the mid-1950s at meetings of the Heritage Society at Oxford University. Back on Tyneside in 1957, he started attending the Marlborough Street Jazz Club in Newcastle, where he saw a young lad called Johnny Handle doing a spot at the interval singing blues numbers. When Johnny was away from the club for a spell, up steps Louis to fill the slot, and you can imagine the discussions when Johnny returned! Thankfully, both men set aside their egos and collaborated. This event led to the pre-eminence of Tyneside and the North East in the coming Folk Revival which continues to this day.

After a few weeks running a night at the Jazz Club, they opened their own folk club, called Folksong and Ballad, in February 1958 at 'The Sink', the universal nickname for the Barrass Bridge Hotel. And the man who got Membership Number 2 was none other than Jack Elliott, the pitman from Birtley, then in his early fifties. Jack volunteered to sing, entranced the crowd with two of his favourite songs, 'Little Chance' and 'Old Johnny Bucca', and became a legend overnight. Although he and Pete were already singing political songs, and some American ones, they realised that the pit songs were theirs, and that people wanted to hear them. From then on, Jack scoured his own memory, and visited pitmen that he'd known from the singing sessions in the local pubs and clubs. He was also given songs by local folklorists Frank Rutherford, a Durham librarian and collector, and Walter Toyn, the local headmaster with an interest in dialect songs. So when the likes of Ewan MacColl and Bert Lloyd came a-visiting, he had a fascinating repertoire of local pit songs.

# The Big Hewer

Ewan MacColl, the co-architect of the Folk Revival, came to the North East in 1961 with a specific purpose. He had by then produced several of the ground-breaking 'radio ballads', starting with *The Ballad of John Axon*, the story of a Lancashire engine driver's self-sacrifice which prevented a trainload of schoolchildren being killed, then *Song of a Road*, about the making of the London to Yorkshire motorway (the M1), and going on with *Singing the Fishing*, about the herring fishing industry. The man behind the radio ballads was the BBC producer Charles Parker, who commissioned MacColl to write them, and who in turn involved the young American folk singer Peggy Seeger to direct the music. They would record working people talking about their work and their life, and put this 'actuality' together with songs written by MacColl based on what he'd heard from the contributors. ('Actuality' was BBC parlance for using a recording of a real working person expressing thoughts about his or her work, rather than putting the words into the mouth of an actor.) There had been a constant struggle with the BBC hierarchy over the radio ballads. Despite their universal critical acclaim and the winning of the Italia Prize for radio documentaries, they were very costly to produce, almost as expensive as TV programmes, at a time when radio audiences were dwindling. The sheer personality, imagination, doggedness, and dedication of Parker in particular kept the show on the road. He also cut down on the expense by working almost 24-hour days in the studio, something that might easily have got him the sack!

By now, the three people, MacColl, Seeger, and Parker were working as a unit, and were thinking about their fourth programme. Ewan, writing in his autobiography *Journeyman* (1), explains how the theme was decided. "For over a year, Peggy and I had worked for the National Coal Board film unit, one of the largest and most productive documentary-film units in Europe. I had written songs and music for the *Mining Review*, a magazine-type film programme, which was shown regularly in cinemas throughout the coalfields, and our visits to the coalfields had whetted our appetites. We told Charles, 'It's coal-miners or nothing.'"

They had first gone to South Wales and then Nottinghamshire, and were now ready for the North East. What MacColl was after was articulate pitmen who could talk about their work. He already knew Louis Killen and through him met Johnny Handle, then working as a surveyor at the Rising Sun Colliery in Wallsend. Johnny himself gave MacColl some good material for the programme, including some very thoughtful, even philosophical observations, or 'actuality'.

> "The silence in the pit, it's like infinity...or the bottom of the ocean. It's peaceful, and yet...it's sometimes frightening. You could be driven to panic with it, I think. You've never known absolute blackness, there's always stars and a moon. But there, there's nothing. And you can feel this pressing on you, the darkness."

Johnny Handle had tried to get songs from pitmen, but with little success. Every time he fixed up with a likely singer to get songs from them, in such rugged places as Stanley and Ashington, they'd get dressed up in a suit and sing him 'Cara Mia Mine' or hits from the shows. So much so that it drove him to write some excellent songs about the pits and local customs, such as 'Farewell to the Monty'. This was about the closing of the Montagu pit at West Denton, Newcastle in 1959, an event that caused both bad feeling and nostalgia in the community, and the song later became very popular in the early stages of the Revival. Johnny wrote the words, and Louis Killen gave it its fine evocative tune. However, Johnny knew that Jack Elliott was special, and promptly sent MacColl off to Birtley.

When MacColl met the Elliotts, it must have been like all his birthdays coming at once. I think that in Ewan's mind, the working man had been endowed with dignity, fierce pride, great honesty and openness, a keen sense of the unfairness of the capitalist system, and a political drive to replace it with a fair, humane, and sensitive brave new world in which the workers would be at the same level as the bosses. In doing this, it would be the community culture that would make it possible, and songs, particularly those of protest, would put the fairy on the top of this idealised Christmas tree. The Elliotts, although far from typical of their community, had quite simply fulfilled all his dreams.

Accordingly, Ewan, Charles and Peggy became the first of several teams to set up their cumbersome recording gear in Brown's Buildings. During the course of a week in March 1961, they recorded their 'actuality', mainly from Jack and Reece Elliott, pitmen all their lives. As we saw earlier, there is wonderful material here about the traditional games the miners played, the terrible conditions, wriggling through a 16-inch seam, the dangers of roof fall and water in the pit, Jack's two accidents, and living conditions at home.

A great deal of this was used unedited in the ensuing radio ballad, *The Big Hewer*. The programme had as its theme the pit's superman, the one who outshone all his mates, could fill two tubs to the others' one, and hold up the dodgy roof with his back. MacColl had come across this in several of the coalfields, and thought it a myth, a John Henry figure. However, there were real men who were like this, and most pits had one. As with every job, there was always somebody who could do it better or faster than the rest. Jack and Reece had known Bob Towers, who came from a family of exceptionally big men, and one of the delights of the radio ballad is Jack and Reece describing him, with the sort of comic exaggeration of everyday conversation.

Jack: "This Towers, Bob Towers. He was a big man, strong. Oooh, he was as good as two men, no doubt about that, he was as good as two men. He didn't even have to set the stand, the drillin' stand, between the top and the bottom of the face. He used to put his foot in his hand to drill a hole. He kept hisself for the job."

Reece: "He was a big man, could you imagine? 18 stone. That was his weight. No fat at all. Eighteen stone of man, and no fat. They called him the County Durham Big Hewer. You never saw any little Big Hewers in the County Durham. They were big men. Big strong men."

Jack: "He used to eat three chops while he was WAITIN' of his dinner, if his dinner wasn't ready. Three chops. Pork chops, while he was waitin' of it. An' he was in bed at 9 o'clock at night, everybody was in bed at 9, so he could get his sleep. And he had a gallowa and trap, that's a pony and trap, to take him to work, and it was there, when he came out the pit, to bring him home again. He never had a marra, because there was nobody could keep up with him. He was always on his own, down the pit."

Reece: "And the butcher cart had to be at his door. Fresh meat. Fresh meat every day. He could eat a pound of steak. Every day."

Jack: "Man and a half."

Reece: "By, he was a big man."

Jack: "He always had a putter to hisself. He was like a machine when he was hewin. He was regular as a clock, you could hear him going 'pick pick pick'. Never stopped."

Reece: "Never stopped."

Jack: "He was finished before the machines, I mean it was all handwork in those days. Hand drillin' even."

Reece: "He came from Bowburn to here, Harraton, (Jack: "There wasn't any transfer fees in those days"), and he finished at Birtley E pit. Pride in his work, big man, big family."

Jack: "Aye, that was the Towers."

Jack's wonderful language here exaggerates for the story, but Towers was definitely real. The men of the family were enormous, with a bit of a reputation. (A later member of the family, the amateur boxer Liddle Towers, died in police custody in a notorious case in the 1970s.) The notes to *The Big Hewer* suggest that MacColl thought the man's surname was a symbol (as in tower of strength). Actually, it's quite a common name in the area. As Doreen says, "you couldn't hoy a brick without hittin' a Towers", and there are still at least two of them living in Birtley. Don Stokoe, one of the Birtley all-time regulars, a major player in the Elliotts' story, and the son of a pitman from mid-Durham, says his dad talked about *The Big Hewer*, and was talking about the same man. Bob Towers had originally been at Bowburn pit but had moved to 'Cotia, the Elliotts' pit, and Don's dad also had the tale about the three pork chops waiting for his dinner.

Other legends in the Durham coalfield included Tempest from Herrington, and Tommy Roseberry, the "Big Putter". Of course, these were men who thrived in the days before the mechanical cutters were introduced in the 1920s, when your rate of pay was determined by how fast you could work with a pick and shovel. In the conversation above, Reece says, "They called him the County Durham Big Hewer", a phrase MacColl could hardly resist. One of the things the brothers commented on regarding Bob Towers is the accuracy and rhythm of his pick as it hit the coal. "Like a ticking clock," says one of them. This sound was incorporated into *The Big Hewer* script, an aspect of MacColl's cleverness at this work. Early in the radio ballad, we hear Jack's voice describing this, then the sound of the "tap tap tap" of the pick, which is gradually joined by some accompaniment on drumsticks, the music to the title song '*The Big Hewer*', and then Ewan sings the verse:

*"Three Hundred Years we've hewed at the coal by hand, Go Down!*
*In the pits of Durham and East Northumberland, Go Down!*
*Been gassed and burnt and blown asunder, many more times than I can number*
*Hewin' the coal, away in the hole, Go Down!"*

This technique was pointed out to me by Bill Elliott, who, in common with many others, regards the man as a genius. The programme was extremely clever in its production techniques, and is still as vibrant now as it was nearly 50 years ago.

Jack and Reece also sing 'Celebrated Working Man' in the programme, which was unusual for the radio ballads, which normally only used songs written specially by MacColl, a testament to the quality of the material and the people of the North East. However, the notes do not name the Elliott brothers, a serious omission I feel. The programme makers came to Durham after South Wales and Nottinghamshire, where they had already got some splendid material, and were only six weeks from completion.

Somehow the Elliott miners added something extra, which simply had to be included. The programme had been planned for nearly a year with the title *The Collier's Rant*, but within a week of the interview with Reece and Jack on 14th April, Charles Parker was informing the BBC programmers that it had a new name. The programme had its title, its theme, and its key song, '*The Big Hewer*'. It is also interesting to see the draft scripts for the programme, with alterations showing how the Elliotts' conversation had been inserted in preference to actuality from other coalfields. In another instance Reece's words had been typed up in an 'anglicised' form, but then this was replaced by the exact original words. Their conversation lived, it had a raw power that came from their experience. The dialect was an important part of this, of course, but I think they were special as well. In writing this book, I found exactly the same. When I tried summarising their talk in my own words, and then compared it with the original, there was no contest.

Bill and Doreen Elliott remember clearly how the whole family, bairns and all, gathered round the wireless in Brown's Buildings on 18th August 1961 to listen to the broadcast of *The Big Hewer*. Imagine the pride they felt. And, of course, the broadcast introduced them to the growing number of folk song enthusiasts up and down the country. The Elliotts had arrived. The family's reaction to the programme, notably including the pitmen, was "a bloody good programme", "great", "true", "the best programme yet" (2). The press was unanimous in its praise. Here is one comment by a correspondent who attended the press preview in London, "It grips your imagination by the scruff of the neck, thrusts it deep into the bowels of the earth, and brings it back sore of limb and gasping for fresh air."

The meeting of Ewan and Peggy with the Elliotts led to a friendship that would last for life, certainly between Peggy and Doreen, and there is little doubt that politics was as important as the songs in attracting both parties to each other.

Peggy remembers the kitchen, with Jack holding court in an intriguing atmosphere, quite different from anything she'd met before. "The Elliotts were all so equal, and I was so green. Ewan did the talking, and I ran the machine," she says. (This magnificent lady is now in her seventies, and still doing solo concerts in places like the Sage at Gateshead.) She also observed that the men were 'more equal' (my phrase) in that whilst Ewan was talking she'd keep quiet, and when Jack was talking, the Elliott women would keep quiet. In those days, even women as sparky, enlightened, and freethinking as these seemed still under that spell of male dominance.

So enthusiastic was MacColl about his 'find' that in an unguarded moment he said their speech was "pure Chaucer". There was much amusement about this from the Elliotts behind their hands, despite him being an important and impressive personality and big in the media. (It now looks as though he was probably referring to the 'pitmatic' in Alexander Barrass's *Pitman's Social Neet*, of which more anon; but for most outsiders the Elliotts talked the same 'lingo'. (3))

Some people say he manipulated Jack Elliott into getting songs, telling the family that they were special people, that they were now "traditional singers", to an extent that in the opinion of some people it started to go to some of their heads for a short spell. In Louis Killen's opinion, Ewan politicised their songs (they of course needed no politicisation of their beliefs). But the Elliotts have never seen it this way. Ray Fisher puts it another way. Ewan had "stoked the fire", bringing to the fore feelings that were already there. As a result of meeting him, they understood more about the bigger system, rather than just relating their sense of injustice to their own situation. Colin Ross, commenting on their singing at the club, saw more a pride in being working men than being political agitators. Their independence was kept throughout, whatever the outside world wanted to think.

# The Folkways LP

During their time in Birtley, Ewan and Peggy actually went down the pit, knees and elbows in the seam. Peggy comments that it was very scary, but she felt that she had to be especially brave to show that a woman could also take it. Although they had come up for the radio ballad actuality, they had not expected to hear so many fine songs. It seems they had recognised something very important here, an 'industrial family' who were singing kids' game songs, two hundred-year-old local pit songs, and Child Ballads. The like had never been heard, and it had to be recorded. Within a matter of weeks, they returned to Brown's Buildings to record the family's songs and conversation, which resulted in an album which many regard as the most important one of the British Folk Revival. It was called *The Elliotts of Birtley: A musical portrait of a Durham mining family*, and was released on the American label Folkways the following year (4).

Folkways had been set up in 1948 by Moses Asch to record and document sound not only from America, but the whole world. The Elliotts'

The Elliotts of Birtley *LP released in Britain in 1967*

record was an early foray into England. Their albums were lavishly produced, with copious background notes on the songs and the singers' background, of a quality that British records did not have. The Elliotts' album was well up to that standard, with a heady mixture of individual songs, groups of kids' songs and nursery rhymes, and the most fascinating chat from Jack, Reece, and the family. It remains an exemplar of how to present traditional music in context, and it set a standard of production for the whole of the Folk Revival.

The only negative aspect of the LP was that it was only issued in the States, and so did not have an immediate impact here. It could be got, but only if you were in the know, and determined. It took another five years before it appeared in Britain on the Transatlantic 'Extra' label, by which time Jack was dead. A great pity, but by then the family had established themselves worldwide, even without the LP. However, that was only with the folk people. Their neighbours and the working-class communities of the North East had not seen it, but here is what Dave Douglass, a friend of the Elliotts and prominent Union man, had to say about the album.

> "The impact of that early Folkways recording *The Elliotts Of Birtley* was profound. It was a treasure of Northern culture, a statement of community, of class and of unending struggle against social and

economic injustice. The voices were 'wor' voices, the voices of 'wor folk' – real folk. The first record me and my Dad ever enjoyed together, when all else had been features of an all-consuming generation war. The class and the culture of folk like the Elliotts finally brought home to me that this dad of mine was one of those workers I waxed so lyrical about, a lifelong miner and trade unionist. He had appeared only as the enemy generation imposing authority and restricting freedoms. That record got me listening to The Elliotts as spokespersons for their generation."

A couple of years later, in the summer of 1963, Bert Lloyd, the other architect of the Folk Revival, paid a visit to the Elliott family, mainly to record songs and a discussion for a programme, *Songs of the Durham Miners*, which was broadcast on the BBC Third Programme (now Radio 3). Remarkable to find such a highbrow station taking a working-class heritage seriously, and a clear sign that the burgeoning folk movement was a broad church encompassing everything from protest songs from America, countless Bob Dylan imitators and those exploring their own musical heritage. A lot of the songs he heard from the Elliotts also appeared in the second edition of his book *Come All Ye Bold Miners*, a book that was very important to the repertoires of the many new singers joining the growing folk movement, and which is discussed later in this book (5). An interesting aspect of this visit is the immortal comment by ex-pit deputy and local songwriter of political songs Jock Purdon that "We did not know we sang folk songs till Mr. Lloyd came up here and told us we did."

> *"We did not know we sang folk songs till Mr. Lloyd came up here and told us we did."* **Jock Purdon**

# The First Gig

The time came when the Elliotts were considered important enough to be asked to sing for somebody else, i.e. be guests at the only folk club then operating in the North East. In the spring of 1962, some time after the MacColl visit and *The Big Hewer*'s broadcast, the Elliotts were asked to sing at the Folksong and Ballad, Newcastle (from now on referred to as 'The Bridge', whatever its venue). It still surprises Doreen how matter-of-fact they were about it. "Me Dad come in and said we've all got to go through there and sing our songs. It wasn't a booking, nobody called it a booking, and we said 'Oh Great!' Not a flicker of nerves or anything. It was absolutely amazing. Oh, we're ganna go and sing, in Newcastle, you know, that was it. Well what we're gonna sing? Well, what we normally sing. And that was the rehearsal. That was all there was to it. There we were, round the table, ten or twelve of us. If we sang one song each, that would be the whack. But we thought it was great. Mi dad did more, like. He was the chairman, the raconteur. He always led the band. The lads used to say Jack's as good as his master and you doff your cap to nobody. We never had any fear, we didn't think 'we're going to sing in public.' Mi dad said we're going to enjoy it, and we did."

*"What'll we sing?*
*Wae, what we always sing!"*

The Newcastle club was at its third venue by then, the Liberal Club, a rambling old-fashioned place where the waiters wore "Basil Brush waistcoats", as Ed Pickford described them. There must have been at least nine Elliotts, up on the stage in a line like the Last Supper, with Jack doing most of the songs and the rest perhaps one each. It was a significant night for them of course, but there was another group of people there that night, Fra', Len, and Ed, lads still at school in Washington who were into rock-climbing, singing, and socialism in a big way. For them, this was their first folk club and their first sighting of the Elliotts. One of them, Iain 'Fra' Fraser, says, "it was like a book being opened". For Fra, these were the songs of working people, with work and song combined, not like in a book or a record.

Ed Pickford, famous later as a singer and songwriter, had mixed feelings about the people running the club, but was fascinated by the rawness and energy of the guests. They both felt an instant kinship, and started regularly to visit the Elliotts' houses in Birtley where they got crack, politics, tea, and songs. To this day they feel like one of the family. Though both of these lads were of working-class background, and fiercely political, they'd never seen anything quite like this. The third member of this gang who fell under the spell of the Elliotts was Len Wilson, sadly no longer with us, and it is no surprise that on the opening night of Birtley Club, 7th May 1962, again there were nine Elliotts, these three lads, and less than half a dozen others.

*"It was like a book being opened."*
**Fra Fraser on seeing the family for the first time.**

# Private Faces

Charles Parker, the producer of *The Big Hewer* and the other radio ballads, had a colleague at the BBC studios in Birmingham who had moved from radio into television, and was interested in politically slanted films of ordinary working people. The Elliotts fitted this bill perfectly, and so he too made the trip to Barley Mow and recorded material for a BBC TV programme called *Private Faces*. His visit is remembered very vividly and affectionately by Doreen Elliott. His name was Philip Donnellan, and on the surface he did not seem to be what you'd expect for such a calling. His accent was "posher than posh", and when you listen to his interviews with the family, the contrast is mighty. The family of course mocked his accent, but it was all done with great affection, and they all got on like a house on fire. For Doreen and Bryan in particular he and his wife Jill became lifelong friends, and they paid several visits to Birtley "for holidays". Plummy-voiced and upper class Donnellan might have been, but when it came to film-making he was ruthless, and in his ability to get messages over, he was first class. The programme he made of the family in 1962 is in a class of its own.

The family was no newcomer to the media, what with the radio ballad and the LP, but it seems that they'd already enjoyed film stardom. The film starts with John and Len Elliott fixing a broken pump in the pit, a scene which came from the NCB series *Mining Review*, which was then regularly shown at the cinema as a short before the main film. The family of course got a free trip to the pictures when that was shown at the Odeon in Newcastle. Doreen Elliott was also the subject of another of these films, called *A Miner's Daughter*.

Donnellan then leaves the subjects of the film to talk in a natural way about their jobs and the community life. It's mostly Jack and Em, with Jack talking about his first day at the pit, the 1926 Strike and the hardship that came with that, and both of them making great philosophical and political observations. Em "would love to travel, but the chances were nil. Good things should be shared and enjoyed, not just by the favoured few." She thought, "High Society need educating ... appallingly ignorant about life. The middle classes have lace curtains and kipper dinners...all show." Jack talks about his atheism. But it's Em who stresses the importance of ballads and folk songs. "Pop is a romantic, a knight in shining armour, it talks about being in love, not loving. Moon in June doesn't tell the real story." In the last scene, Jack sits astride a chair, saying little, but letting John, Pete, and Len lead a great discussion of the importance of community in the pit village, philosophy, and politics in a virile, articulate, and highly knowledgeable manner. At that time ordinary voices were not usually heard or given the opportunity to express themselves in such a way.

Pete: "I've detected in the last few months that miners are fearful of a return to hard times again. The NCB has been soulless in closing a mine and practically killing the community spirit, which is the essence of mining, this close-knit society, and it's destroying it."

John: "In a pit village you get the majority of the men, possibly nine tenths of them working at the pit, the same pit, and the fortunes of that colliery affect the fortunes of practically everybody in that village. If the pit's doing badly, the village is doing badly. So folk share the hard times. If the pit's doing well, then they enjoy that. Now if they close the pit and they go out to various industries, you get the picture, where one industry's doing badly, which'll affect perhaps a tenth of the village. But the other nine tenths are doing all right, and they say 'Well, it's hard lines like, but we're OK.'"

Pete: "I think this feeling of belongin', of a continuity with the past, a feeling of 'this is your kind', this is what we're losing, and this idea of the world becoming smaller. But is it? Do we feel neighbours with say France? I know I don't. Not the sort of neighbourliness that Pop was talking about. Mind, it has its disadvantages, with folk walking into your house all the time without even knocking. But this feeling that if things go wrong, your next door neighbour will stand by you."

Len: "I think this is something that's been lost. What should happen is, you should start with a small community, go out to a big community, go out to your country, go out to the next country, but that's not happened. The neighbours in the big cities don't know each other."

Pete: "You can take this village, this community and build it to a universal community and build it to incorporate the whole universe then."

The film ends with some pithy comments on class. The sons are happy to be working-class, whereas Jack hates the word, thinking himself a "working man", and Pete typically takes things further. "What people mean by working-class is lower class, but I consider myself to be working-class, which is the top class!"

The great pity about this splendid documentary is that the 'highups' at the BBC thought that it was not the sort of thing they were after, and refused to schedule it. Too left-wing, too anti-religious, it was not seen, even by the family, until well after Jack's death. Fortunately, there was some redress when Donnellan made the later film *Death of a Miner*, which did get shown, and included in it a lot of the scenes from *Private Faces*. The second film is discussed in Chapter 3.

*We will bring you bread and wine*
*Ee, ee i-over*
*We will bring you bread and wine*
*We are the Roman soldiers*

*We don't want your bread and wine,*
*We are the English soldiers.*

*You must send your captain now,*
*We are the Roman soldiers.*

*We will send our captain now,*
*We are the English soldiers.*

*We've got your Roman soldiers.*

# The Club

Before the Birtley folk club started, the only regular folk club in the North East was Folksong and Ballad, then at the Liberal Club, and about to move to the Bridge Hotel in Newcastle. There the residents sat on the stage ("the platform") and monopolised the night, only allowing floor singers of the highest quality. There is no doubt that the drive for quality that Johnny Handle and Louis Killen had was what gave the North East its early lead in the Folk Revival, and the club spawned several professional folk musicians as well as the High Level Ranters. Johnny also makes the point that in the early days, volunteers from the floor would do the same song every week, which was boring, whereas the residents actively learnt new songs to sing at the club. The down side was that they got a reputation for elitism and discouragement of other performers. Even if you were allowed to sing, the "platform" behind the singer was intimidating to many, even people like Ed Pickford. By now, a number of people were coming round to the Elliotts' houses for a chat and a sing, and it became a natural next step to start a club.

Doreen takes up the story,
"A meeting was held at Number 7 Brown's Buildings round about the middle of March 1962, to find out if we thought we could start a folk club. We had never considered it, but it was Ewan MacColl who suggested it, and as the Newcastle Folksong and Ballad Club closed for the summer and it was the only club in existence at the time, we decided to give it a go. We then had to decide on venue, policy etc so Pete, Jack, Em, John, Tess Stobbart (a lad from the back lane who was a keen singer and worked at 'Cotia), Malcolm Henderson who was only there for the crack (I think as he never came to the folk club), and myself. It was decided that a Wednesday was a neither nowt or summat night. Nobody had much money left, so Wednesday seemed perfect. I was elected treasurer and secretary. We thought that the Barley Mow Workingmen's Club would be the venue, Dad being a founder member etc. We could have the room for free, which was a big plus so the first meeting was two weeks later."

And so, with everything decided, they went ahead with the first night.
"The format was a singaround, no embargos on origins of songs and all instruments welcomed, an admission charge of 1 shilling (5p), students and unemployed free. The main reason for the singaround policy was that, despite there being 11 singers in the family there was no way that they would always be there every week, and we knew we didn't know sufficient songs to run a folk club. Despite MacColl's enthusiasm. But we also wanted to hear other singers. We only met one night at the Barley Mow club, and it was chaos. We may have had the room booked, but the policy was that paid-up members were allowed to roam freely. Entrance fees were a no-no, and keeping quiet was, which wasn't on. We were glad to get out in one piece!

We applied next to the Birtley Welfare club, and again no problem getting a room for free. It was certainly quiet, big, but cold and soulless; and of course DRY. What a fiasco that was, a DRY folk club! Unheard of. We had about 17 people, but lost some of them at the interval, as the British Legion was straight opposite. So, we had an extended interval. Those of the members who didn't drink (and surprise, surprise, there were some) had coffee I made from a bottle of Camp coffee and chicory essence and a tin of evaporated milk as part of my duties as Hon Sec."

Doreen still remembers a lot of the characters from those early days at the Welfare Club.

> "The people I remember at the first gathering at the Welfare were Maureen Craik who went on to become a great folk singer, but unfortunately died very young; Len Wilson, Ed Pickford and Iain Fraser, the trio from Washington Grammar School; Tess Stobbart; Mrs Henderson, Bryan's mother, who didn't ever come back (think it was Tess singing his song about the old woman's ass, a bit too dirty); Vi Gill, a visitor from Canada; Mr Fred Anderson and nine Elliotts. Len remembers singing 'Geordie's Penker'. Nan would sing 'Harraka Harraka' or 'Little Bird' and of course Jack sang 'Busty Fields'. This venue was not suitable either, so we realised that if we wanted a successful venture we would have to book a room in a pub, and we as a family would stand the cost of two pounds which the Red Lion was going to charge. We got membership cards printed, and opened there, at the beginning of May, the first night proper of the club, and as they say the rest is history."

It was probably MacColl who suggested that they run it "like you sing around the kitchen". Again it is ironic that the Bridge, like the Wayfarers' folk club in Manchester, had a format that was based on the Singers' Club in London, where there was a stage, with performers entertaining an audience. Here, MacColl was suggesting something different, obviously recognising that this family had something unique. They didn't put on a show. They were just singing in the pub instead of the kitchen. The singaround format was born. Some see this as the forerunner of all those singing sessions at Keele, then Loughborough, and subsequently every other folk festival in the country, where the singaround can go on for days! But of course, there's nothing new, is there?

At the Eel's Foot public house in Eastbridge in rural Suffolk in 1939, Bert Lloyd found part of what he had been looking for; a living tradition of rural English folk song. Titled *Saturday Night at the Eel's Foot*, the resulting programme was broadcast on 21st July, 1939. This was A. L. Lloyd's first substantial contribution to the Folk Song Revival, a radio broadcast demonstrating that English folk song had not died out but lived on, in full vigour, in the villages of East Anglia. The difference between this and the folk clubs of the '60s was that this was not a club, it was simply what they did every Saturday, and had done for as far back as anybody could remember. When the Chairman, Philip Lumkin, banged the cribbage board onto the table and started singing, then people in the room had to "sing, say, or pay," a policy which certainly stimulated people into having a go. This tradition carried on for a few years after the war.

The collector Keith Summers revealed an even more vigorous session to the outside world in 1953 at the nearby Ship at Blaxhall. So although Suffolk did not feature in the First Revival, it was offering the coming '60s Second Revival a taste of how things used to be done. Looks like the Elliotts, without knowing all this, had continued a tradition that had just held on in East Anglia. The Suffolk people used the pub as a focus for their community, to sing, just as the Elliotts had the family as a focus, coming together to sing as a communal activity. The Folk Revival has continued this with their community in the singaround that we find at clubs and festivals.

In the Red Lion days, the club was so popular that snug, bar, passage were all full, and even Doreen had to be there at 7 o'clock to make sure of getting in! Some remember this time as the club's best days. Ed Pickford in particular thinks that the club was not the same when they left it, but admits that this was probably due to its being very crowded, and to the exciting atmosphere of the explosion of folk music, something Birtley shared with many parts of the country at that time. After about a year at the Lion, it was inevitable that they should find somewhere else, so they moved to the Three Tuns, just up the main road. The room there has been described as a 'ballroom', but they needed it, as they were getting up to 200 people a night.

Doreen again recalls those busy times,

> "It was mainly through word of mouth that we took off, and the fact that you could go along and be invited to sing certainly hit a button. We never had to finance the club because we had so much money coming in. We had to start and book singers, and the list reads like the *Tatler* of the folk world: Pete Seeger, The New Lost City Ramblers, The Spinners, Jackie and Bridie, The McPeakes, Packie Byrne, Joe Heaney to name just a few. The Red Lion soon became much too small, people queuing at 6.30pm, so we moved again, to the Three Tuns, in a room that was big enough to hold ceilidhs. So we had a dance once a month, and got Graham Binless to be caller, as we had no idea of ceilidh music or the dances, but it became another part of our learning curve. Somewhere in the archives of the BBC and Tyne-Tees TV are films made at the Tuns. I must also say that lots of romances flourished at the folk clubs and these couples still come to Birtley Club."

Jack, writing to Bob Davenport, speaks with enthusiasm about the guests, "... Nigel Denver last week, Davy Stewart next week, and Tom Paley in April ..."

Despite what some people said about the "platform" at the Bridge, the residents of that club gave great support to the Birtley club. Johnny Handle, its organiser, talks of the period between Birtley and the first Keele Festival in 1965 as a time of great community spirit amongst the growing numbers of folk people and folk clubs.

Ray Fisher and Colin Ross would come down often to the club in the Three Tuns days, and remember the effect, if anybody was a little noisy, of all of the Elliott men standing up instantly, that's Pete, John, Len, and Bryan. They didn't have to say anything; the offenders were instantly quiet! Ray recalls there being very few women singers, herself and Pat Elliott probably, but rarely Em or Doreen. It seemed to her to be something of a male bastion. (Despite Jack's conviviality and spending time with his mates in the pub, Em did not approve of drink, a factor which caused some friction between the pair in later life. This was probably the main reason for her not having been seen very often at the folk club. Doreen points out that she was usually on door duty and often too busy to sing.) Of course, Ray was already well established as a Scottish folk singer at this stage, and the Elliotts regarded her as a source singer and learned some of her songs, which in some cases became Elliott songs. Ray did not resent this, but found it a compliment, and as she remembers, there were times when the boot was on the other foot. Louis Killen had given the song 'The Weary Cutters' to Pat, and as nobody was singing it, Ray got it from Pat, and sang it for many years.

Roy Harris, a fine singer from Nottingham and a major influence on many during the Revival, is typical of a guest's reaction to the club at this time.

> "My first ever gig at the Birtley Folk Club was circa 1964 or '65. I'm not sure of the exact date but I can say that being booked there gave a big boost to my confidence. I figured that if I was good enough for a famous place like this I stood a chance anywhere. It was at the Three Tuns, and I remember that the room was packed to capacity. I was under no illusion that the crowd was there because of me, an opinion that hardened when I heard the standard of the singers present. It taught me a lesson. If a club is well enough run audiences will come regardless of how famous or otherwise the guest artist might be, or even if there isn't one. They will consider a night at the club worthwhile, and not be put off by an unfamiliar name, because they trust the organiser's judgement. A valuable lesson, one that I bore in mind in anything I ran thereafter. Over the years I went to the club many times. I always looked forward to going and I was never disappointed. I shared with Pete a love of New Orleans jazz. For some

years we swapped quiz tapes of various bands and blues singers, where we each had to identify the performers. I also admired Leadbelly, and the pop singer Frankie Laine, as did Pat. We sent each other Christmas cards addressed to/from 'Huddie Laine'. In my time in folk music I've been lucky enough to meet some exceptional people. None more so than my friends The Elliotts of Birtley."

*"Some people think the singaround was a weakness of the club, but I think it was a strength."* **Ed Pickford**

Although the Elliotts are seen by folk people as representing a mining community, they were not typical, and very few of the pit folk and other neighbours came to the club. In truth, the people of Birtley en masse were just the same as everywhere else, so it was Elvis and the Cliff they wanted to hear. What the club attracted was young people who wanted somewhere to sing, or at least to share in the growing Folk Revival, as well as political people who relished the club's anarchic attitude to establishments of every kind. As Doreen recalls, "When we started the Birtley club there were no other folk clubs apart from Newcastle in existence in the North East. I think South Shields would be next, then Redcar, but they mushroomed overnight, and yes, we went to as many as possible. (Stockton actually came first, started by Johnny Handle in 1961.) Singarounds were still unusual. We never had a stage and we didn't have residents as such. When

*Doreen*

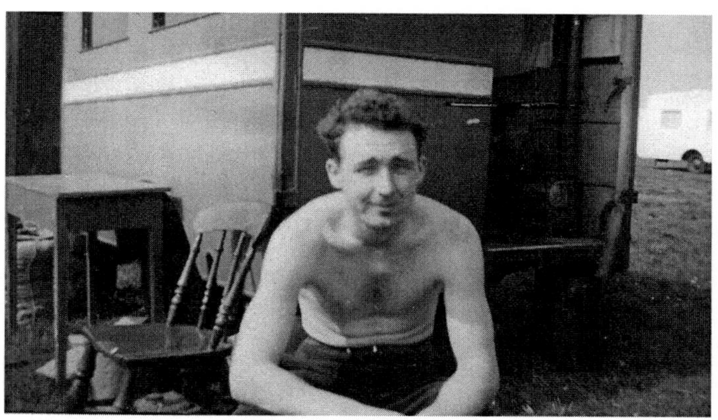

*Pete*

the club started, we knew we didn't have the repertoire to hold it then. Maybe four or five hours we could do, but that wasn't enough, to be doing it every week, and there were so many eager and good singers just waiting to sing and us so keen to hear them that we have never felt the need or desire to change the format. There were lots of other folk clubs in other parts of the country who through word of mouth had heard of the club and asked for a hearing and /or a booking. After about three months one of the first guests were Ewan and Peggy and after that it became practice for a monthly guest."

"The key to the Elliotts was the club, because it was a singaround, democratic, everybody included, at the same level," was a widely held view according to Ed Pickford. Peggy Seeger remembers the club with great affection. She doesn't remember who suggested the singaround concept to them, but thinks it was a great idea. On their visits to the club, she felt "part of the circle", that it was an honour to be there, and was very nervous. Praise indeed from such a highly experienced professional folk singer! Ed states, "It gave people like me a chance we didn't get at the Bridge or elsewhere. Some people think this was a weakness of the club, but I think it was a strength." Ed is very emphatic about these points. He not only got a place to sing, but found himself one of the family as did so many others. Em in particular encouraged him with his songwriting. He doesn't remember the first night particularly, but does remember getting the bus or walking from Penshaw (buses were the norm then, but they even came from Peterlee and Whitley Bay by bus!). Don Stokoe came about 18 months after the club started. He emphasises how embarrassed he was at the idea of singing. "How did these people like Len Wilson, just turn round and sing an unaccompanied song like that, off the cuff, and with no embarrassment?" He liked the way the singing was natural, not like the way they forced you to sing at school, a process that had seriously put him off.

Teesside songwriter Graeme Miles used to go back to Brown's Buildings after the club for a session, then walked to Sedgefield (must be 20 miles!) to get back for work at six in the morning. "It's just the way you did it," he says. At that time, Graeme was teaching at West Hartlepool Arts College, with students who were mostly miners' kids from the Durham pit villages, and from whom he says he got "whiffs of miners' culture". This was nothing very tangible until he saw Jack Elliott, when he realised how very real this culture was. Moreover, he was deeply impressed by Jack's familiarity with poetry, classical music, Darwin, and that he could quote spontaneously from Marx and Engels. No ordinary pitman, this. He clearly had a great intellect, but this was matched by his experience of real life. For Graeme, the songs were "sheer poetry", and "definitely not Owen Brannigan".

Prior to the 1960s, most recordings of folk songs had been done by professional 'arts' singers, with very produced voices, usually accompanied by a bright piano, the product bearing no relationship to the way the songs had originally been sung by traditional singers. This parody of a style was also lampooned by Cecil Day-Lewis (writing as Nicholas Blake), "... one of those extras dressed up to look like rustic ancients for a British quota film, who enliven the proceedings by bursting out every now and then into Somerset folk-songs in perfect harmony and Portland Place accents." Many people blame this way of singing the songs for the almost complete lack of interest or awareness of the culture among ordinary people from the 1920s to the 1960s. They were instead swamped by American music during most of that time. Although a Geordie, the opera singer Owen Brannigan, prominent in the '40s and '50s, personified this style of singing.

The Elliotts' club and the emerging folk clubs were the complete opposite of this approach and they opened a floodgate of enthusiasm for the simple natural way of singing that traditional singers had kept alive.

References for Chapter 2

1. Ewan MacColl, *Journeyman*, Sidgwick and Jackson, 1990
2. From a letter from Louis Killen to Charles Parker in late August 1961, Charles Parker Archive, City of Birmingham Library
3. Alexander Barrass, *The Pitman's Social Neet*. J. Dent, Consett, 1897
4. *The Elliotts of Birtley: A Portrait of a Mining Family*, Folkways inc. FG3506, 1962, and Transatlantic Extra 1967.
5. A L Lloyd, *Come All Ye Bold Miners*, Lawrence & Wishart, 1st edition 1952; 2nd edition, 1978. (CAYBM)

# Chapter 3
# The Folk Revival

It's worth pausing at this stage to review the music and song in the family. Doreen's descriptions of parties at the house talk of lots of music, as do Pete's of listening to records and the wireless with his dad. Em's family had been musicians in the theatre, and Jack's mother's side, the Greens, had had a band. Jack's father Lance was a melodeon player (the one who kept bursting the bellas!), and so there was no shortage of musical ancestry. Reece was a fine singer, as was Jack, and although it is a pity that in the many interviews Jack did before he died, he was not asked where his songs came from, we do have some wonderful memories from Reece in this regard.

In an interview on tape carried out by Pete and Doreen he talks about his youth. He talks first of how they made dancing dolls, how you needed lots of practice to get "knack of the rhythm", and then how he and other kids would take them into the pubs to entertain the men drinking there. The annual trip to South Shields in a horse-drawn brake set Reece off with many memories of songs. His version of 'Oh Canny Man Ha Your Happeny Out' was learnt off the South Shields kids on one of these trips. On a chapel trip on a coal lorry to Saltwell Park, he remembers singing 'There Was a Man Up a Tree', but didn't know the source. At the time of recording he still sings several songs his brother ("Uncle Len") used to sing, which include 'The Chinese Song', and 'Candy Man'. Interestingly, when Pete sings one of Jack's songs 'No Booze Today', Reece cannot remember it, but he does remember a very unusual version of 'Roll the Old Chariot Along'. The whole interview again shows the variety of song that the family absorbed, most of it in the oral tradition.

Reece also picked up songs at the big celebrations, all part of the pitman's life. This was the case with another favourite of his, 'I Love You Better Than You Knew'. He got it as follows.

> "The first sentimental song ever I sung. I learnt it at Durham. I only sung it once in the folk club. I was exactly five year old, when Gunner first took me to Durham Big Meeting. And I remember him, in the market place yonder, wae peglegs were very common then. Well, this feller had a pegleg, and he was playing a violin, and ya bugger, he had

a hatful of coppers, an Aa've never seen a one since. Buskin', that's playin' and singin'. He was playing like the Canadians, fiddle down on his hip, like, and singin'. Wae, he had a crood around him, singin this song, 'I loved you better than you knew'. It was a favourite song of your mother's (Em). An that's the first sentimental song ever I sung."

This was 1899 and Reece was five years old at the time. The song had been written by an American professional songwriter only a few years previously. It had clearly travelled fast, in those days before radio or records, and may have spread by sheet music. But the method by which Reece acquired it seems as traditional as that of any folk song. When Reece was asked about whether there were lots of buskers, and what they played, he says,

"Wae aye. Mostly concertinas. There was a great concertina player in Browns Buildings, lived in Number 7, I think it was (eventually Jack's house). He was in my grandfather's string band (the Greens). Grandfather was on bass fiddle, him on concertina, two small fiddles, and a melodeon. Nae drums, mi grandfather used to keep time with his hobnail boots."

*Reece Elliott, c 1960*

He recalls many other local musicians in the pit community, including "a canny few fiddlers, John Swailes, Geordie Towers ..." and there was 'Piccolo Bill', who played in his grandfather's band, Joe Fargieson who played tuba, and his Uncle Peter on trombone. Interestingly, his niece and nephew, the interviewers, found some of this new. Whistles were home made, and lads got mouth organs for Christmas. There was also clog dancing, which in that area was learnt off Johnson Ellwood of Chester-le-Street, the most successful dancer of the day. He can remember men dancing on flat iron sheets at the bottom of the pit whilst waiting for the cage.

"In them days, they danced in the street all the time. He used to play in the streets, he didn't mind where he was playin'. Middle of the road sometimes if he was half tight. They would dance in the street, old fashioned dances, such as waltzes and schottisches, And country dances; jigs and reels, like ' Flowers of Edinburgh', I know a canny few of them tunes. 'Cos I mind when our Meg was married, to Uncle Joe (she was the furst un of course) it went on for fower days. I remember Alfie, that's the only one that's left of my uncles on my mother's side, he was sittin' on the top of them drawers, playing a chella. Joe used to be generally conductor."

Next on the recording, Reece sings 'German Band', which reminds him of the German street bands of the Edwardian period. They used the hurdy-gurdy (with monkey), and "small fiddle" (violin). It's probable that here Reece is referring to the barrel organ, then common with buskers, and often called a hurdy-gurdy, rather than the French folk instrument, which is quite different. He mentions the fiddler Bob Hepple giving Jack lessons and his own two lessons on the instrument (including his dad's reaction, which was not altogether complimentary!).

Reece's memory stretches back even farther than that when he remembers his granddad as a child. He remembers his grandfather singing the broadside about Nelson ''Twas in Trafalgar Bay', and being so drunk that he sang the song all night, from 11p.m. till 5a.m. Eventually, Reece starts to sing it, and the others join in.

*"Twas in Trafalgar bay,*
*We saw the Frenchmen lay,*
*Each heart was beating then;*
*We scorned the foreign yoke,*
*Our ships were British oak,*
*And hearts of oak our men"*

Next, he sings a couple of music hall songs, including 'Rosie O'Grady', a Boer War song. Reece sang with great dignity, a quality he afforded just as much to innumerable kids' songs, music hall snatches, and other short songs. He sings a somewhat crude version of Old King Cole on the tape, which Doreen sings as well!

It was still recognised both within and outside the family that Jack was at the centre of all this music. Jack played a lot of instruments. Although he gave up on the fiddle, he was good on guitar, banjo, mandolin, melodeon, mouth organ, and Jew's harp, all widely used in folk music. We have already seen that the pitmen in Birtley sang a great deal. Jack, according to Pete and Doreen, probably picked up his traditional songs in the working-men's club and pubs from men in his own community. The men sang at the pub regularly (no musak in those days), and as we saw earlier, the kids would often stand outside the open window on a Saturday night in summer, and hear the songs getting more and more lively as the drink mounted. Probably the family was not exceptional in their taste in songs, but they sang even more than the people around them, and were special in character, 'crack', general liveliness and commitment. They'd sing when walking round the house doing everyday tasks. They had legendary parties, family celebrations of one kind or another where "the mats would be rolled right back".

## *"The mats would be rolled right back."*

Jack was a great character down the pub, his love of life being a driving force. His humour was catching and unique, but without malice. No wonder the house was always crowded with visitors and friends well before 'folk music' came along. As Bryan Henderson commented, the Elliotts might have a night where the songs and jokes were the same as a night ten or more years previously, but they still enjoyed it. Enjoyment was the norm, otherwise there was something wrong with you. Jack passed on his enthusiasm for music to his family.

Jack had discerning taste, and songs had to have some wit and meaning to them. He was not very fond of popular songs and he didn't think much of Gracie Fields or George Formby, famous northern variety and film artists in the 1930s, who he thought had sold out their class. He preferred American 'Hillbilly' singers like Jimmy Rodgers, Vernon Dalhart and Frank Crummit. But he had catholic tastes, and also bought records of Caruso and Gigli as well as those of Duke Ellington and Louis Armstrong. Pete Elliott recalls his father Jack's musical tastes.

> "At that time, although he had smoked from childhood, Pop didn't drink, preferring to spend his spare cash on records. He was acquiring a taste for opera and classical music from Mam, so his collection was very varied. She could have made a career in the singing profession, given a more caring parent, for she had a beautiful singing voice. She knew how to harmonise too, which Pop quickly learned. They went in for esoteric forms of music, way off the musical beaten track, like the aforementioned Jimmy Rodgers and others like him, Sol Hoopii with genuine Hawaiian music, Frank Crumit who specialised in numerous songs, and jazz performed by the likes of Duke Ellington. He also collected records by The Mills Brothers, who, with only a guitar accompaniment, sang and imitated instruments of a jazz orchestra. They loved the songs of yesteryear and Mam always made much of her love of folk music. The only intolerance over any kind of music that we imbibed at our parents' knee was rejection of the second rate. Why

listen to crap like Secombe, Lanza, Joe Toss (Loss) or Hank Marvin when you can have Gigli, Pavarotti, Louis Armstrong or Django Reinhardt?"

Everybody agrees that Jack was the best singer and was the natural leader. People say this only because he was so exceptional. He had undoubted charisma, was popular in the bar, a natural, entertaining singer, and you knew when he was in the room. He had that great elusive quality, 'presence'. Part of this was his voice. Even his speaking voice commanded attention. He might have been talking about the most trivial or comical things, might have been telling a rude joke, or talking about some disaster in the pit, or coming out with some political invective, but he had a dignity and power and attractiveness that drew the listener to him. Even Reece, his older brother by thirteen years, and who "worked marras wi' him" said he had something special. And when he sang, he was totally in command of the song, hardly ever a waver or a hesitation; and if one did occur he could carry it off with such wit and aplomb that it increased his stature even further. As Ed Pickford says, Jack was a good singer because of his timing, but also his strong belief, with nothing false in what he did. MacColl, rather parsimoniously in my view, called this "stagecraft".

The family's singing style, which eventually came to be widely known, was mainly unaccompanied "because that's how we sang at home". Many first-time visitors were impressed by this, at a time when other clubs were

*The Skiffle Group, late 1950s*

full of guitars. Pete sometimes used the guitar, and though Jack could play several instruments, he had difficulty in singing and playing at the same time. The harmonies in the group songs were done mostly by the women, Em and Doreen. In fact the songs they sang the most were the ones that they could harmonise to. A regrettable feature of the family's songs is that the women hardly ever lead a song, and yet both have excellent voices of real character. Jack sang a great number of other songs, of all sorts, and played many tunes, but these were not the songs the family sang when together as a group.

A remarkable feature of the Elliott 'clan' is that all the people who married into it have been good singers, and have sung with the family either straightaway or eventually. John's wife Nan was a Gateshead lass, who brought along not only a good voice, but songs from her own patch. (The Elliotts regarded Gateshead, of course, as foreign territory, so these were exotic songs!) Nan would go to the Club regularly, but didn't go on bookings. Bill says she sang when she was comfortable, not wanting to be a performer. John's second wife, Pam, who came along in 1980, is a very good singer, having more of a trained voice than the Elliotts, and experience of singing Irish songs in particular. Pete's wife Pat had a strong voice full of character, and tended to do songs from the Revival rather than local songs and pit songs. Pete and Pat's daughter Laura remembers her mam practising for the Club, singing a song over and over while she was trying to do her homework. Pete clearly went head over heels in love with her, because "she came off a Tory family", though those of us who knew her later would never have guessed. She matched the Elliotts in that you definitely knew where she stood, and you didn't want to be on the wrong side! As her family were also church-goers, it's hard to imagine a more unlikely match! Pat had the driest sense of humour with a wit that could be very scathing. Always plenty of crack! At Pete's sixtieth birthday party at the Club, he went round the room, asking every singer to sing a particular song, one of theirs that he liked. He asked me to sing 'The Snows They Melt the Soonest', a song I'd recorded with the Ranters, but I couldn't remember the words. I was the only one the whole evening who couldn't manage the song he chose, and I still squirm at the memory. At the National Festival, after Pete died, there was an hour devoted to Pete's memory on the Sunday lunchtime, and when it was my turn, I told them the story of Pete's sixtieth. Quick as a flash, before I could start the song to make belated amends, Pat quipped "It's all right, he forgave you just last year!" Typical.

Bryan Henderson is the longest serving "married-in", and a great source of material for this book. He was obviously attracted to Doreen Elliott, because they married in 1953 and remain a happy couple still living next to Brown's Buildings. But he came initially for the 'crack', playing blues and jazz with his mate Pete. And it wasn't just music. Lively political discussion was also a feature of the kitchen. The Elliotts' was "the place to be". It was this same atmosphere that eventually attracted Ed Pickford and his mates to come round in 1961, before the Club started, and later the collectors arrived – the MacColls and the Lloyds of this world.

No sooner were they wed than Doreen and Bryan went off to Hamilton in Canada, where Em's family had emigrated, and stayed with them for two years

> "We, Bryan and I, had decided to try Canada before we wed. One of the reasons was his reluctance to join the armed forces. Over there we lived with my Aunty Vi, Mam's sister and that's when I realised that our love of singing came as much from Em's side as Jack's. Oh what harmonies. Two guitar-playing cousins, western songs, hymns, wonderful nights when the singing could go on for hours. The downside of Canada was that there were no libraries, and no political parties. This was the height of the McCarthy witch hunts in the nearby United States, and the people in the area said the Elliotts were communists. You couldn't even mention Charlie Chaplin. Bryan loved Canada and he did eventually get a good job in the foundry, but I had already miscarried with one baby and discovered I was pregnant again and wanted to be at home for my baby's birth. So at seven months pregnant after frantic saving we sailed for home, and actually it was as cheap for two of us to sail home as pay the hospital expenses. No NHS there, so Kay was born at home. We lived in at Number 7 until Kay was about seven months, a very happy time and I was so glad we came home, as Mam had suffered a bad heart attack while I was in Canada and she had decided not to tell me, being in that delicate state. We bought our first house at 9, Waggonway Terrace, Fatfield."

Bryan and Doreen are now the mainstay of the Club and still have a great zest for life. Bryan has a lovely, quiet, relaxed style and a wide range of great songs both local and from elsewhere, including recently some of Terry Conway's songs like 'The Bus to Morpeth'.

The political element was never very far away with the Elliott family. In the early part of the Folk Revival, political songs were very much to the fore, and the ban-the-bomb movement in particular generated many new songs. Even in the early '60s, it was bearded men in duffel coats and banjo-toting pigtailed young women in dungarees that set the popular image of folk music. The establishment probably saw them as "lefties and probably Soviet spies". As Vic Gammon of the Folk Music Degree Course at Newcastle

University remarks, "The movement was complex and never had one single idea or approach, although alliances of convenience were common and a left-wing impetus was present in some aspects. The music performed varied from revived traditional music to political and protest songs, to comedy, to pure self-indulgence."(1) Actually most "folkies" very quickly gravitated towards traditional song, in all its many forms. There were the lyrical southern songs all about May mornings collected by Cecil Sharp and others; shanties, greatly helped by Stan Hugill, England's last shantyman and foremost collector of shanties; the great border ballads; bawdy songs which allowed you to say things you couldn't have got away with anywhere else; Napoleonic war songs; and Irish rebel songs.

But there were very few industrial songs. It seemed, even to the scholars, that the tradition was entirely rural, maritime, or military, a thinking which predominated in the English Folk Dance and Song Society. It's interesting to note that many of the first people along to the Club from the area, such as Hebburn and South Shields, had never heard a mining song. There were mining terms in the general North East vocabulary, but few songs. Even the Elliotts themselves sang few songs about pit life before the Revival. The songs they sang before the Folk Revival were not, in the main, overtly political, nor did they dwell on the hardships of the mine. Pitmen were sensitive to the dangers and the sheer barbarity of the conditions they worked in, but singing about them or whinging in the pub was not the way they coped with them. Humour was their weapon, and it permeated their chat, their home life, and their songs. The family songs were mostly cheerful, happy snatches, a mixture of pit songs, music hall, bits of kids' rhymes, and popular songs of the day. There were also songs that we would now classify as political, but they didn't dominate. Some were local, whereas others might be considered national. They weren't political weapons, but things that held the family together.

Both Bert Lloyd and Ewan MacColl were keen to prove this assumption wrong, possibly because both had an agenda due to their Communist backgrounds. There were few people interested in folk songs in those days, and the tradition appeared to have disappeared beneath the ice for good. But there was a hidden spring, and in the late '50s and early '60s, the meetings of MacColl and Lloyd with the Elliotts revealed so much more material, particularly in the North East coalfield. Bert asserted that the creation of rural folk songs had ceased by about 1850, whereas urban songs continued to be made. He had published his *Come All Ye Bold Miners* in 1952, instigated by the National Coal Board, and dependent on miners sending in songs to Coal, the NCB magazine. It was a slim volume indeed compared with the second edition in 1978. Meeting the Elliotts helped convince Lloyd and MacColl that there was a culture of industrial folk songs. Thus the second edition of Bert's book was much bigger, and was heavily dependent on the North East, and on Jack and Reece Elliott in particular. Significantly, Bert's 1967 magnum opus, *Folk Song in England*, included both industrial and political songs for the first time in a serious study of folk song. (This significant work has recently been selected by Faber and Faber for inclusion on their print-on-demand list 'Faber Finds'.)

*"The Elliotts helped convince Lloyd and MacColl that there was a culture of industrial folk songs"*

By the mid-'60s, through the interest of MacColl and Lloyd, and the wider media world, the Club and the family rapidly became well known in the region and nationally. In 1964, Bert Lloyd made a two-part radio programme called *Songs of the Durham Miners* for the erudite BBC Third Programme (now Radio Three). Lloyd took the opportunity to broadcast some of his theories using recordings of an evening at the Birtley Club interspersed with academic commentary from himself. The programme is remarkable for Bert's erudition and imaginative tales. He went on to say how mining areas throughout Europe often have the oldest and deepest of folk cultures, such as sword-dancing, which seems to have been associated with mining from a very early time in history, and that the song culture of North East England is as strong as those of Silesia, Carinthia, and the Carpathian mountains. The standard of singing, with the Elliotts at the height of their powers and supplemented by the elite of the Bridge Club, i.e. Johnny Handle, Louis Killen and John Reavey, is superb. All the classic North East mining songs are here, with Jack, Louis and Johnny doing most of the singing. 'Little Chance' is sung by John Elliott, and described thus by Bert; "hybrid though such songs are, they mean a good deal to the men who make and use them. Though traditionalists may wince, they're worth far more study than they've had till now."

It is interesting that out of the twenty songs in the programme, only two are sung by a woman. Pat sings 'Bonnie Pit Laddie' and 'A U a Hinny Burd'. It's a pity that Bert mistakes her for the daughter of a Gateshead miner, when she came from Jesmond (the posh area of Newcastle). In Em or Doreen he could have had the real thing. The blurb written by himself for the Radio Times shows Lloyd demonstrating the existence of a modern, breathing industrial oral tradition fully aware of its past.

> "English miners in particular have for centuries been making songs out of their daily lives – old songs about encounters with the Devil in the pit, nineteenth-century songs bubbling with industrial ferment, new songs full of today's stresses and enthusiasms. A characteristic modern form is the farewell song to pits closed by the National Coal Board, with words expressing the divided emotions of colliers who hate working in obsolete mines but are sad to have to leave them. Last summer, Douglas Cleerdon and I visited part of the Durham coalfield to record these songs. Some of these recordings will be heard in two programmes of *Songs of the Durham Miners*."

He also uses the description to emphasise an underlying theme of his work; that folk song was the true antidote to the mass commercialism being foisted on the masses.

> "There's much talk nowadays of 'the Mersey sound'; 'the Durham sound' is another matter. It has more fibre than frenzy, and speaks of real experience in a way that rouses no screams (though some may wince at its force). I invite you to listen to the colliers singing choruses over their beer-mugs, in the Three Tuns pub in Birtley, County Durham. You'd think the place was full of Cossacks."

*"I invite you to listen to the colliers singing choruses over their beer-mugs, in the Three Tuns pub in Birtley, County Durham. You'd think the place was full of Cossacks."* **Bert Lloyd**

After this there was a special programme on Tyne Tees Television called *A Richer Life*, in 1964 or 1965, and the BBC flagship arts programme *Omnibus* put out an issue on the Birtley Christmas party. Besides these commercial productions that they were involved in, there were many others who beat a path to Jack and Em's door during those years. The School of Dialect Studies at Leeds had at least two students doing final year dissertations on North East songs, in 1962 and in 1965, which involved recordings of Jack (2), and many recordings done for Beamish museum, for the FED, by Doc Rowe for his archive, and others for private use. Notable collections of North East songs published in this period used Jack as their primary source of several songs (3).

*Mary-Anne Teacake, how do you like my hat?*
*Upset the tea-pot and nearly killed the cat,*
*The cat start to bubble, I hit it with the shovel,*
*I knocked it in the corner with the rhubarb-pudding.*

# London

Some time in the early '60s there was a Club trip to the Singers' Club in London at the request of Ewan and Peggy. A 40-seater coach was duly filled and down they all went. Some have mixed feelings about the trip, saying MacColl was arrogant and didn't let them sing. They had thought they were taking over the Club for the night. In fact, however, it was just the Elliott family that had been asked to go. Imagine the effect of these boisterous Geordies, all het up and raring to go, on the staid Singers' Club audience of that time!

However, as Bob Davenport, the Gateshead singer long exiled in London, comments, Jack was told what to sing at the Singers' Club. It seemed he was there as a performer, obliged to pop up from time to time in order to illustrate a point from MacColl's 'lecture'. He was delighted to find that when invited to sing at the Fox Club in Islington, he could sing anything he liked when he liked! (Different approach, different people, the Folk Revival had it all.)

Jim Bainbridge, long-exiled singer and musican, and member of the legendary Marsden Rattlers of the 60s and 70s, has this to say:

> "Tolerant folk clubs taught many of us that, given the opportunity, most singers improve with time and experience, and that this serves the tradition much better than the quality control exercised at Ewan MacColl's Singers Club. MacColl was a wonderful songwriter and promoter of the tradition as he saw it, but as a man of the theatre - with little time for imperfection - his ideas for improving the quality of singing were applied via technical advice and analysis rather than absorption by exposure to the perceived inadequacies of unbelievers. No less a singer than old Jack Elliott of Birtley was once castigated by this crowd - after a return visit to the Singer's Club, disappointment was expressed that his singing hadn't "improved" since his last visit - What a damn cheek!"

There was also apparently a comment by either Ewan or Peggy that Jack "hadn't moved on", implying that they expected him to develop a stage act, much as they had done. It's sad that they didn't see the true value of such a natural singer who had such a wide appeal without artificial devices. Certainly the way the Elliotts' visit to the Singers' Club was treated looks like that, but for Graeme Miles there was something more. For him, doing it that way was just as artificial a way of presenting the material as was the Owen Brannigan/Peter Pears approach. It seems the essential point here is the different reasons for singing. Both McColl and Brannigan were professional singers, and in my opinion therefore professional entertainers, and they needed a worked-out stage act to make a living. So folkies like me can take a lofty view of Brannigan's style as decidedly 'art' rather than 'folk'. But then McColl didn't sing like a working man or a traditional singer either. (This area will be taken up in more detail later.) But like most things involving McColl, it was never as simple as that.

In 1965, the English Folk Dance and Song Society, or EFDSS, ran a concert at the Royal Festival Hall in London, called 'The Sound of Folk Music'. The concert was a belated recognition by a rather stuffy body of the arrival and importance of a second Folk Revival. The vigour of the young people now becoming thoroughly immersed in the tradition was somewhat hard for the largely dance-orientated EFDSS, and there was a feeling of them jumping on a bandwagon that was rushing by rather swiftly. Peter Kennedy, an established collector of folk songs and son of a scion of the Society, Douglas Kennedy, organised it. He certainly knew what he was about when it came to the choice of performers. Ireland had the McPeake family and Paddy Tunney (both from the North), Scotland had the émigré group the Ian Campbell Folk Group together with their Aberdeenshire parents, there were the Watersons from Yorkshire, and the Coppers from Sussex. The West Country had Charlie Bate, Cyril Tawney, Lewis Johns and John Steele. This is hardly an even geographical representation of the British Isles, but the region with the most guests was the North East, with Louis Killen, Bob Davenport, Jack Armstrong, Patricia Jennings, the Stockton Blue and Gold Rapper Team, and Jack Elliott. This was a tribute indeed to the importance of the region, and with Jack as one of only six source singers on the bill, a mighty tribute to him and his songs. It was at this concert that he made the famous one-liner "It's Jack Elliott. Not Ramblin' Jack Elliott, but Stumblin' Jack Elliott."

This line came from the fact that when Ray Fisher moved to Tyneside in 1962 and was told "You've got to hear Jack Elliott, he's a regular at the Club", she naturally assumed this was a reference to the American singer of Woody Guthrie's songs, known as "Ramblin'" Jack Elliott. In fact, the American Jack had appeared at a one-off concert at the Sink pub sometime in 1960 or 1961, and the Birtley Jack had stood up to sing, and referred to himself as "Shambling Jack" for the sake of the rhyme. By 1965, however,

*"It's Jack Elliott. Not Ramblin' Jack Elliott, but Stumblin' Jack Elliott"*

his health had caused him to change the adjective. He was already not well. Soon after, on 28th June, he had not been paid for the concert. He says in a letter to Bob Davenport "The EFDSS would hardly expect folks to travel all the way from Newcastle for nowt."

## Death of Jack

In another letter, dated 30th January 1964, Jack reports to Bob, "I've been to hospital for a check-up last Saturday, 4 or 5 X-Rays, and have to go again tomorrow to see Mr Rowbotham the nerve specialist. I've been told quite frankly that I've got to get out of the pit and get a desk job. I've been doing too much manual work this last two years, and it's telling now. I've been a bloody fool for doing it. We'll hope for the best, anyway."

He did retire soon after this, and started making a living cobbling shoes, which he'd always been good at, and this was often being close to full time. He often used to remark, as other retired pitmen sat aimlessly on their hunkers waiting for the pubs to open, "Jesus, Just look at those buggers; don't know how to fill their time in. There aren't enough hours in the day for me." He told a tale of cobbling "a pollis's geet big, size fourteen boots, using almost a hide of leather in the process." When the Plod's wife returned for them, he said, "Aa'm sorry it's tacken see lang pet, but Aa had t' wait forra a fine day, 'cos th' were an ootside job." She was not amused!

However, the success of the record and the radio ballad had brought Jack to the notice of the burgeoning folk club movement, and he started to get paid for doing what he enjoyed most. One idea that was tried out about this time was a group consisting of Jack and two North East music maestros, John Doonan the Tyneside Irish flute and whistle player, and Billy Pigg, the finest living Northumbrian piper. This could have had a tremendous impact on the Revival, but ill health prevented that happening. He took on a vastly increased number of folk club bookings around the country, salting away every penny, which along with his cobbling money was to pay for the great Canadian adventure. In early 1966, Jack and Em went on a trip to Canada, which was intended to culminate in his singing at the Newport Folk Festival. Not long before setting off for Canada, they had appeared on a Philip Donnellan documentary on Westminster Abbey. In retrospect, according to Pete, he looked well below par in health, leaning far more heavily on his stick than usual. He still managed some pithy remarks though, his best being "Ye knaa Em, every bloody war but the class war is commemorated there!" At the farewell drink before they set off in April, he seemed to the family to be quieter than usual. They put it down to trepidation about flying, although this was not his normal reaction to a new experience.

Unfortunately, he took ill half way through the trip and had to come home. This is the saddest part of the whole of this book, so I'll let his eldest son Pete tell the story.

> "At first the vacation seemed to go terrifically well. They visited all the relations on the Eastern seaboard and were feted wherever they went. They then made a boring four-day train journey across the width of Canada to Chilliwak, where they met up with Doll and Cess, their neighbours, and a number of expatriate Geordies. Pop celebrated his fifty-ninth birthday at Doll's, and she made him a cake in the shape of, and decorated like a banjo. Back home we were delighted for them. Then the bombshell struck. We received a letter telling us not to worry,

(always a certain signal that you should), but Dad had been taken to hospital for a check-up, after experiencing acute stomach pains. The concern deepened when we learned that part of the examination was with a bronchoscope. Whatever else its uses might be, they certainly have nowt to do with the stomach. The final alarm struck home when we were informed that they were cutting short the holiday in order for Pop to have treatment in the UK.

I drove to Newcastle Airport to pick them up and take them home, almost beside myself with worry. When they got off the plane, it was a grey, haggard, old man I saw coming down the stairs, clutching a two hundred pack of cigarettes under his arm. I hardly needed Mam, who looked almost as ill as he, to take me to one side and tell me he had cancer of the lungs, and it had spread and was terminal.

I drove back to Birtley on auto-pilot, trying to come to terms with the fact that this big, smiling, affable man I'd known all my life, and regarded as indestructible, especially after what he'd been through, was a mortal being like the rest of mankind. I also made a solemn vow on that journey never to smoke another cigarette in my life. I felt a loathing for the killer tubes for having struck my old man down that has never left me.

I dropped them off at Number 7, made sure they were as comfortable as we could make them, and then went down to our Doreen's, where the pair of us broke our hearts. Even writing this now, I can feel waves of sadness pour over me. It was a depth of sorrow I would never again be capable of experiencing. The first loss of someone central to my existence. We were also grieving over the fact that his suffering might be of long duration, and devoutly hoped it wouldn't be."

In retrospect, he must have been ill for some time before going to Canada. He hadn't said anything and nobody, not even Em or the family doctor, had realised. But as Doreen says, "It was obvious that the man was dying. When I saw him without clothes one day, there wasn't a pickin' on him." In those days, nobody talked about cancer, it was the 'unmentionable disease', but as he lay dying Jack told John and Doreen to "pack those cigarettes in now".

Pete continues the story.

"On the Monday they took him into the R.V.I. After a week of watching him visibly go downhill, and the Infirmary doing nothing, and Dad knowing they were doing nothing, they called us into the Ward Office and informed us there was no help for him and they were sending him home. I was told that he broke down when he entered the house, then put the best face on things that he could, but I'm certain he knew the score. By the end of the week he was obviously in tremendous pain. The doctor took Mam to one side and said he could keep Dad hanging on in that condition for a few weeks longer, or he could make his time shorter, but a lot easier. After agonising for a few minutes, Mam agreed that his going should be helped. From then on, as soon as Pop moaned in pain as consciousness returned, the doctor would inject him with a massive dose of morphine. He died late on the Tuesday night, at nine-o-clock, the sixth of July, and when I arrived at the house, the downstairs back room was already beginning to smell of death."

Given about six weeks to live by the consultant, he in fact died two weeks after his return, on 6th July 1966. The funeral was a very moving affair, with hundreds of people packing the Birtley crematorium and overflowing outside. His family and the Birtley community were there of course, but there were also people from the North East folk community and beyond, including a striking number of young people. The turnout amazed the family, who had no idea how famous he and they had become. Jack being an atheist, the eulogy was given by the socialist humanist Bob Griffin from Newcastle. It was a remarkable tribute to a remarkable man, of which this is an excerpt.

"In these later years, the ability of Jack to get on with everyone has manifested itself in the growth of the local folk music movement: which spread out from Jack, Mrs. Elliott and family, like a ripple in a pond into which a pebble has been cast, until the movement has spread all over the North Country. In this movement we have cultural links with the past of the Birtley area, allied with pleasant music-making, whether round the fire on a winter's evening, or to a wider audience on radio and television.

We cannot leave Jack today without making mention of his atheism and his freethinking. These views were held without heat or rancour, but they were held firmly, and he would want us at this time to make this clear, so that his passing would be in keeping with his living convictions. It is something of a wonder that, while he held these views so uncompromisingly, it did not lessen his ability to make and to keep friendships with all kinds of people, especially amongst those younger than himself."

This particularly impressed Ray Fisher. "Such a straight description of an individual person, his personality, his singing. Not the token stuff you got from priests at the crematorium at other funerals. It was quite remarkable." And her husband Colin Ross was there along with fellow piper Foster Charlton, to play the coffin from the house, and afterwards at the 'do'. The Elliotts really loved the Northumbrian pipes, and later Colin was there to play at both Em's and Pete's funerals.

There were also resounding tributes from the media who had so taken him to their hearts. Here is one of the many obituaries for Jack, written by Karl Dallas for *Melody Maker*.

> "When I heard he was to go to Newport, I thought at the time there was hardly anyone who could better represent us. As Louis Killen said to me only this weekend, to have him sit in a room with you, even if he was deliberately taking a back seat to allow someone else to take the floor, was to be aware of his presence, filling the room. He was not only a great traditional singer, whose stock of mining songs and stories made nonsense of the belief that folk singers have to come out of rural surroundings. He understood what the Revival was all about, and his club at Birtley, which started as a family gathering, became internationally known as the best in Britain."

Fortunately, we can see the funeral in the second film made by Philip Donnellan, by now a great friend of the family. Donnellan combined Jack's funeral with the death of 'Cotia pit, where Jack had worked for 42 years, and which by a remarkable coincidence was being demolished at that same time. The result was *Death Of A Miner*, and although the family were happy with the film being made, not everybody in the 'extended family' that had grown around the Elliotts in the previous few years agreed. Jim Irving, self-confessed "angry man" at the time, saw it as an intrusion into "our grief" and got upset with the TV people, although he now agrees that it was a good thing it was done, and has a cherished copy of his own. This gritty, sympathetic film, commemorating the end of an era in two senses, still makes compulsive viewing after forty years. The family went back home to the traditional pit ritual of a ham and pease pudding meal, prepared by Em's neighbours, and purged their grief by sitting the whole afternoon swapping stories about his life. Later, all three generations would meet again at Brown's Buildings to watch the film shown on television, feeling great sadness but enormous pride, just as they'd done for *Mining Review* and *The Big Hewer*, but had been deprived of doing for *Private Faces*. Fortunately, as observed earlier, the new film included a lot of the material from the banned one, and it's this that sticks in many people's minds: Jack, Em and the boys talking so eloquently about things that really mattered. The new film also included a lovely piece on Doreen, while on playground duty, talking about the death of the village, and remembering how she and her brothers went to the pit to watch her father going up the ramp to the cage as he started yet another shift. Doreen had been impressed with *The Big Hewer*, but describes this film simply as "sensational".

Doreen was asked to deliver the eulogy for Donnellan at his memorial service a year after his death in 1999. Here is the final paragraph from that moving tribute.

> "Finally I would like to say that I hope when this film was first shown that it altered some people's perception of working-class families and if it just made a few people think that perhaps life isn't fair to the havenots, and if today people who are seeing it for the first time feel moved forty years after it was made, then Philip Donnellan was a craftsman and a forerunner of today's documentary makers."

*"It was obvious that the man was dying. When I saw him without clothes one day, there wasn't a pickin' on him."* **Doreen**

Jack's death was felt deeply by many in the North East. The family and the Club had built up a tremendous following, with huge numbers attending every week. Many people had sung for the first time at Birtley Club, and some had gone on to become established singers. Everybody wanted to do something to recognise Jack's importance, and a number of things came out of the discussions with the Elliotts and one or two friends like Don Stokoe and Jim Irving, who suggested a solo LP of Jack.

Meanwhile, the North East representative of the EFDSS, Graham Binless, saw that the time was ripe for folk music in the area to be a bit

*The family at Jack's concert*

more organised, and in December of 1966 set up the North East Folk Federation, always known simply as 'The Fed'. Chaired by Tony Wilson, with Pete Elliott and Jim Irving as joint secretaries, the Fed was set up to promote folk music in the wider North East, and had people from the whole region on the committee. At the inaugural meeting, at the Bridge Hotel in January 1967, it was agreed that a Jack Elliott memorial concert should be arranged, specifically to fund the making of Jack's record, and to fund cancer charities in the North East. The concert took place in April of that year in the 2000-seater City Hall, at that time the major concert hall in the region. It was organised by Don Stokoe and a sub-committee of the 'Fed', and was an invitation concert, with guests including Bob Davenport with the Marsden Rattlers, the Spinners, the High Level Ranters, the John Doonan Trio, the Watersons, and Alex Campbell, as well as the family themselves. It also had Uncle Reece, who hadn't joined in the Club much till then. For Don Stokoe, however, the hit of the concert was Billy Pigg, who dazzled the audience with his sheer dexterity on the Northumbrian pipes. (A great pity that he too had not long to go.) The concert was a sellout, and a large profit was made, enough to fund Jack's record and to donate a handsome sum to cancer research.

The 'Fed' grew from strength to strength in the next two or three years, taking over the fledgling Hexham Festival, organising workshops, starting the Morpeth Gathering, running a second Jack Elliott concert in 1968, and eventually having a major involvement in the Newcastle Festival of the early '70s. The 'Fed' was undoubtedly a significant force in the folk music of the North East at that time, and did much good work. One of its lasting legacies was to purchase a tape recorder and organise field recordings of notable performers, such as Billy Pigg and the Elliott family themselves. These recordings, many made by the late Phil Ranson, form an invaluable part of the North East musical heritage, and feature prominently on the FARNE website (4). Soon, however, there were clashes within the Fed, and people such as Pete Elliott and Jim Irving did not approve of a lot of the 'professional' newcomers. There were too many meetings, and too much bureaucracy. The organisation had probably just got too big, and perhaps lost some of its original ethos. Pete Elliott left the Fed and formed the Durham Folk Alliance, reflecting a divide between the Tyneside and Durham folkies which to some extent remains to this day.

Undoubtedly its finest legacy was Jack Elliott's solo LP. However, the production of this proved somewhat problematical. It had been decided to use mostly amateur tape recordings from friends and folk enthusiasts all over the world, including a number from Canadian relations of the family, who had been in Birtley the previous year. They had been in the habit of visiting Brown's Buildings on Saturday afternoons, and had taped Jack's singing. The tapes had been sent off to Canada on the Monday, and so quite a collection had built up. There were technical difficulties with transcription, and complex financial considerations. However, Don Stokoe organised the project, and Bill Leader agreed to do the technical business.

Bill was one of a handful of good recording engineers who liked folk music. As the Revival grew in the mid-'60s he recognised the demand for traditional song and music, which the big commercial labels were unwilling to touch. The pioneer, Topic Records, had its beginnings in the Communist party in the 1940s, specialising in political songs, but now, under direction from Bert Lloyd, it was putting out many albums of British traditional music. Bill Leader, having worked for Topic, decided in the late '60s to start his own business. He would have one label, the 'Trailer', which would cater for the growing number of 'Revival singers' such as Nic Jones, the Dransfield Brothers, Tony Rose and others who came to make a career as singers, and another, the 'Leader' label, which would issue albums of authentic, source singers. Significantly, for his first album on Leader, LEA40001, his flagship, Bill Leader did not choose one of the established rural singers from Southern England, Scotland, or Ireland. He chose Jack Elliott, the pitman from Durham. *Jack Elliott of Birtley* came out in 1969; it was a great success, and it gave Bill the impetus to challenge Topic in the importance and quality of folk music productions (5). It was launched at Bates Colliery in Ashington, by Lord Alfie Robens, Chairman of the NCB, and Sid Chaplin, well-known local ex-pitman author, who did one of the eulogies that went with the record's sleeve notes. Here is a review of the record by Mike Yates from the *Folk Music Journal*, 1970.

"The Jack Elliott record is sub-titled "A memorial album assembled from recordings made by his friends and admirers" and one would be

*"Jack's solo LP went like snaw off a dyke"*

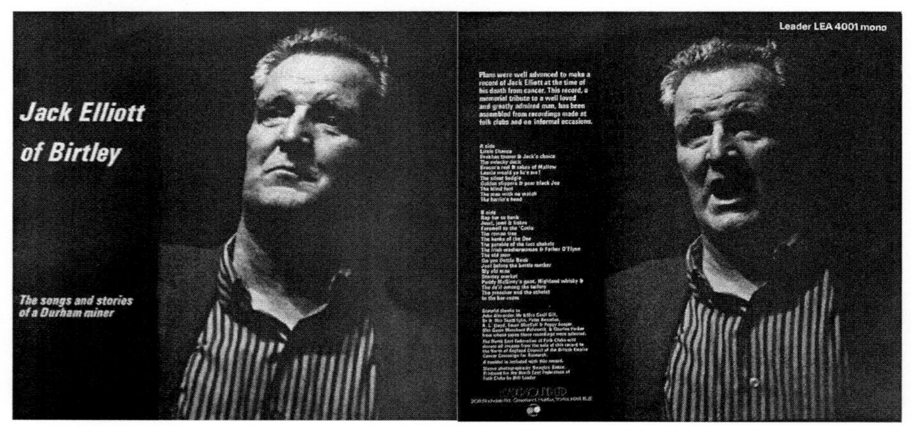

> hard put trying to think of a finer record for a new company to begin with. Bill Leader, whose name has been synonymous with some of the finest folk music recordings of the last decade, has edited over twenty tracks of vocal and instrumental music linked together with stories and speech. In many ways it is similar to the earlier Folkways record *The Elliotts of Birtley* and several of the songs are on both records. Industrial Durham is a far cry from, say, East Anglia, or Donegal for that matter and the songs on this record are likewise different. One does not expect to find Fair Phoebe and her amorous swains sporting about the Durham pits, but rather some hard-cut mining gem fit for a throat well lubricated on Newcastle Brown. A society does not necessarily lose its culture (and I include its folk culture in that) with its transition from a rural to an industrial state. Rather, it may be said to change and Jack Elliott stands out as the epitome of such a change. It will be hard to find a better memorial to such a fine man."

To use one of Jack's own expressions, "it went like snaw off a dyke". Although this solo LP is seen as a landmark record, it is notable that his voice had lost a lot of the quality heard in his singing just four years previously on the *Elliotts of Birtley* record, and must reflect his hitherto unsuspected illness.

After Jack died, it was clear that the Elliotts had lost their patriarchal guiding force, a man who simply could not be replaced. For the first few weeks following the funeral, the family were too upset to go to the Club. However, he had started something that was hard to stop, and Don Stokoe ran it while they got themselves together. As Jim Irving puts it, "Jack's seat wasn't allowed to be empty", and when they did return, Pete moved into it by comment consent.

*I saw a mouse run up the wall,*
*Pit lie idle, pit lie idle,*
*Saw its arse and that was all,*
*Pit lie idle, pit lie idle*

Several people started going to the Club at this time, and became lifelong enthusiasts. Benny Graham, now a professional folk singer, first started going to Birtley in 1967 when he was fifteen, the year after Jack died. It is interesting to note that these were the prosperous '60s, and folkies were better off. Whereas in 1962 Ed Pickford had used buses or walked to the Club, Benny now rode down from Stanley on his motorbike! Transportation was clearly an issue with Birtley, as Jim Irving used to fret about having enough petrol for his car, and on cold nights he used to take the spark plugs into the Club so they'd be warm enough to start the car afterwards! Anyway, Benny paints a very clear picture of the Club at that time. It had by then moved from the Red Lion to the Three Tuns, where they had a massive ballroom. All the family was there, with Pete in the Chair in the corner with Pat, John and Nan, Doreen and Bryan, and Len. Uncle Reece, who hadn't previously joined in with the folk club, was now a regular. Perhaps it was the huge reaction to Jack's death that made him realise what a big thing this was, and he rapidly and deservedly achieved "grand old man" status. He was still a very enthusiastic and charismatic singer, and took a keen interest in songs from Alexander Barrass's *The Pitman's Social Neet*, the epic musical play written in the 1890s, and a great reference point for dialect and the life led by pit families. Although Reece shared many songs with Jack and his family, some were original to him rather than 'family songs' ('The Other Fine Day' is an example), and he was a significant contributor to Lloyd's second edition of *Come All Ye Bold Miners*. It's said that 'My brother Sylveste', sung by Jim Irving and others in the North East, and more widely by Mike Harding, came from Reece.

For Benny, the format at the Club was always the same. Pete and Pat would start, then pass clockwise round the room with the Elliotts doing individual songs. He remembers particularly Doreen with 'My Son David', and Len's famous 'Gallowa' Hills'. Although the family might finish with 'Miners Life' or 'Wild Mountain Thyme', there was a strict regime. If he didn't get round to you, that was tough, no matter who you were. So there were nights when the likes of Bob Davenport, Johnny Handle, and Louis Killen didn't get a song. In those days, Pete ran it rigidly, with no favourites. As Benny says, "there were no stars at Birtley, unlike the Bridge where the platform provided entertainment for an audience." Generally, most songs were unaccompanied, and the politics was "worn lightly". Pete wanted a place where everybody had a chance to sing, especially local songs, they being guardians of the tradition.

There were also ceilidhs once a month, with Graham Binless calling, and a band, which was often supposed to be the High Level Ranters or the John Doonan Band, but more often than not was the Marsden Rattlers or Jimmy Irvine's band, due to the others having 'gigs'. It is interesting that both Benny and Ed Pickford before him became well-established performers, and both extol the great encouragement they got from the Elliott family. Benny was "encouraged beyond belief" by Pat and Pete. Many years later when he produced *The Pitman's Social Neet*, Pete came no less than five times, saying characteristically that it was the only way to understand the play.

By this time, John Elliott's son Bill, who had been on the record and allowed on some of the family gigs, was old enough to go to the Club. His strongest memories are of Andy Irvine and Allan Taylor on their first North East tours, when Allan was still singing traditional songs (and very well too, says Bill), Martin Carthy, and the McPeake family. The McPeakes' night was always a special night at the Club, not just due to the music, but also because of the affinity and friendship that developed between these two "folk families". Doreen describes having the McPeakes to stay with them at Number 7 Brown's Buildings as "the meeting of soulmates, Old Francie the patriarch, middle Francie his son, and young Francie, as well as 16-year old Kathleen."

Bill had never seen the Uillean pipes before, and he was even more knocked out when Finbar Fury guested at the Club. He too remembers the ceilidhs, and in particular the Christmas parties, which were so good that he even took his mates along! These parties were legendary, with everybody letting their hair down, dancing, and the centrepiece, the "Fyece to Fyece". For southerners, this is the face to face competition, where two contestants sit facing each other, nose to nose, eyes open, singing different songs, the dafter the better, until one cracks, either by messing up the song or, more often, by dissolving into hysterical laughter along with everybody else in the room. Doreen remembers this being first performed at Number 7 Brown's Buildings by Bill Pearson at the 1950 Christmas Party. He won the contest by singing 'The Lost Sheep on the Mountain' and just mimicking a sheep by baa-baaing. Pete had heard something similar performed by a workmate in his youth, a fitter from Houghton-le-Spring called Hedley. For a pound or so a man, two singers would stand as close together as they could get and sing two different songs. The first to show any expression was adjudged by a neutral referee to have lost. Pete says, "Hedley reckoned that for years he was the local champion, and I could well believe it. They'd have found it impossible to hide the pain! I was to remember Hedley and his singing twenty years later when we were looking for folk entertainment at our folk club Christmas party."

The fyece to fyece at the folk club party is always hugely popular, and there have been many stars over the years. Jim Mageean, already getting a reputation round the country as 'Shanty Jim', won it three years running, until John Elliott, always a totally biased and grossly interfering referee, banned shanties. It was only then that we realised that Jim didn't know any other songs! This has of course been remedied in spades, as now he is one of the best exponent of Joe Wilson and JP Robson songs you'll ever find.

Terri and Eric Freeman (who later were to start the Davy Lamp Club at Washington, and in the late '60s were running clubs in Sunderland) regarded Birtley as "hallowed ground", having heard of its great reputation. They remember very clearly their first visit to the Three Tuns in 1968. The awful weather meant a much lower turnout than usual, so they got asked to sing, which they did with trembling knees, terrified. But it didn't stop them having "a fantastic night because of the crack". The family were "larger than life", with Len in particular telling great stories (Help! Were they supposed to talk as well as sing?). Like others before and since, they were hooked on the family, and became regular attenders, as well as part of the family. To this day, Terri is like a daughter to Dot, and her kids are regarded as the Hendersons' grandbairns.

Jim Irving says that people were frightened to miss Birtley, "you should have been there last neet ...". It was thriving along with the rest of the folk clubs at that time. "You had lads coming down from Northumberland, lads up from Yorkshire and Teesside. The guests ... well ... they were up against it." And he's talking about the likes of MacColl and the Stewarts from Blairgowrie. There were high old times indeed! Jim didn't see such a fixed pattern to the nights as Benny had. On a good night the Elliotts might not sing, but on a poor night they'd steer it through. It's notable that John, for instance, would often sing a short quick one in order to give another singer some space. These people always put the importance of the night above any personal vanities.

Meanwhile Em, who had stopped going to the Club some time before Jack's death, and had been suffering from angina, retreated into herself, despite the best efforts of the family to cheer her up. In truth, the death of Jack had left her without much interest, and the spark had died. Em was nearing the end of her life, as Pete describes.

> "On July twelfth of 1968, John, Len and I and our partners went out for an Indian meal at a restaurant in the Bigg Market in Newcastle. Afterwards we all went back to our house in Sandyford for a drink and a crack until around midnight. At nine-o-clock next morning the doorbell rang and our Len and John were standing on the step. I almost knew before they told me. Mam had had a massive heart attack and died during the night. She'd had four or five minor attacks since Dad died, but this was a monster. Like Dad we had her cremated at Birtley, and again we had Bob Griffin do the eulogy. Colin Ross was in attendance to play on the Northumbrian pipes a couple of tunes she loved, 'The Rowan Tree' and 'Sweet Hesleyside'. Our ineffable sadness was tempered by the fact that in many ways death was what she wanted after Dad had gone."

There is no doubt that the death of Em so soon after Jack, probably from a broken heart, marked the end of an era. So much life gone. Although there's a lot more story to tell, this is the place to quote one of the best tributes ever paid to the Elliott couple. It was written for the cover of Jack's LP by a great friend of his, the great County Durham writer Sid Chaplin.

> "It is that he, a rank-and-file miner with a family to bring up, and what is more, working to bring them up at the hardest job in the pit at that time, on the cutting machines, made himself the embodiment not only of the Durham miner of his own day but of every Durham miner who has ever lived and toiled, dreamt dreams and saw visions, loved, jested, hated and knocked back a jar. What enabled him to do it was enduring love for his kind and the three weapons of voice, curiosity and memory – a memory sharp and as clear as a magic crystal. What I treasured most about him was his continuous flow of witty, humorous, often caustic 'crack', which all added up to a picture of the counter-environment and communal spirit that mining folk painfully built up against the brutal framework of their existence.
>
> As an artist in words he could hit off a voice, a situation or a period to perfection – spot on. As a human being he was big and generous, brimming over. He gave and gave. Em, his wife, would need as many other words again. I'll try to sum her up. She was a little woman, burning. I shall always remember her in her chair, smoking cigarette after cigarette, and burning with a zeal that could never be damped. She was Jack's helpmate. They brought a family up. They remembered their roots. They sang in their lives, and I shall never forget them."

## References for Chapter 3


1. Vic Gammon, Introduction to *The Folk Handbook*, EFDSS 2007
2. Maureen Atchison, BA Thesis, 1963 and Maxine Baker, BA Thesis, 1965, both Leeds School of Dialect and Folk Studies, Brotherton Library, University of Leeds
3. Gwen and Margaret Polwarth, *North Country Songs*, Frank Graham, 1969; Dawney, Michael, *Doon the Waggon Way*, Galliard, 1973; Dawney, Michael, *The Iron Man*, Galliard, 1974
4. FARNE, Folk Archive Resource North East, www.asaplive.com/FARNE/Home.cfm
5. *Jack Elliott*, Leader Records LEA 4001, 1969.

# Chapter 4 Politics, Class and Religion

## Politics and the Elliotts

The Elliotts have always had a reputation as proud standard-bearers of the working class, with passionately left-wing views, often seen by some as Communist in nature, although they would say "socialist". Their views and attitudes have meant most of the time that none of the political parties in this country could ever match their particular take on socialism. From the 1930s onward, Jack and Em found problems with the Labour party, and all of the family have been disappointed, to say the least, with Labour governments from Attlee to Blair. (The feelings of the remaining members regarding the Blair regime of recent times would be embarrassing to put into print.) People have seen these views as being inextricably linked with their songs, and yet, as indicated earlier, this was not always the case.

There is nothing in the historical record about strife or industrial militancy in the Elliott family before Jack's time, no family heritage of politics or activism. The pit had been in full production since he'd started just after the First World War, his father had been a deputy, and his brothers and sisters were in work. However, great events both locally and nationally were going to change things and radicalise the family forever. Global economics following the Great War had led to the 1926 Miners' Strike and the subsequent Depression, which lasted for several years, as described in Chapter 2. The hardships both during and after the 1926 Strike were intense, with many memories of hard bosses and indifferent blacklegs, although, as Reece proudly says, "There were no blacklegs at 'Cotia".

In 1925, Jack had fallen in love with Em Wilkin, had married her quickly, and she was expecting. Jack the Lad was about to become Jack the Dad, with family responsibilities now the priority. He needed his job, and a house, and wasn't about to go looking for trouble. Em was a quiet, fairly naive girl, who had escaped a drudgery that we have already seen, and yet she was far from politically aware. She had no experience of what it was like to be a miner's wife, but soon she came to realise it wasn't Jack's fault that things were bad. Together they became aware of the injustices of the system and the unchanged attitudes of the pit owners and managers. She told a vivid story of the time there was an accident at the pit, and a man's body was brought home "in a sack, on a handcart, and dumped at his widow's door, as if he were a dog". The supervisors reinforced the miners' sense of injustice. On one particular occasion, Jack and Reece had failed to make their target, and were taken before management. Doreen tells the story, "Reece was a big man with a broken nose, crossed muffler and cap, who only shaved once a week, 'Satda' when he was goin' oot the pub. A gentle giant, but he could look quite intimidating. They were on foreshift, but had to go and see the manager in their own time, 6 o'clock. Two giant men walking up the path, dejected, standing with their caps off, to see this get of a man. 'Tojo, Uncle Reece called him, after the then Japanese Emperor. I was still a kid, but felt the injustice, and was politicised by it. It was always Them and Us."

There were no strikes in the '30s, as the pressure on your job was too great, and they were illegal during the War. Jobs outside the pits were scarcer than ever, and a Union man on a bike with a crake (a football rattle) would often come round the house to tell them "The pit's lyin' idle" (no work). It was common for the owners to insist on a three-day week, because if it was less than that the men would qualify for dole payments, which looked like the owners were working with the government. There was plenty of work, although after Jack's problems with his back during the war, they were "as far back as ever".

## *"There were no blacklegs at 'Cotia."*
**Reece**

Certainly, these events are the sort of thing that will turn people political. As Em famously remarked in the film *Private Faces*, "You've got to keep a little bit of bitterness inside you. Don't be complacent. The depression could come back." (Her fist was clenched and raised slightly as she said this.) Well, in a way Em's words were prophetic. The 1926 Strike had been about loss of sales of coal, as were the 1973 and 1984 strikes. In 1926, whole communities were often dependent on one local coal owner for employment. Though this changed, and by the end of the century this dependency was no longer the case, the last strike in '84 was, of course, terminal. There is now virtually no industry left.

Ed Pickford says, "Miners' wives were usually non-militant until the '73 strike, when they were much more politically active, but Em was different. She was strong, and a thinker." Em expressed her political views very clearly in the film, "I hope that the day comes, I won't say a fairer distribution, but a fair, an even distribution so that there would be no distinctions whatsoever no matter what the man's work was. He could be a roadsweeper, a doctor, a musician, a gravedigger, there would be absolutely no difference in earnings. They're all important people, and they're entitled as human beings to enjoy the good things of life."

She and Jack were both in the Labour Party, Em more seriously than Jack, but both were really too left-wing for the Party, and did not get on any committees. Em was elected on to the Parish Council, for the sole purpose of getting political books into the library; Victor Gollancz had arrived in Birtley!

Jack was in the Union, and had a political passion, but was less happy with local organised politics. He went to meetings, but brought back mocking comments, which read like a comic script. The Chair at one meeting during the war had asked the committee if they knew where "Random" was, as its pit was getting bombed every night! When the treasurer at Fatfield Parish Council had given his financial report, a hand went up and asked what were these "sun dries" (rhyming with pies), to which the Treasurer replied, "Aa's not ower sure, but Aa think it's the little bit o' jam atop the butter."

Jack found more kinship for his beliefs with the International Workers' Association. He was not happy with the Labour Party, and since no other party was offering what he wanted, he spent a lot of time talking atheism and politics with Yankee Jim Roberts, the Geordie miner who gave him 'Celebrated Working Man'. Jim had been chased out of the USA for his politics, and had rescued him from the roof fall after his accident in the pit. Through him Jack and Em became aware of the "Wobblies", the International Workers' Organisation.

The IWW started in the USA in 1905, a loose amalgamation of socialists, anarchists, and radical trade unionists, mainly miners, which must have been part of the attraction for Jack and Em. The Wobblies emphasised that all labour struggles were part of a wider class struggle requiring organisation. The badge motto reads "An injury to one is an injury to all". They rejected the idea of labour leaders bargaining with employers of workers, and Jack had a similar antipathy based on his own experiences. They were less in evidence in Britain, but had been prominent in the 1926 General Strike and the 1947 Dockers' Strike, and it would seem that Jack and Em's association with the Wobblies informed their political viewpoint.

The added attraction must have been the Wobblies' penchant for song. When management started sending in the Salvation Army band to cover up the Wobbly speakers, Joe Hill wrote parodies of Christian hymns so that Union members could sing along with the Salvation Army band, but with their own purposes (for example, 'In the Sweet By and By' became 'There'll Be Pie in the Sky When You Die (That's a Lie)'). The *Little Red Songbook* was still available when the Folk Revival started in the early '60s, with performers like Pete Seeger and Woody Guthrie reflecting Wobbly views. While the family singarounds were at this stage a personal expression away from the hardship of the mines, here was an organisation that used song to express its issues and principles; to be fashioned into a tool to be used in the struggle. How could they resist?

*Old Joe Badger had a little Indian,*
*Old Joe Badger had a little Indian,*
*Old Joe Badger had a little Indian,*
*One little Indian boy.*

*He had two, he had three, Little Indians;*
*Four little, five little, six little Indians,*
*Seven little, eight little, nine little Indians,*
*Ten little Indian boys. (etc.)*

# Nationalisation and the NCB

After the Second World War, change was in the air, with the Labour Party winning a landslide victory in the 1945 election. For the Elliotts, as for so many people at that time, it seemed as though their time had come. The capitalist system had let everybody down in the '30s, and had led to a titanic battle between the democracies and the fascist dictatorships. Now the people had voted for change, giving the Labour Party an overwhelming majority. Surely now socialism would come at last, with nationalisation putting power in the hands of the people who had previously had to work for a privileged class, especially the miners. Pete Elliott wrote,

> "That crafty old git Churchill – who was as popular with my parents as a dose of' pox, principally because he turned out the army on striking miners in 1910 – he called a snap election, hoping to skate in on the strength of his premiership during the war. There was a Labour landslide. We all thought that Utopia was just around the corner. What optimistic dopes we working class can be!"

Attlee's post-war Labour government was an alliance of democratic socialists, trade unionists right through to radical Marxists, but in practice it was unwilling to contemplate any change that would challenge the sovereignty of the familiar parliamentary system. Labour's manifesto had called for the "socialist commonwealth of Great Britain", free, democratic, progressive, and public-spirited. Orwell's 1941 essay *England your England* echoed the belief in a better life of welfare plus nationalisation; "This war, unless we are defeated, will wipe out most of the existing class privileges. There are every day fewer people who wish them to continue." His dream of a new kind of socialist society was widely shared among Labour supporters.

Labour's first challenge came from the ending of American money under the Lend Lease scheme. This was replaced by a loan under the Marshall Aid Plan that saddled Britain with a crippling debt it was unable to pay off for the next fifty years. The money needed to be spent on rebuilding Britain's transport and industrial infrastructure, but the Attlee Government spent much of it on the Welfare State.

Part of Labour's plan was taking into public ownership, or nationalising, a sizeable chunk of the British economy, particularly coal and other power sources. Among the criticisms of nationalisation was the fact that there was little coherent planning to relate it to the economy as a whole. Also, the casual appointments to the nationalised boards allowed ministerial interference, which underpinned unrealistic policies.

When Labour won the election in 1947, there were street parties in Birtley, the sort of thing the rest of us only had on VE Day. The Elliotts saw "Vesting Day", as the date of the nationalisation of the coal-mines in 1947 was known, as leading to Utopia. They had a list of wants: the land first, then the banks ... The family didn't see themselves as Communists, but assumed that if they got socialism, then Communism would follow! An extract from the NUM official website gives the flavour of the time.

> "Vesting Day, January 1, 1947, saw the nationalisation of Britain's coal industry, and miners and their families marched in thousands behind banners and colliery bands to the pitheads where they saw new plaques declaring 'This colliery is now managed by the National Coal Board on behalf of the people.'

All the mining communities around the country believed this was the beginning of a change that would bring decent wages, family security and public ownership of the coal industry. Soon, however, hopes and dreams began to sour as miners became increasingly aware that private ownership had been replaced by State rather than common ownership. It was now apparent that control and management of the industry had been left in the hands of those who had previously been either managers or actual owners of private mines."

The Elliotts shared this disappointment. In the first place, they strongly resented having to pay the owners for the pits, and to add injury to this injustice, the new nationalised coal industry was also forced to pay compensation to former owners for pits which had already been closed! And it all seemed a bit of an anti-climax, with the managers all being the same people, the conditions just the same, and with competition between the coalfields just as before. Pete talks about this time in characteristically robust terms.

> "The first thing that went wrong was that a whole bunch of macky-on socialists got most of the top jobs. The premiership job for instance went to Clem Attlee, with fruity voice and public school education, eventually to become Lord Attlee – going into the House of Lords that the Labour Party had sworn to abolish once they got into power. They introduced the free National Health Service and before the next election had begun to dismantle it by introducing prescription, dentistry and optical charges. They nationalised the gas, coal and electrical industries, then put the same buggers in to run them as had been there when they were in private hands. They also significantly failed to nationalise banks and the land, which they had promised to do in their manifesto. More failed dreams!"

An example of the negative effects of government interference came when the newly created National Coal Board (NCB) was instructed to sell its coal at less than the commercial price applicable throughout Europe. This meant that a potentially extremely profitable industry consistently showed a loss on its balance sheet. There was also a widespread feeling that an opportunity to give workers genuine control had been missed. Bryan Henderson observes that the NUM didn't embrace nationalisation as they didn't want to be involved with a management that was the same old order as before. He contrasts it with the sort of workers' control seen in Communism, or at least with workers' involvement, as in Western Europe where bosses and workers were on the same side (i.e. the side of getting more work rather than losing it through industrial action!). In a way, he was foreseeing one of the main causes of Britain's economic troubles in the '60s and '70s. The Elliotts as a family believed that "we never even had socialism in this country".

Mind you, it wasn't all perfect harmony, and fierce debate was often a feature of family life. In fact, even when they agreed, they'd have the fiercest arguments. Onlookers in the kitchen would be highly entertained as well as educated by the honest and invigorating rows, which for the Elliotts were commonplace. Here's a snapshot of such an exchange involving all four of the Elliott children, when they were in their thirties and forties, recorded by Charles Parker in 1967.

Doreen: "I've seen a terrific change, not only in the miners themselves, but their wives."

John: "'Cos the telly's come on man. Bingo."

Doreen: "It isn't even the telly John. They've got more money. Life has been made easier for them. They've got material things they never had before."

John: "They've been seduced by the good life. What good has it ever done them?"

Doreen: "John, I know people that haven't even got a television."

Len: "The majority of human beings are apathetic. They do not care."

Doreen: "I think they do care, I think they care about the wrong things."

Len: "You want your cake and eat it. Caring about the wrong things is worse than not caring."

Doreen: "Oh My God, no Len."

John: "The vast majority, they're not capable of thinking any higher."

Len: "They will not stir themselves."

Doreen: "If you're talking about bingo. It's not my form of entertainment at all. But I think for a lot of people it's the only entertainment that they're capable of doing."

Len: "But that's what I'm saying."

Pete: "But what's wrong with it is, it's something for nowt. It's sheer bloody stupid materialism. They cannot see beyond the acquisition of … stuff."

Bryan: "But what was the gaff, in the old days?"

Doreen: "But that's what I'm saying."

Pete: "They've been seduced by the good life."

Len: "Socialism is unnatural. If you go back as far as mankind goes, it's survival of the bloody fittest. Socialism is unnatural."

Pete: "Balls. It's just as bloody natural to help each other. Don't give me that, that every bugger is a selfish swine, who … I don't accept this."

John: "In 1000 years of civilisation we've had no system that remotely approaches what they say is a basic."

Len: "I didn't say it was a basic."

Pete: "We had this community thing in this bloody street, when I was a bairn, people helping each other."

Len: "What about the buggers that were forcing these conditions on us? That forced you to help each other out?"

Pete: "You weren't forced to help each other. You helped each other because you wanted to."

And these were the bits which could be picked out, as a lot of the time they were all shouting at once! So by 1967 the family had become more politicised, much, much more so than most other people in their community. The same was true of the music, and both aspects attracted people to Brown's Buildings.

Their mutual political involvement drew Bryan and Doreen together. They met as teenagers at social meetings of the Labour Party's League of Youth, in the late 1940s, and well remember the Newcastle Youth Parliament, to which the political parties sent delegates to discuss specific issues for a day.

> "We were very very political, and that had a big influence on our life. We formed the League of Youth years before, which occupied most of our time. We used to sing then, go away for weekends, a whole gang of us. Pete used to take his guitar. We sang all sorts, even opera, from my dad's opera records, and we'd sing an aria from Nabucco, with our own words! We were very catholic in our music (catholic atheists!)."

## *"It was always them and us."*
**Doreen**

Later, in their early twenties, they spent a week at Butlin's in Filey, with League of Youth people from all over the country, where Labour Party luminaries would come and talk politics at them. (They were, however, free after 5 p.m. each day for whatever else took their fancy!) Lots of their holidays were spent camping in Northumberland with other young people from the League. There they would dress up and act out plays. This would be in the early '50s, before TV and computer games, of course, when people made their own entertainment. They attended political meetings and borrowed books from the Left Book Club.

Doreen and Bryan still remember some of these influential characters from their youth. One focus for socialist interest was Newcastle market on Sunday nights, where there were fiery political speeches from people like Jack Brighton, the "Atheist Bishop", whom we met in Chapter 2, and the heckling was mighty. "Very very exciting," says Doreen, still remembering it with great fondness over fifty years later. The Elliotts' passionate views on politics and religion could be very infectious. Charles Parker, for example, a very cultured and religious man who along with MacColl had produced *The Big Hewer*, became a Communist and an atheist as a result of meeting them. Similarly, as Bryan Henderson says, "Philip Donnellan was a frustrated brickie" (Bryan's own trade). Donnellan had been responsible for filming *Death of a Miner*. Here is an interesting observation on Parker from MacColl's autobiography *Journeyman* (1).

> "For Charles, meeting miners was a shattering experience. Up until this time he had managed to hold on to the Panglossian view that everything was all right (or nearly all right) in this best of all possible worlds. The coalfields changed all that. Before we were half-way through the fieldwork, he confessed to feeling utterly uneducated in the presence of miners. Prior to this he had maintained a fairly formal relationship with his informants. During our first days of recording miners, Charles would talk more than the person he was recording. In a way, he was trying to justify his beliefs, his presence. It was Dick Beamish, an articulate and militant Union shop steward, who finally silenced Charles in a series of brilliant outbursts. After that, Charles learned to listen."

Ewan, on the other hand, found nothing surprising in their ability to express themselves. "After all, I had been brought up among people who talked about important things like politics and revolution, and who referred to Burns and Tanahill as if they had been members of the family circle. Furthermore, I had been fairly familiar with miners and their families ever since the days of my childhood." It seems that there is little that is ordinary here, with either the Elliotts or their visitors!

*"You've got to keep a little bit of bitterness inside you."* **Em**

Unknown to the family, their appearances in *The Big Hewer* and the LP of the early '60s had helped them become an inspiration for young socialists, and political icons for at least one young Geordie.

Dave Douglass is a fascinating character, the son of a Jarrow pitman who as a 14-year-old was rabidly left-wing, active in the most militant of the Tyneside political factions, and by his own admission something of a tearaway, always "on the hoy". Small wonder that he didn't get on with his strictly Methodist father; but when Dave played him the Elliotts' LP, his pitman dad was overwhelmed to hear his own culture on a record. It was something he had never imagined possible, and a bridge was formed between father and son. What an amazing achievement for the music! It is ironic that Dave, who was storming around Newcastle demanding rights for the workers of the world, had not thought of his dad as one of the workers for whom he was trying to campaign.

In Dave's opinion, the regional flavour, their culture, the "spirit of the community" was an essential ingredient of the socialist programme, and the Elliotts were in the socialist vanguard. But the Elliotts didn't sing many overtly political songs, so did he regard the songs as political tools? No, he says, it was just as important that they were from the area, from their culture. For Dave even the Northumbrian pipe tunes, such as 'Derwentwater's Farewell', recalled political battles of the distant past. If the Bridge Club didn't allow political songs, nor Eddie Pickford singing 'Johnny B. Goode', well, Birtley would allow both. He remembers going now and again to the Three Tuns by bus, as a pilgrimage, and finding it incredibly difficult to get in. They were acting as role models for the politicos, as was Ed Pickford, though Dave thinks that neither knew this at the time. He talks about a wild social scene in Newcastle, gatecrashing parties, and playing Elliotts' songs. (We do have to remember, however, that for Dave free sex was a political statement, whereas for most of us it was just fun.)

Dave later became a pitman, and immediately got involved with the NUM. Being transferred to South Yorkshire following the Robens pit closures of the '60s, Dave and his politico mates soon established an active coterie in the Doncaster area, setting up the Red Star Club, probably the most political folk club ever. Politics was in the air in the '60s, but in 'Donny', Dave found a culture stuck in the '50s, the men in the pit villages still wearing the drapes of the Teddy Boy days, and the girls in bodices and frilly skirts. It was inevitable that the Geordie folkies would guest, and sure enough, Jack Elliott, The Northern Front, and Tony Corcoran made regular appearances. Later, after Jack's death, the Elliott family continued to travel to Donny. They also did gigs in the outlying pit villages, and the Yorkshire miners' gala. They made a great impact there, and several pit families 'covered' Elliotts' songs, adapting them to Yorkshire. When I commented to Dave that the family was very unusual in their community, he told me that they were "like the Geordies – honorary Irish". By this he meant that they shared a culture of song, dance, and crack associated with the Irish traditional culture. In common with the Doonans, who were often visitors in Dave's mother's kitchen, they talked about the "owd songs" rather than "folk songs", a term seemingly not in any lexicon before the 1960s.

The Doonan family came from Hebburn, descendents of Irish immigrants from the mid-19th Century who had come to seek work in the burgeoning shipyards on the Tyne. The family had passed Irish music down from father to son, in this generation with flute and piccolo player John Doonan, soon to be joined by sons Michael on Uillean pipes and flute, and Kevin on fiddle.

*Salvation Army free from sin,*
*Went to heaven in corn-beef tin,*
*The tin upset and down they fell,*
*Instead of going to heaven, they all went to Hell.*

# The Robens' Pit Closures

Pit closures in the '60s would threaten many North Eastern communities. It became clear that British deep-mined coal was far more expensive than opencast coal from abroad, and Britain was forced to allow cheaper foreign coal to be imported. The consequence was wholesale pit closures, and Alfred Robens, the then Chairman of the NCB and architect of the closure programme, has forever been linked to hardship and unemployment in the less productive parts of the British coalfield. The North East was squarely in this category, and many pits, particularly in the west of Durham, closed at this time. This in turn led to the infamous 'Category D' classification of some villages whose pit had closed. This meant there would be no development allowed, and the community would be left to wither. It happened at West Cornforth, Cornsay Colliery, and many other places like that. And all this was happening under Wilson's Labour government! Robens, who was later elevated to the peerage, achieved more widespread notoriety for his callous comments regarding responsibility for the Aberfan disaster. In 1966, 116 children were buried alive by a pit heap that fell upon their school, which Robens described as a "natural event". A man with very little conscience, it would seem. Robens was the target of several North East songwriters, notably Ed Pickford with his immortal 'Pound a Week Rise', still a favourite with many singers such as Dick Gaughan.

*Come all of you colliers who work in the mine*
*From England to Scotland, from Tees up to Tyne*
*I'll sing you the song of the pound a week rise*
*And the men who were fooled by the government lies.*

*Chorus:*
*So it's down you go, down below Jack*
*Where you never see the skies*
*And you're working in a dungeon*
*For your pound a week rise.*

*In nineteen and sixty, a long time ago*
*The mineworkers' leaders to Lord Robens did go*
*Saying, "We work very hard, every day we risk our lives*
*We ask you here and now for a pound a week rise."*

*Then up spoke Lord Robens and made this decree*
*Saying, "When the output rises, then I'll agree*
*To raise up your wages, give to you fair pay*
*I was once a miner's man myself in my day."*

*The miners they went homeward and worked hard and well*
*With their lungs filled with coal dust in the bosom of hell*
*The output rose fifteen per cent and eighteen and more*
*Till after two years had gone it rose above a score.*

*The mineworkers' leaders went for their hard-won prize*
*To ask Lord Robens for their pound a week rise*
*But Robens wouldn't give a pound – he wouldn't give ten bob*
*He gave them seven and six and said, "Get back to your job."*

*Come all of you colliers and heed what I say*
*Don't believe Lord Robens when he says he'll give fair pay*
*He'll tell you to work hard and make the output rise*
*But you'll get "pie in the sky" instead of a one pound rise.*

(words and pie courtesy *The Ed Pickford Songbook* (2))

For mining folk like the Elliotts, it felt like the pre-nationalisation days. The owners were still there, still calling the shots. For example, there was no provision for dealing with redundant miners, as there was in Europe. In Durham, the pits that were closed were the older ones in the west and north of the county, which were generally less efficient. However, the coastal pits such as Dawdon, Easington and Vane Tempest were still good, efficient pits with plenty of reserves. (Note the name of the last pit; it was the family name of the Marquis of Londonderry, one of the major coalowners at nationalisation. It has always amazed me that the NCB was not forced to change its name.) These deep pits at the coast ran out several miles under the North Sea, and when they were eventually shut in the early '90s it was said that the seams ran as far as Norway! In some areas of Durham, following the Robens closures, there were as many buses ferrying miners from west to east out to the coast, as there were taking kids to school.

However, many miners were not given this option, and they were given the choice of the midlands coalfields like Nottingham, or the dole. Jock Purdon's song 'Farewell to 'Cotia', which got sung by both Jack and Reece, spells this out rather well.

*Ye brave bold men of 'Cotia, The day is drawing near*
*You'll have to change your lodgin's lads, You'll have to change your beer*
*But leave your picks behind you, You'll ne'er need them again*
*Off you go to Nottingham, Join Robens' merry men.*

*Ye brave bold men of 'Cotia, The day is drawing near*
*You'll have to change your language lads, You'l1 have to change wah' cheer*
*But leave your picks behind you, You'll ne'er need them again*
*Off you go to Nottingham, Join Robens' merry men.*

*Ye brave bold men of 'Cotia, The day is drawing thus*
*You'll have to change your Banner boys, And join the exodus*
*But leave your cares behind you, Your future has been planned*
*Off you go to Nottingham, Lord Robens' promised land.*

*Ye brave bold men of 'Cotia, To you I say farewell*
*And maybe someone will someday, The 'Cotia story tell*
*But leave it all behind you, The death knell has been tolled*
*'Cotia was a colliery, Her men were brave and bold.*

Jock's comment on the song was, "Aa knew the pit was closin' and that a lot of the lads would be movin' away to pits down south, so ah wrote 'Farewell to 'Cotia' for them, and put it up in the pit head baths." In fact, the 'Cotia men were offered Dawdon or Vane Tempest at the coast, but, to this day, there are still sizeable bits of a Geordie diaspora in Nottinghamshire, South Yorkshire, and Staffordshire.

The closure of 'Cotia in 1965 after 366 years was a great blow to the people who worked there, from a practical point of view but also an emotional one. Jack Elliott had just retired, as had Reece a few years earlier, but John Elliott and Jock Purdon were still in the prime of their working lives. When, along with many of his mates, Jock asked to buy his lamp, he was refused. The men really hated the manager for saying no, but Jock's son Gavin, who wrote a book about 'Cotia in the early '70s, has recently come across letters from the colliery manager begging his boss to let them have the lamps. Actually, says Gavin, the manager had told Jock to

*The Closure Notice*

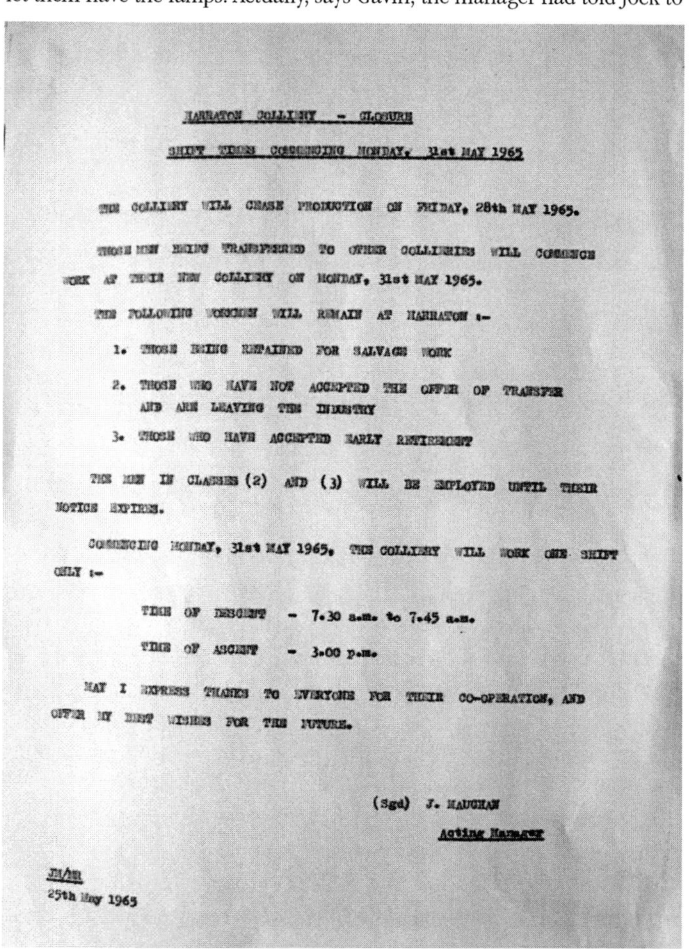

HARRATON COLLIERY - CLOSURE

SHIFT TIMES COMMENCING MONDAY, 31st MAY 1965

THE COLLIERY WILL CEASE PRODUCTION ON FRIDAY, 28th MAY 1965.

THOSE MEN BEING TRANSFERRED TO OTHER COLLIERIES WILL COMMENCE WORK AT THEIR NEW COLLIERY ON MONDAY, 31st MAY 1965.

THE FOLLOWING WORKMEN WILL REMAIN AT HARRATON :-

1. THOSE BEING RETAINED FOR SALVAGE WORK
2. THOSE WHO HAVE NOT ACCEPTED THE OFFER OF TRANSFER AND ARE LEAVING THE INDUSTRY
3. THOSE WHO HAVE ACCEPTED EARLY RETIREMENT

THE MEN IN CLASSES (2) AND (3) WILL BE EMPLOYED UNTIL THEIR NOTICE EXPIRES.

COMMENCING MONDAY, 31st MAY 1965, THE COLLIERY WILL WORK ONE SHIFT ONLY :-

TIME OF DESCENT - 7.30 a.m. to 7.45 a.m.

TIME OF ASCENT - 3.00 p.m.

MAY I EXPRESS THANKS TO EVERYONE FOR THEIR CO-OPERATION, AND OFFER MY BEST WISHES FOR THE FUTURE.

(Sgd) J. MAUGHAN

Acting Manager

JM/[illegible]

25th May 1965

take the lamp, put in a chit to say he'd lost it in a fall of stone, and he would sign it, but Jock was of such moral rectitude that he would not go along with the plan! Gavin also has recently acquired the full details of all the men and what was to happen to them, as well as a copy of the paper that was pinned to the board at the colliery giving notice of closure.

HARRATON COLLIERY – CLOSURE

SHIFT TIMES COMMENCING MONDAY, 28TH MAY 1965.

THOSE MEN BEING TRANSFERRED TO OTHER COLLIERIES WILL COMMENCE WORK AT THEIR NEW COLLIERY ON MONDAY, 31ST MAY 1965.

THE FOLLOWING WORKMEN WILL REMAIN AT HARRATON:-

1. THOSE BEING RETAINED FOR SALVAGE WORK
2. THOSE WHO HAVE NOT ACCEPTED THE OFFER OF TRANSFER AND ARE LEAVING THE INDUSTRY
3. THOSE WHO HAVE ACCEPTED EARLY RETIREMENT

THE MEN IN CLASSES (2) AND (3) WILL BE EMPLOYED UNTIL THEIR NOTICE EXPIRES.

COMMENCING MONDAY, 31ST MAY 1965, THE COLLIERY WILL WORK ONE SHIFT ONLY: -

TIME OF DESCENT – 7.30 a.m. to 7.45 a.m.

TIME OF ASCENT – 3.00 p.m.

MAY I EXPRESS THANKS TO EVERYONE FOR THEIR CO-OPERATION, AND OFFER MY BEST WISHES FOR THE FUTURE.

JM/MR (Sgd) J. MAUGHAN
25th May 1965 Acting Manager

The pit closed in May 1965, and Gavin's book has a photograph of an old man wheeling a pram up a muddy lane towards 'Cotia the colliery with all the buildings and winding gear (3). The photographer was Norman Anderson, a pitman, the old man was his father, a retired miner, and the baby in the pram was his son. A week later the pithead had been razed to the ground. This must have been just before the film *Death of a Miner* in which we see John Elliott looking through the rubble at the 'Cotia pithead and picking out those old records.

A couple of extracts from Gavin's book illustrate the bald matter-of-factness of the situation facing the men at that time.

"The last coals were drawn out of 'Cotia on Friday February 26th, 1965 and 'Cotia lads rode to bank for the last time on Friday May 20th 1965.

*Cotia pit a week before closure in May 1965*

The work cage was taken off and Harraton's swift turning pulley wheels, a familiar sight to generations of miners, were stilled forever. 'Cotia was no more."

"When the colliery closed in 1965, I was one of the last men riding out of Harraton before the' took the cage off, one Friday in May. The' was five of us down the colliery that day. The shaft man, Mr Wilkinson, Alan Geoffries: assistant, Ronald Gibson: blacksmith, Joe Elsdon and myself. We were the last five men out of 'Cotia on the Friday dinnertime, just before the' took the cage off. It was the first time I'd ever seen a cage removed in 48 years I'd worked at the colliery. That was the finish of 'Cotia. On the following Monday I started at the Vane Tempest." *Jack Johnson*

Jock went to Dawdon where he was a deputy for a few years before spending the rest of his career as a civil servant. John Elliott was down for Vane Tempest, but in fact left the pits at that point.

*My lad's a canny lad*
*He works down the pit*
*He never comes to see us*
*Unless he wants a bit.*

# The Elliotts and Class

Jack and Em's political viewpoints were passed on to all of their children, but particularly so with Pete and Doreen, who became more extreme and active than their parents. As we have seen, when Jack died, Pete took over the chair of the Club, and although very set in his ways, he was still fiery in his politics. "There was no arguing with Pete," says Ed Pickford. He was proud to be called a humanist, socialist, and folk singer, and it showed in his every reaction to the things he saw around him. As a socialist, Pete could never understand why working-class people who were intelligent and knowledgeable suddenly became middle-class. He wanted people to come down to the working-class level, rather than him move up! Achievement was a personal goal rather than a means to abandon one's roots.

One unique achievement of Pete Elliott has nothing to do with singing, politics, or unions. By virtue of his work in the laboratory at the University he had his name on a research paper in Nature (Vol. 199 pp 1242–1244, 1963, entitled "A working model of the mechanical escapement in Su Sung's Astronomical Clock Tower" by Prof. Aubrey F. Burstall, W.E. Lansdale and P. Elliott). There are eminent scientists the world over who have spent a whole career failing to get a paper in the world's leading science journal. To Pete it was a matter of interest and a job well done.

When Pete grew up, he stayed clear of the pits, but loved everything about the community surrounding the industry. He was also ambivalent about the pits, thinking they should all be closed down, and was very angry with his brothers and other lads for going down the pit. There was no pit romanticism for him. But then this was a widespread view in mining communities. Men went to the pits most often because they had no choice.

Solidarity with the Union was always important to him. Quite late in life, when watching a man from the Confederation of British Industry talking to the TUC, the miners' delegates walked out, but his own Union didn't. When quizzed by Pete later the man could not justify his position, so Peter tore up his Union card. This from a man who had always said he would die a union man.

He took his Union responsibilities very seriously, so much so that his two bouts of depression were in part due to his activities as shop steward. Although he had managed to save many of his colleagues' jobs, there were still two people made redundant, something that clearly preyed on his mind.

His family were always expected to follow his political lead. Pete reserved his most consistent and vitriolic disdain for the Tories, and his kids certainly knew this. As his son Pete says, "Politics was everything in the house. Once our Paul threatened to vote Tory, and Pa said 'You fuckin' vote Tory, you're out son'". When I asked Pete and Laura whether he tried to teach them politics, the answer was an emphatic yes. "Don't believe them, son" was a common utterance. Laura became political when she saw her dad shouting at the telly over Northern Ireland.

It seems that young Pete was ambivalent about the Folk Revival, reluctantly admitting that the working class didn't want it, and that it wouldn't have happened but for the middle classes. Although the family were famous in folk circles, these did not permeate working-class Tyneside, and their neighbours and workmates in the town were rarely seen at the Club.

Most of all he treasured the family he had been born into, and their contribution to the Folk Revival in which they played such a significant part. He wasn't the world's best singer or musician, but he had an intense interest in all things musical that came down through at least two generations of Elliotts, particularly his father, with whom he'd shared all sorts of musical tastes, most of it via the shellac 78s on the wind-up gramophone.

Doreen also was highly aware of the issues of class and culture. She says, "I was always for the underdog, being one myself, the odd man out, taught me with a vengeance at the secondary school. No uniform, no religion. Just needed to be vegetarian and we'd have been expelled! In my younger days I helped form unions at three places I worked in, two of them in shops. USDAW was the union – the management wanted to search our handbags! We stopped that, and got tea breaks and a rise. At Vickers Armstrong in Scotswood Road – trade unionism at its most militant, but it was a different story in the offices where I worked. Well, together with an aristocratic man called Fred Reed and with great support from the men in the yard, we soon formed a union." In later years, when on holiday in Cyprus, she spent time on the picket line of the striking hotel workers! "People's needs are the same the world over," she comments. Following in her mother's footsteps, Doreen later stood for the local council, notably as an Independent Socialist. Like their parents, the Elliott children did not find any political party quite fulfilled their expectations.

*"No uniform, no religion. Just needed to be vegetarian and we'd have been expelled."* **Doreen**

This political legacy has been carried into a new arena by one of the next generation of the family. John's son Bill Elliott remembers the general political awareness in the family, with his grandma, Em, being very well read, Nye Bevan her big hero, and that she was a politician herself. He also comments on the strong disagreements between members of the family, particularly between his Uncle Pete and his Uncle Len, of which we saw an example earlier in this chapter. These disputes did not lead to any falling out, but it is worth noting that there have been several serious and long-term rifts in the family, which seem to be more about personal chemistry than political differences.

Nowadays, Bill Elliott teaches in Wallsend, an ex-shipbuilding area, where the kids still have working-class values, something that can easily be recognised. He talks about these matters with his sixth-formers, using *Death of A Miner* to show some 1960s attitudes to class. His grandmother, Em, had a strong working-class feeling, and disliked the middle classes more than the upper classes. To Em the middle class were all about pretension, about forgetting where you came from. If you were a miner you were working-class whether you liked it or not, and Em in particular used the word a lot, as when she talked about the blacklegs as having "sold out their own class".

> "She used the word class then, about blacklegs selling out their own class, the working class. And then she uses the term middle class, which she doesn't have much time for. Blacklegs should remember that people go on strike for the betterment of their own class, and they are selling out. I mean, she'd no time for blacklegs at all, and there wasn't a blackleg at 'Cotia pit. And basically she talks about that structure in society, and she knows what part she belongs to, and has strong views about other parts of that society. So what I try to show the kids is that at the end of the 20th Century, beginning of the 21st, there is an argument that the class structure has changed, and changed quite dramatically. Other people would say there's no change, so I'm trying to get the kids to think this through, through the two arguments."

Bill's use of the film is a far cry from its original message in some respects, but in others his examination of the views held by that culture is as relevant now as when the film was first made. When asked about his dad's political views Bill comments that whilst Pete and Doreen had inherited their mother's fiery political passion, their brother John took after Jack. Yes, his dad talked a little about pit life, but was not the type to express his troubles. He always had a view, as we can see as he leads the argument about the politics of the pit village in the film *Private Faces*, but wouldn't follow it up with a letter to the council, the press, or the local MP. He'd made his point, but things were the way they had to be. But, like Jack, it wasn't that he didn't care. He had his own way, and if he could find a humorous aspect to a matter, he'd take that route. Again, in the film *Death of a Miner*, it is his dad John who is showing us round the ruins of 'Cotia Pit, with all the job cards lying around in the rubble, pieces of paper which management had told them were so vital to keep, now blowing around in the wind. Sometimes people thought he didn't care, that he was making it all a joke, but as we've seen, this was far from the case. Bill uses his personal history to teach the kids.

> "So they're given a view on this from the 1960s, so when you're looking at sociology as we do, you go back as far as Marx in terms of theory, but what social changes would their parents, their grandparents be aware of. Well these are my grandparents and these are the views they held. Now are they still relevant, are they accurate? This is the question being posed by the film. And it's a novelty for them (the kids) 'cos I'm in the film, a 16-year-old at Birtley Folk Club, and I'm listening to Foster Charlton playing, with Colin Ross, I think it's 'Derwentwater's Farewell', and then Don Stokoe gets up and sings the Jock Purdon song, 'Farewell to 'Cotia'. This was a special night at the Club, for Phillip Donellan to film, and all the family were there. So the kids can see me there, a 16-year-old, and if you like it's a bit of light relief, a bit of a novelty. But with a serious edge. It's different, it's not a textbook."

Bill Elliott considers both his Uncle Pete and himself to be middle-class because of their jobs, and that the whole class thing has become blurred. "Look at Tony Benn, first an aristocrat, then a Labour 'grandee' unveiling the new 'Cotia Banner. Definitely a man of the people."

As Dave Douglass pointed out, the Birtley Club always had politics at its core. By the time Jim Irving, South Shields singer, musician, and later to be organiser of Marsden Folk Club started going to Birtley Folk Club in 1964, there was certainly a political flavour to the evening. "It was the biggest political platform we'd ever had." He had never mixed with middle-class people, but at Birtley there were university people from Durham and Newcastle. There were consultants and clergy! "We didn't think we had a chance of getting any further in life, because we knew nowt. We heard political songs like Leon Rosselson's 'Diggers Song'; great, but who were the diggers?" (Leon Rosselson is a professional folk singer and songwriter, who is noted for his political songs, many of which have been recorded by eminent artists such as Martin Carthy and Dick Gaughan.) Jim cites Pete Smith, a working-class lad from Manchester, as an example of somebody who had risen through the Union, worked his way into academia, and was now a tutor at Durham. Despite having been a Merchant Navy officer of some standing in the community when he was home, Jim felt out of his depth outside the area or with educated people. It was folk music which decided him to get an education, which would help him overcome a feeling of inferiority. Birtley Folk Club had opened his eyes.

There were lots of political songs, including Irish rebel songs, which after the Troubles started in 1969 became too sensitive to sing. Jim remembers lots of arguments about singing these, including some with soldiers on leave from Ireland who happened to be in the audience. This is another illustration of how unusual Birtley was as a folk club, where political debate could break out at any time, whereas in most clubs it would have been swept under the carpet. Eric Freeman, great friend of Doreen and Bryan and organiser of the Davy Lamp Folk Club at Washington, says that there is now very little politics at the club, but thinks that for Pete, Doreen and Bryan, it has always been the be-all and end-all. They were the most political. "In the old days, anything right-wing would be stopped, or challenged. Doreen still goes on marches." He jokingly says she only asks about the cause once she's started marching!

# The '84 Miners' Strike

If there was one event in recent history that crystallised the stance of the family's politically active members, it was the Miners' Strike of 1984. The Conservative government under Margaret Thatcher had returned to power in 1979, determined to break the back of the entire trade union movement and in particularly the union responsible for their double humiliation in the strikes of 1972 and 1974. As Seamus Milne wrote in The Enemy Within, "The NUM's unique industrial position, its unmatched radicalisation, and the Conservative Party's spectacular humbling at the miners' hands left little question as to which union would become the new government's most important target … The overriding aim of the British government's entire energy policy from 1979 onwards was to destroy forever the power-base of the National Union of Mineworkers and exorcise the Tory nightmares of the early 1970s." (4)

In 1984, the National Coal Board, under its chair Ian McGregor, announced that an agreement reached after the 1974 Miners' Strike had

*'The Six' campaigning in North Staffs*

become obsolete, and that in order to rationalise the subsidies the government gave to the industry they intended to close 20 coal mines. The proposed pit closures represented 20,000 jobs, and miners became sensitive to the threat to their livelihood. On the 12th March NUM president Arthur Scargill declared the various separate miners' strikes to be a national strike and called for action from members in all coalfields. Thatcher referred in Parliament to the striking miners as "the enemy within" who did not share the values of the British people. "We had to fight the enemy without in the Falklands. We always have to be aware of the enemy within, which is much more difficult to fight and more dangerous to liberty."

From this viewpoint the government responded to the miners' dedication with increasing savagery, and a massive co-coordinated police operation was set up to combat effective picketing. "The coalfields of Britain became battlefields in which civil liberties and human rights were smashed by the truncheons of riot police. Scenes at the Orgreave coking plant in South Yorkshire in May, June and July 1984 horrified participants and observers alike. At the height of the picketing, 10,000 miners faced 8,000 police equipped with riot gear, horses, dogs and motorised vehicles." (NUM Official Website.) On the following day, Thatcher said in a speech, "I must tell you that what we have got is an attempt to substitute the rule of the mob for the rule of law, and it must not succeed. It must not succeed. There are those who are using violence and intimidation to impose their will on others who do not want it ...The rule of law must prevail over the rule of the mob." Arthur Scargill's response to the incident was, "We've had riot shields, we've had riot gear, we've had police on horseback charging into our people, we've had people hit with truncheons and people kicked to the ground ... The intimidation and the brutality that has been displayed are something reminiscent of a Latin American state."

By then, the Durham coalfield had very few pits left, all at the coast, and most of the action was in the South Yorkshire area. However, the Elliott family still felt a great loyalty to the action being taken and went to great lengths to support the miners. Doreen and Bryan involved themselves by marching and supporting the miners' women's groups, and the whole family did many benefit concerts during that period, not just in the coalfields. They also performed in the big cities like Manchester and Liverpool, where the support was very strong. As Pete and Pat objected to Scargill's stance as leader, Doreen and Bryan were the only ones in the family who went on marches. "We knew this was the big one. About survival, keeping your job. For Durham, it was do or die. We knew we were doomed, but it didn't stop us marching from Day One." They marched and they marched. They marched to Sheffield, London, Manchester, and Liverpool. But it was near home at Easington that they became aware of the seriousness of the situation.

> "The feller that took us, Paul, says 'Have you got a muffler?' 'No, why?' 'Well you want it to cover your face, because you're on camera, see those? and they're filming you all the time.' I wept, well, I never ... All the buildings, the pityards and the surrounding houses, there were cameras. It was frightening. And there were stormtroopers, dressed head to toe in navy blue, no numbers, no insignia, nothing. Don't know where they came from, but there were hundreds of them. Frightening."

They didn't use the batons at Easington, but Doreen and Bryan got the sense of what happened at Orgreave.

The struggle of 1984–1985 revealed a new dimension in British political life, with the creation of women's groups in mining communities, which not only staffed food centres and collected cash but also took their place on picket lines in defence of jobs and what was obviously a fight to save the National Union of Mineworkers. Doreen was heavily involved with the women's groups and concentrated on helping miners' families. "When we were going round the country in the bus to support the miners," says Doreen, "we were stopped and searched all over the place by the police. During that time, we lived off Bryan's wages, and mine went on parcels for the kids. We'd leave them on the door, or leave food. But I was determined that they weren't going to have second-hand toys. It wasn't the bairns' fault that there was a strike." And yet Bryan feels that they had "let them down. We weren't starving. We weren't on the bottom." During this time, locally the men were on picket duty, but the women were active as never before, marching and collecting and supporting the families.

The political effects spread beyond the strike itself and occurred in all sorts of situations. Doreen was then working in Chester-le-Street, in the office of a local bus company, and learnt that the company was planning to bus in scabs to the pit. She crept down to the garage and confirmed this, and felt a strange atmosphere. When she looked out of the window, the police were in the allotments waiting for the pickets. "There were hundreds of them. I was shouting to the pickets. They were going to beat the shit out of them. I was never so angry in my life. I felt like I was going to collapse." In the end, the pickets themselves were by now used to these situations, and refused to fight the police, as that was what they seemed to want.

Pete and Pat's daughter Laura remembers going with her mam, Pat, taking soup to support striking ambulancemen and firefighters at Concord in Washington prior to the Miners' Strike. This was the first time she'd been aware of political things. She was only 11 at the time of the strike, but remembers her dad being very angry. She recalls the school dinner ladies going on strike, and she arranged to go to a friend's house for lunch. There she discovered that her mate's dad was working at Dawdon pit – Blackleg! Needless to say, when she told her dad, she was immediately stopped from going there again. "But dad, I'll be out on the street!" She remembers other girls who were sent to Coventry because their dads were scabs.

The Elliotts had been to Liverpool before the strike, having done the Liverpool Folk Festival twice, as well as the Folk Club. Bill was involved in both of these, but there was certainly no question of nepotism. The family was a big hit with everybody, and Bill was held in some awe, often being asked "Is it true that you are one of THE Elliotts?" They'd had a problem with the Club, as it was on Wednesdays, which of course clashed with Birtley. It took some doing, but they finally arranged special dispensation for one night. Bill remembers a great night, packed with people, and he recorded a piece on Stan Ambrose's weekly programme on Radio Merseyside. So, when the Unions and the folk clubs organised a miners' benefit night in 1984, the Elliotts were a must. It was a Saturday, with lots of busking and bottling during the day, with the family and the other guests involved. Such an impression was made, I think mainly by the Elliotts, that a man came up to them in the street and gave them a cheque for £250. And at the concert that night, held at the Neptune Theatre, Doreen Elliott was able to announce both this, and that a newly-wed couple in the audience had donated their honeymoon money! Everybody who was there will remember the final number, led by the family: 'Miners' Life', of course.

The 1984 Miners' Strike marked not only great hardship and a brave fight against hopeless odds, but also a clear cultural change in British society. Although everybody in the country admired the miners, and gave them great support, particularly when people saw the ruthless way in which the police and army were deployed by the Thatcher government, they lost the battle. The Thatcher government had their way, with massive closures and lots of miners thrown out of work. Pete "cried his eyes out when they went back. They'd been shafted, it was the end." This was the end of an era all right, and as Jock Purdon remarked, "Pity about nationalising the pits. We could beat the owners on occasions. We could never beat the government." As Seamus Milne puts it,

> "Estimates of the full economic cost of the war on the miners – including those of the 1984–5 strike, pit closures, redundancy payments as well as the wider economic and welfare costs – run into close to £30 billion at current prices. That war, it is now evident, was an act not only of class revenge, but also of national vandalism. A generation on, the economic and social rationality of the miners' resistance could not be clearer. The events of the mid-1980s will continue to be a focus of controversy, because they cut to the heart of political and social power and how it is exercised." (5)

Doreen and Bryan talk bitterly about the effect of the loss of the pits on the Durham pit villages. They went to the Miners' Social Club at nearby Lumley recently, but it was closed. Even on a Saturday it didn't open until 7p.m. The community had gone, vanished forever. In Easington, the site of the chilling confrontation with the police, "The kids are running wild with no discipline, and the police are never there, relying on CCTV alone."

The official NUM website describes the '84 Strike as follows, "The strike had not been about wages, better conditions or any material gain. It had been waged on principle; the principle that miners' jobs were held by each generation of workers in trust for those who would come after them, and must not be wantonly destroyed." And again, "The strike had set a new example in working-class struggle, marking another milestone in a long road. It had been hard, bitter, painful and, as in 1926, there were those who said that never again would the British trade union movement see such a conflict. As in the aftermath of 1926, only time will tell."

*A flyer for the 1984 Liverpool concert in support of the miners' strike.*

MERSEYSIDE TRADE UNION, COMMUNITY
AND UNEMPLOYED RESOURCE CENTRE

MINERS' BENEFIT

AN EVENING WITH

THE ELLIOTTS
OF BIRTLEY AND
KEITH ARMSTRONG

Songs, stories and poetry from a
Durham mining community.

– WITH –
• SYLVIA HIKINS • HAROLD HIKINS • BACCHUS
• SOCIALIST SINGERS • MUSICIANS COLLECTIVE

AT: THE NEPTUNE THEATRE
HANOVER ST. L'POOL 1.

SATURDAY 24th NOVEMBER
7.30 pm.

TICKETS FROM: M.T.U.C.U.R.C.
HARDMAN ST. LIVERPOOL 1.
– INFORMATION – PHONE – 051 734 4839 –
– ADM. £2.50 (waged). £1.50 (unwaged) –

# The 'Big Meeting'

One salient aspect of the politics of the North East is the fact that the Durham miners' gala, "The Big Meeting", still survives, long after similar miners' gatherings celebrated in Yorkshire, South Wales and other coalfields have faded into memory. Although there are no pits left in Durham, many of the lodge banners are still paraded, with new ones still being made, and the procession still takes all morning to pass the Royal County Hotel where the political bigwigs watch from the balcony. In particular, there is a splendid new banner for 'Cotia Pit, organised by Doreen and Bryan and unfurled at the 2004 gala. Even that caused controversy, because it depicted Jack Elliott and Jock Purdon. Some NUM diehards at Durham objected because neither man had been a strong Union man, and, to compound matters, Jock had been a deputy. When asked about the gala's role, then and now, and why it's still going, Doreen says, "Aye. It's still smoulderin'. It was always political. There's still a lot of interest from the older people, with vivid memories of the '84 Strike, and many local groups are still politically active. The agenda is broader than it was, but it's still political."

*"The gala's still smoulderin'."* **Doreen**

That same gala in 2004 attracted the attention of Man Booker prizewinning writer D.B.C. Pierre, author of *Vernon God Little*. In his article in *The Guardian* (5) he writes how shocked he was at the state's onslaught, and yet he still saw the continuing spirit of the North East on display.

"Through an entire childhood, adolescence and early adulthood living in the world's largest urban concentration of people – poor, spirited people – nothing prepared me for the sight of a nation's police machine so bitterly deployed against tens of thousands of young men trying to stay employed. England showed me that. This year marked the 20th anniversary of the great Miners' Strike. I returned to Durham to see what had become of the country's only surviving gala, and the people whose voice it had written so large. While Thatcher's government may have destroyed many things in the North East, the mineworkers' unions, and the defiant pride of the region, weren't among them. This year saw the 120th Gala storm through Durham's ancient streets, and it throbbed as it ever did.

George Robson, tireless Gala co-ordinator for the last 27 years, told me over a pint in the Royal County Hotel, 'It's as if the Gala's been through ten years of mourning. But this year there have been new banners commissioned, and labour organisations from all over the country are here to march. It's back, and growing. Still said to be the biggest political gathering in Europe.'"

Pierre goes on to speculate about the future of the Gala in light of the absence of an active mining industry and its struggles;

"Back it clearly is. But while the Gala remains a great day out, I wondered whether the same sharp edge, the sting of miners' causes, their struggle, their politics, would be missing from what may have become a simple celebration of heritage. Where might its future lie?

I found one answer on the hotel balcony. Applauding alongside union dignitaries stood South Africa's high commissioner, Lindiwe Mabuza; accompanying her in the weekend's festivities was South Africa's AngloGold choir on their first trip to the Gala. In a world quickly turning right, it seems the Gala's arms are wide open."

He finds that the spirit and humour of the miners hasn't changed and is still a challenge to New Labour;

"As I jostle past the balcony with the crowd, I sense something in the composition of assembled dignitaries has changed.

I turn to one of the marchers.

'Isn't the leader of the Labour party usually invited to preside from the balcony?'

'Aye, we've had Attlee, Wilson, Callaghan ... '

'So where's Blair?'

'You're joking, man,' laughs the marcher, 'he wouldn't bloody dare.'

In a classic demonstration of mineworking spirit, one pit community has set out to ensure that New Labour doesn't miss the flavour of the cause. As if delivering sandwiches served in a napkin, it's made a habit of marching a brass band and a handful of banners to Blair's back yard in Sedgefield ... for a full-blooded performance of The Red Flag!"

And one of the banners he would have seen would have been the new 'Cotia banner, with Jack and Jock. One thing's changed though; there aren't so many bands around, so they cost a lot to hire. No problem for the 'Cotia banner with Doreen and Bryan in charge; they'd have a folk band, led by the redoubtable Jim Bainbridge, whom we met earlier.

# Atheism and Religion

The family is well known not just for its strong political views, but also its atheism. Bertrand Russell's statement, "Religion may, in most of its forms, be defined as the belief that the Gods are on the side of the Government," would have been a truism to Jack, born of many years experience. Jack came to his atheism very early in life, and when

*John and Doreen with the new 'Cotia banner*

Phillip Donellan asked him "Do you believe in God?" in the film *Private Faces*, he described how he formed his views at such an early age.

> "No. Not now, maybe up to 12 year old, then I started to read the Bible and I rejected it as absolutely untenable to the things I'd read. I started to read about evolution, I read Darwin's *Origin of Species, Martyrdom of Man*, and I found that I just couldn't believe in the Bible any more. I read it through, and it was just a lot of legends to me."

However, this didn't mean that he lacked a strong moral sense, which he passed on to his children.

"I brought my children up without religion, I've had four children, and not a one's been in any sort of trouble. Morally they're second to none. I've had a wee bit of ostracism from people, knowing that I was an atheist, but it didn't really bother me at the finish. I used to teach my children this: 'If you hurt society, you're hurting yourself for the simple reason that you're a member of society,' and that's the only way to teach children. If they want to do a bad thing, let them do it, but don't kid theirselves that it's a good thing. Make them face up to it. They're part of society, and whatever they do, it must have some bearing on the happiness or otherwise of society."

Graeme Miles asks, without irony, "Did Jack have his own God?"

"If Christianity was as powerful as it's supposed to be, there wouldn't be any need for policemen, and if all Christians were as good as they're made out to be, the prison would be full of atheists. But that's not the case; they're full of Christians! If I had to rely on help down the pit, it'd be my marras."

Em certainly shared Jack's moral views, but found it difficult to give up religion at first, as Doreen recalls.

"Mam really didn't have time to think about the causes of the conditions of other people, being too busy surviving until she married, and me dad knew he couldn't go on being Jack the Lad. I remember when I was little and the six of us were all in the one bedroom, my mam kneeling at the bed side saying her prayers and even getting out of bed if she forgot them. Gradually it stopped, and my dad started getting books from the left-wing book party, brown coloured dust jackets they had."

It was Jack's friend Jack Brighton who said that things are "negative till proved positive. You need to prove there is a God, so assume that there isn't." The result of this and so much other discussion was that Jack and Em made the decision to become atheists and joined the National Secular Society. This was after much discussion and going to meetings and meeting other like-minded people.

Jack and Em's views on religion did cause problems for Doreen at school.

"They never wavered in their beliefs, and decided that they would take us out of religion education at school, which I think they realised was maybe not such a good move as time progressed and we changed schools and met blatant discrimination from the teaching staff. Never from neighbours or friends, but oh dear, the teachers! I often wonder if they thought my parents were anti uniform, as we never had a uniform. My dad had had a bad accident at the pit and boy, was money short."

Doreen still believes that these differences only strengthened their identification with other people or groups who were treated differently because of their opinions.

"However, we were never allowed to join Boy Scouts or Girl Guides. He didn't believe in either of those two organisations. However, in retrospect I don't think it damaged us. It made us very sympathetic to other minority groups and made for a very close relationship at home. I might add though, that I allowed my children to take religion, as I still didn't know if the teaching profession had overcome their prejudices. We didn't have our children christened, as we thought it a bit of a liberty to choose one for them at such an early age. Being without a religion has made life so much easier. Nothing to give up, no soul searching to do. Easy peasy."

Despite their atheism, it's worth noting that Em and Jack sent the kids to Sunday School. There's a running joke in the North East and no doubt elsewhere as to the reason parents sent their kids to Sunday School, but Em swore that it was to allow her time to get her chores done! As usual, we turn to Doreen for a choice story.

"Sunday siesta – that was also standard practice. I realised much later in life that it was also the time for nuptials. In fact, lots of men demanded it as their right. I remember when I was about fifteen and reading me book very quietly, when a neighbour came in, full of her news. 'By, Emmie,' she said, 'Aa fettled him the day. He finished his dinner and made ti gan up stairs sayin as he went "Thoo be up in ten minutes." Whear Aad had enough Emmie, so A took aal me claes off doon the stairs and galloped up there nyeeked and stood at the bed end and says "Noo whats thoo gan a dee?" and he was so shocked he could dee nought.' I can still picture her and me mam laughing till the tears came."

If the children questioned what they'd heard at Sunday School, the parents would give their views, but leave it to the kids to work it out for themselves. Certainly Jack was an atheist from chidhood, but Doreen and

Pete both remember their mother praying before bedtime when they were little, though that changed later. It would be surprising if the family's experiences of the '20s and '30s did not lead to a socialist political interest and doubts about a God.

Pete Elliott was, if anything, more fervently atheist than his mam and dad, both fierce and vocal. Dave Sutherland, an ex-regular at Birtley and very actively involved in the North East folk scene of the '60s, wrote in an obituary for him in 2000, "Pete cherished his socialism and atheism in the way a conformist feels about their particular deity. When asked to take part in a carol concert at Hexham Abbey by a well- meaning but naïve young lady he said, 'What! I'd rather sing for the Tories!' There's also a story that when he was doing his National Service in the Royal Navy, an admiral had died and they came for volunteers to attend the service, like, 'You, you and you,' and unfortunately Pete was one of the 'you'. He refused to go on the grounds that he didn't know the man and he was an atheist, so he didn't want to participate in a religious service. He peeled spuds for a week for his defiance!"

Being an atheist gave him a problem being married to Pat, who was from a strongly religious family. He allowed the kids to be christened until the last two, Pete and Laura, when perhaps the more enlightened atmosphere of the 1960s allowed him to put his foot down. Young Pete, the first affected, comments that he nearly died at birth, and this might well have had something to do with the change of heart. When asked if they were ever tempted to rebel against their dad, Laura's reply is unequivocal. To her, religion means nothing. She can't understand why people want it, as it never played any role in her life. Both she and Pete know about current atheists such as Richard Dawkins, and their Dad had given them The Golden Bough, humanitarian tracts, and books about evolution when they were younger.

When I mention their Aunty Doreen's experiences at school concerning religious studies, Pete and Laura have different stories. Young Pete had much the same experience as his Aunty Doreen, with an alcoholic headmaster who resented them being excluded from RE lessons, and the other teachers making them stand out, to be shown to be different from the rest. It was, remarkably, the same experience as Doreen's, and this in the so-called enlightened '60s. Yet it's interesting to note that by the time Laura was at school in the 1970s, RE was off the curriculum and her headteacher was an atheist! The thirty years between Doreen and Pete saw no change, and then, in ten short years, things were completely altered.

Mind you, mindless conformity also exasperated Pete, and, with Laura, her dad had found something else to rebel about. She was not allowed to wear a school tie, which made her feel excluded, something not welcome for a kid of twelve or thirteen. Pete was certainly a man of principle, as he'd refused to wear a tie at work, something which delayed his promotion until "the tie-wearing, compliant arselicker had popped his clogs … If you can prove to me that a piece of cloth round my neck makes me do my job better … "

Their older brothers having been through the school, they got the withering look from teachers as soon as they gave the name Elliott. Some of it was because these older brothers Paul and Bruce had been a bit troublesome. There is a story about one teacher having hit Bruce for not wearing a blazer. He had no blazer due to a lack of money in the house. Pete went round and, despite his size, pinned the teacher against the wall, and threatened to "fill him in front of the entire school if he ever did it again". Imagine this angry dad, all five foot nowt of him, outraged at the injustice of it all, against an ex-Sergeant Major! The Elliott kids became famous in the school forever.

*"Being without a religion has made life so much easier. Nothing to give up, no soul searching to do. Easy peasy."* **Doreen**

It is worth looking at one person who was a particularly important influence on the family's atheist views, Jack Brighton. He has been mentioned a couple of times earlier, but here is Pete's description of the man.

> "Apart from my parents, the person who had most seminal influence on my life was Jack Brighton, known widely as the 'Atheist Bishop of Durham'. He came to live in our street when I was around twelve years old, and his reputation went before him. 'Aa see that bloody heathen Brighton is coming to live here,' and 'People like that should be bloody well locked up,' were a couple of sample observations from our neighbours. My parents, particularly my Dad, were already asking unanswerable questions about religious dogma and, since we were a very open family, so was I. This drew my parents and me to Jack like a magnet. We soon were regular attenders at his debates and lectures on religion and morals in society, and from them a close friendship developed. My father saw him most, since they both worked at Harraton Colliery."

Pete also remembers Jack Brighton's considerable skills as a debater and orator out on the streets;

> "Jack, like my Dad, spoke with a broad mid-Durham accent, yet his debating skills and his depth of knowledge were phenomenal. Many a debater with an upper-class accent found to his cost that you patronised Jack at your peril. His wit could be cutting and devastating. A sample of his debating skills comes to mind. He once asserted, quite truthfully, during an opening speech, in debate with a Christian Fundamentalist, that the human body is 75% water. His opponent, in his answer, poured loud and belligerent scorn on the idea. In reply Jack said, 'However distasteful my friend may find this statement, it remains a fact. The only pity is that so many people have their H2O above their shoulders.' Everyone laughed except his adversary, who merely looked bewildered!

Jack guided my reading habits towards such books as Tom Paine's *The Rights of Man*, Darwin's *The Origin of Species*, Foote's *Bible Handbook* and the Left Book Club publications. In response to my questions about the nature of the universe, he turned my thoughts towards an interest that still consumes me today – Astronomy and its first cousin cosmology. He further taught me that although socialism and a caring society are beautiful ideals, they could never be realised, owing to nepotism and organisations like the Freemasons, secret or otherwise. Under this heading of course came monarchies and other kinds of inherited privilege; so I became a republican at a very early age.

His advice was to 'always ask questions', particularly on matters of dogma, either religious or political. 'You need to prove there is a God, so assume that there isn't,' he'd say. It was certainly his guidance that kept me from joining the Communist Party, which almost actively forbade questioning. In all his life he only used his intellect and oratorical skills for the enlightenment and betterment of his fellow man. In his late fifties he became the first President of the Durham Deputies Association, but I am sure he cherished his appellation 'The Atheist Bishop of Durham' much more."

*"You need to prove there is a God, so assume that there isn't."*

**Jack Brighton, pit deputy**

## References for Chapter 4

1. Ewan MacColl, *Journeyman*, Sidgwick and Jackson, 1990
2. Ed Pickford, *The Ed Pickford Songbook*, nd, www.ed-pickford.co.uk.
3. Gavin Purdon, *'Cotia Pit*, Instat, c. 1971
4. Seamus Milne, *The Enemy Within*, Verso, 1994
5. D.B.C. Pierre, *The Guardian*, 1st September 2004

# Chapter 5
# The Last Thirty Years

*My mother says I never should*
*Play with the gypsies in the wood*
*If I do my ma will say*
*"Naughty girl to disobey."*

## 'Chairman Pete'

The early '70s found Birtley Folk Club thriving, celebrating its tenth birthday in 1972 with a great night and a special feature in Tyneside's *Sunday Sun* newspaper. Whilst the Bridge in Newcastle had residents who were national celebrities, such as the High Level Ranters and Ray Fisher, and a "platform" that singers found difficult to access, the Elliotts continued with the singaround format, where everybody got a chance. The format of the night was one reason for the large audiences, but the other was the character of the family itself. Jack had been a dominant force in the family, and at the Club. Nationally, it was Jack as an individual who was recognised, partly due to his attractiveness as an individual, but also due to his fine singing style. Although the children did not match him in their singing ability, they shared his enthusiasm and strong personality. But it seemed that they needed a new "gaffer", and there was never any doubt as to who that would be: Pete Elliott.

Stu Luckley and the Doonan brothers, Michael and Kevin, remember those days very well. The club was "packed every week, amazing, great crack. Never seen owt like it. It was different, just … different ... almost a working men's club." Stuart remembers, "Half way through the night, in comes a gang of longhaired blokes … lots of different instruments … clattered through the place … how dare they come in here like that?" The group turned out to be the new Scottish group, the JSD band, on their first trip to the North East, just popping in "on spec". The Doonans were already doing bookings in those days, and their band Hedgehog Pie had just gone electric. Surely that was sacrilege in the Elliotts' eyes? But they got the gig, and according to Mick Doonan, Pete said to them at the end of the night, "Ye knaa we'd never book any other electric band." It was a big privilege for them to play there! Stu also comments that "Nobody dared have airs and graces. Aye, you never got above your station there, did you?"

"Chairman Pete", as somebody dubbed him in those Maoist days, was a fiery character indeed, being described as "irascible" and "cantankerous" even by some of his best friends. The phrase "not suffering fools gladly" might have been coined with him in mind, and although he didn't necessarily expect people to agree with him, he was never short of an opinion, and it was always worth hearing. As Barrie Temple, Newcastle folk singer and songwriter, now along with his wife Ingrid a stalwart of the festival scene, says, nobody used the word "shite" with such intensity as Pete.

He was particularly venomous about Ewan MacColl, and took special delight in always calling him by his real name of Jimmy Miller, stressing that the man "wasn't even Scottish". This was part of his more general dislike of professional folk singers, because from where he was sitting, there should simply be no need for this. MacColl, so talented a man in so many spheres, had somewhat of a star's attitude to performance. Whilst insisting that Revival singers sing songs from their locality, he was setting definitive standards in Scots ballad singing despite speaking with his distinct Salford accent. To Pete Elliott, such things rankled as sheer hypocrisy. (MacColl, of course, felt he could justify this because of his Perthshire mother's singing style, which he had inherited.) He and Peggy had also developed an approach to many folk clubs whereby they insisted on doing the whole evening, apparently not wishing to listen to the resident singers. Again, this would be a red rag to a bull to Pete, who had inherited the most democratic folk club in the land. On one occasion at the National Festival, there was a discussion about the emergence of the Second Revival in the '60s and '70s. During the debate Terry Whelan stood up and said, "Let's not forget MacColl." Pete shot up out of his seat, and caused five minutes of chaos, with Pat trying to pull him down and Pete waving his stick shouting "He called me Dad a song-carrier!" (With his strong affection for his father, he was offended by MacColl's dismissal of Jack, or anybody else for that matter, as a mere "vessel" which transmitted the song.) Norma Waterson in the chair was trying to calm things, and Tony Rose trying to disappear. It was ironic that the club Terry had run in Manchester, inspired by MacColl, was called the Song Carriers!

His reaction to false dialect was also characteristic; he strongly defended the Durham dialect, and in my opinion frequently over-emphasised it to make the point. He was incensed when some visiting folk group attempted the local dialect and failed. Although he didn't go down the pit, he could "out-pitmatic" the pitmen. He even typed in dialect, as this short extract from a letter to Jim Bainbridge shows.

> "Dear Jim and Francie, Y'bugger I'm really letting my bloody correspondence run adrift for aa've had lots of words from yourselves & lots from a canny aad wife we exchange letters with who lives in West Yorks. Forst off like, it so happens that I know exactly where and by whom 'The Clippie Mat' was writ, although how the hell it landed up in West Cork, Aa hev nee idea. Best love t'y'byeth, Pete 'n' Pat."

Religion would always be a target. When some years ago Vin Garbutt was in his religious phase and sang his anti-abortion song, Pete, atheist to the core, famously told him, "Not at a folk club son, try it in church on Sunda' mornin'." Dave Webber recalls the time when he introduced a song by saying it was "a bit like a hymn with no religion in it", and Pete chirped up from the front row, "Aye, a bit like me!" Danny and Joyce McLeod, organisers of the Tynefolk Folk Club and well-known characters on the North East folk scene, remember their early dealings with Pete, when they found him to be quite cantankerous on occasion, although it rarely applied to them. However, he made no allowance for a nervous singer, talking loudly and making jokes, which probably compounded the poor singer's misery! He once asked Joyce how long she'd taken to learn a particular song she'd just sung at Birtley for the first time. "Biggest waste of time," he said. Like the rest of the family, Pete had a very fixed idea of how a club evening should run, and once told Danny off for "club etiquette" when Danny had had a little too much to drink. Danny and Joyce also tell of the time the family were booked at the Conservative Club during Whitby Folk Week. It was Pete who turned the picture of Maggie Thatcher to the wall, resulting in a severe admonition by the committee!

But all of these things were driven by the man's passion, and he was often encouraging and helpful. He once complimented Barrie Temple on his song 'Nae wark', emphasising that for somebody who hadn't experienced the phenomenon, he had captured it well. Dave Sutherland, a Tyneside singer active in the FED in the late '60s and Birtley regular long exiled in the Midlands, recalls one Wednesday night in the old days when Pete pinned him to the wall of the toilet in the Three Tuns to tell him to "Dump my mate Alan Patchett as singing partner, choose my material carefully and be more relaxed about it, don't rush everything. Then perhaps I might become something of a singer and find the clubs more welcoming."

He also had a great sense of humour, and usually laughed loudest at a good joke. Sometimes this could be quite elaborate, as happened to me at the Morpeth Gathering in 1975, when I had entered the traditional singing competition. This took place, along with other competitions, in the Town Hall, which was packed solid with local worthies in buttoned up overcoats and tweed jackets. When it came to the singing, it appeared that I was the only entrant, and so demurred, saying there was no point in my singing. "Oh No", came the answer from the platform, "These people have paid good money to hear you sing, so come up". I sang, and thought I'd done well despite being the only entrant!

But the judge seemed to think otherwise, as he and the steward conversed for several long minutes before slowly arriving at a decision. They seemed almost reluctant, but after all this suspense awarded me. . . first prize! The steward was Don Stokoe and the judge who was winding me up for the crack, as you will by now have guessed, was Pete Elliott. Everybody roared with laughter at my discomfort as I was obliged to take away the biggest cup on the table and look after it for a year!

The Elliotts were always interested in the provenance of the songs. It was largely down to Pete as well that when somebody sang a song at the Club, there was often a prolonged discussion about the source of this version versus that, something which was unusual if not unique in folk clubs during the '70s. This was another facet that had been inherited from Jack and Em. *The Elliotts of Birtley* LP has them explaining how and when they learned their songs, where they argue over the authenticity of a text like their version of 'Lord Randal'. But there is a contrast between the Elliotts and the informants of Cecil Sharp and the other earlier collectors.

As Ian Watson observes, "These are not William Allingham's 'slips of memory, omissions, patches and lucky thoughts', not Cecil Sharp's 'unconscious output of the human mind', but articulate, literate working people reflecting on a living cultural tradition which they know to be their own. Against Sharp's picture of his deferential singer-sources (all his informants address him as 'Sir'), the Elliotts offer pride and self-confidence and, in contrast to the increasing rarity-value of the tradition presented by Sharp, the Elliott repertoire occupies a very important place in the family's social life, and, while it is not merely treasured as an heirloom, it is used frequently and enjoyed immensely." (1)

However formidable Pete appeared when running the Club, he and Pat were famous for their hospitality, and during this period it was at their house at Killingworth that guests were put up, along with the six kids, who'd come down every other Thursday morning to find all sorts of people kipping on the floor. At least one other folk "family", the McPeakes, stayed there. The children also remember bank holidays at the Doonans' house in Hebburn, where the song, music and dance would go on "till yon time". (It was Kevin Doonan who, at Pat's request, played 'The Blackbird' at her funeral.) Pete's youngest two children, young Pete and Laura, recently watched the BBC4 series *Folk Britannia* along with their older brother Paul (who unfortunately died in December 2007). Paul kept saying, "He stayed ... and him. That lot were here all the time ... ." Of course, it was some time later before they realised what eminent people in the folk movement these had been. Pete and Pat were also famous for their New Year's Eve parties, which even now are still a talking point. Lots of people remember on one occasion Pat losing her false teeth down the toilet, and about how Jim Irving and others had the drain covers off and found them. "You don't think I'm putting them back in do you?" The consequence of this was that Pat had to take a fortnight off work while she got some new ones!

*Reece's eightieth birthday*

By the '80s, when Laura was in her early teens, her friends would call round and hear the records Pete was playing, which she often found embarrassing. He'd say, "What you listen to is what I call shite." But when she realised who the parents of Kirsty MacColl and UB40 were, that Barbara Dixon started as a folk singer, that Mark Knopfler had been a regular at the Gosforth Folk Club, and that Eric Burdon had been in Pat's Scout group, she started to see the links. It impressed her, and she now wishes she'd got into it earlier. Although she has Pat and Pete's songbooks, she says she can't sing them because she hasn't the tunes. However, at her mother's funeral, when she sang one of Pat's favourite songs, Graeme Miles' 'Over Yonder Banks', there wasn't a dry eye in the house.

# Early Festivals

By the 1970s, the Folk Revival had settled down a bit. After the first wildly exciting learning phase of the early '60s, which had led to a huge number of folk clubs, these had dwindled as the "craze" phase of the movement passed. By now there was a hard core of people who would be "folkies" for life, enough to support a small group of individuals who had elected to have careers as professional performers. Although the clubs were fewer in number, festivals had become a feature of the summer, and the artists could guarantee a reasonable income. Usually running for a weekend, but in some cases for a whole week, many people built their holidays around them. So it was at this time that various members of the Elliott family started to appear at festivals throughout the country and abroad. Sometimes there were Pete and Pat, sometimes there was a foursome with John and Pam, and sometimes, with Doreen and Bryan, a full show with "The Six". In 1976, Roy Harris, by now an established singer in the Folk Revival, was asked to run a folk festival at Loughborough. Roy had some strong ideas as to what such a festival should be.

> "When I was approached by the EFDSS, the Elliott family was the first name on my wish list as I set out to book artists. This was because I had decided to alter the format from having large set-piece concerts to one where the music came in smaller packages, virtually singarounds led by a host singer or group, with a few guests, and the freedom to call up floor singers if they so wished. I wanted the audience to be up close, to be able to see the twinkle in a ballad singer's eye, to feel part of the experience, not merely distant spectators. (I have never thought of folk music as being a spectator sport.) To this end I needed hosts who were themselves artists, people who could deliver great music of their own and inspire and encourage others, including the audience, to give of their best. I had seen this task handled par excellence by the family at Birtley Folk Club. I realised that I wanted every session at my festival to BE a 'Birtley Folk Club'. So I put the family on in two sessions entitled 'Birtley Comes to Loughborough', with guests like George Belton, Joe Hutton, Bob Cann, Charlie Bate, Roger Brasier, Canny Fettle, Frankie Armstrong, John Kirkpatrick and Sue Harris, and Francis Shergold's team of Bampton Morris Men.
>
> Did it work? I quote from the review in the *Melody Maker* of the following week … 'If one were dishing out accolades, it must be the Elliott Family of Birtley who will be most affectionately remembered … there's so much warmth within them that, trite as it may be to say

it, the Elliotts represent the true essence of folk singing ... with a complement of ten, they brought their Birtley club to Loughborough, and what a club it must be.'

My opinion of the Elliotts never changed, so when I started the 'Traditions at the Tiger' club in Long Eaton, Notts., I brought them in as opening night guests in February 1991, and again the following year on the club's first anniversary. The club is still going strongly and the contribution made by Pete and Pat is still well remembered."

*"The Elliotts represent the true essence of folk singing ... with a complement of ten, they brought their Birtley club to Loughborough, and what a club it must be."* **Melody Maker**

Loughborough ran for a number of years as "The National", and the Elliotts became regulars. In 1979 the family ran a workshop there, which Bill Elliott remembers well. Bill, who had so enjoyed the Club in the late 1960s, had played professional football for Darlington for a year, then spent six months in a bank, until the manager told him to get his hair cut. Clearly, hair was a very important cultural statement in 1971, because it forced him into teacher training. He started college in Liverpool and taught there for several years, where he went to the traditional clubs, meeting people like Shay Black and Tony Gibbons, and starting to sing, play, and run clubs himself. He became a full-fledged "folkie", the only one of that generation of Elliotts to do so.

Although he did not sing the family songs at that time, Bill went over to the National and was really impressed with the family's performance, which was recorded for the Radio Two folk programme of the time. As the workshop was about mining songs and pit life, he was particularly pleased with his dad's part in it, as he was the only one there who had worked down the pit, and who could therefore speak authentically about it.

"If you remember the film *Death of a Miner*, it was me dad who was showing Phillip Donellan round the pit, when he went round those rooms. Also, they showed you film of me dad and Uncle Len working underground. That film was made by the NCB for *Mining Review*, shown at the pictures. I know, 'cos we were taken to see it. We'd no interest in the main film whatsoever, but *Mining Review* was on first. Go and see your dad at the pictures – for free!"

In 1976, and apparently without most of the Elliotts knowing, Pete was part of a group of folk people representing Britain at the American Bicentennial celebrations in Washington DC. The rest of the party were the Waterson family, Walter Pardon, Flora McNeil, Angus Grant, Tommy Breckons, Nibs Matthews and the Headington Quarry Morrismen, all in the capable hands of Bert Lloyd. Luminaries indeed! Mike Waterson recounts how several of the party, being either republicans or Scottish nationalists, had refused to shake hands with the Queen, and so were immediately dispatched by Bert to perform with the Yugoslavians for the day. But it seems that Pete overcame his convictions, and bit the bullet, although we haven't seen the photograph! Not only that, but the Duke of Northumberland was there as well, and Pete couldn't resist telling him, "Aa could've saved ye the fare, I only live just down the road." And of course, Washington was not only named after the place four miles away from Birtley, but at home the initials "DC" stood for Durham County, a further irony not lost on the family. What a superb scene; the atheist Communist miner's son commemorating a republican revolution with the aristocracy and the head of the Church of England!

Ted and Ivy Poole are two of the best known and loved folk club organisers in the country, having run the Swindon Club since the '60s. Jack had been booked at the club for late 1966, which of course was just after he died, and so they did not get to see him perform. However, they later met the Elliotts frequently at the National and other festivals and got on like a house on fire, not only sharing the folk interest, but also exactly the same political beliefs. Ted, like Pete, was a strong Union man. He got Reece's song 'The Other Fine Day' from Pete, and was proud as punch when Pat asked him to sing it at the National in 2001 during the session in honour of Pete. They remember being at the National just after the American bicentennial and hearing how exciting the event had been for the singers who'd attended, like the Watersons and Pete.

After Roy Harris had stopped running Loughborough, the atmosphere at the 1980 festival was apparently much less fervent than the first three, but national folk journalist Colin Irwin once again singled out the Elliotts for particular praise.

> "With a dour inevitability creeping over the place, what else could a poor journalist do but follow the Elliotts around everywhere? I've never been there, but I swear the Elliotts' club in Birtley, Durham, is the best in the country. They transported it to Loughborough and the subsequent Saturday night session was a killer. A strange assortment of musicians trooped on and off, each subjected to merciless banter from the seven-strong family grouped around them, who were the real stars

of the show. Flowers and Frolics came best out of the test, giving as good as they got, and playing English country music with magnificent abandon, ending up with the old Bonzo song, 'Mr And Mrs Mickey Mouse'. Not for the first time during the weekend I was moved to wish for the presence of Bob Davenport to top it off. The Elliotts were no less riveting the following day when they conducted a workshop about Durham mining songs."

*There came a gypsy riding, riding, riding,*
*There came a gypsy riding. Why are you?*

*I'm riding here to marry, marry, etc.*

*Will you marry me sir, me sir, etc.*

*You're far too stiff as pokers, etc.*

*Can bend as well as you sir, etc.*

*You're far too black and dirty, etc.*

The 20th anniversary of the club came round in 1982, with great celebrations, as with the 10th, but with a bit less attention from the media, due to the dying away of interest in folk music. However, in an interview published in the Newcastle daily paper *The Journal*, the Elliotts were asked for their views on the folk scene of the early '80s. John expressed the opinion that "We have always believed that the Folk Revival was about getting people to sing the songs, not just listen to them." Pete had his usual caustic assessment of the current scene: "There are too many clubs and too many professional singers. I think it's a contradiction to talk about a professional folk singer. You can't get up on stage every night, and just turn it on, you have to have a proper feel for the music." Pat was more phlegmatic: "The folk scene has its ups and downs, recently it's been in the doldrums, but it will revive again, although not to the extent that it once was. The strong clubs like ours and the Bridge will survive, but I'm not sure about many of the others."

In 1983, the "Six" (Pete, Pat, Doreen, Bryan, John and Pam) were invited by the Arts Council of Great Britain to perform in Berlin. They gave four concerts there in as many days, representing British culture, which was of course a great accolade for them. But the thing everybody in the family recalls is a bit less edifying. At that time, the city was divided into

East and West by the notorious Berlin Wall, with very few crossing places, one of which was Checkpoint Charlie, operated by the Americans and the severe, rather intimidating East German border guards. Pete had always had a problem with his bowels. As a longtime sufferer with IBS his demands for a toilet were both immediate and imperative. But at Checkpoint Charlie? There was nothing worse than to be caught short on a bus waiting to go through the Berlin Wall. So, summoning the stone-faced GDR border guard over he whispered "I need a shite, I need the shitehouse!" "Scheisse? Schiessehaus? Ja," was his reply. Very shortly Pete was frogmarched off the bus and across the tarmac, "nipping his cheeks", as young Pete describes it. The other passengers were treated to the sight of this rather short Geordie, flanked by two large East German border guards armed with automatic weapons, being hustled into the guardhouse. The fact that Pete was struggling with his discomfort made the situation look worse, and there were some fears of an international incident. Not so for the Elliotts, who were fully aware of the situation and were rolling around in the bus, hysterical with laughter.

*Pete and Pat at the National*

Another European appearance found John, Pam, Bill and Roz in Amiens, on a cultural exchange event that ran for two or three years, organised by Durham County Council. They got a tremendous reception, particularly from the students and trades unions, who were showing appreciation of the family's support for the miners at that time. Some years later, in 1986, when the National had moved to Sutton Bonnington, the family (i.e. the "Six"), started attending the festival on a regular basis, booked or not, and they were always great favourites. Many will remember their table in the bar as a focal point, with great crowds gathering, usually resulting in the inevitable singing session. Other festivals where they were regulars, booked or not, were Holmfirth and Whitby.

Another important festival appearance during the '90s was the English Country Music Weekend. This festival is different from most in that it concentrates on source singers and musicians. ECMW had started in 1976 when members of the Old Swan Band, Flowers and Frolics and other enthusiasts of the then current Revival in English country music held a weekend in Cricklade in Gloucestershire for those interested in jigs, polkas and hornpipes. It re-emerged refreshed and renewed after twenty years in 1995, first at Postlip in Gloucestershire and subsequently at various venues around the country. Whilst it is true that singers in modern times have of course listened to recorded songs most of their lives and have not just learned them orally, it is still possible to recognise some as being special. They have been much more influenced by their family or people they knew as children than by records, they usually sing unaccompanied in a simple, traditional style rather than trying to do something novel or flash with the song, and they have not in any way made a career out of it. Thus from the North East, Louis Killen and Johnny Handle have not been guests, but Brian Watson and the Elliotts have.

In the summer of 2000, the festival came to Todmorden, on the Lancashire/Yorkshire boundary. The guests included Brian Watson, the foremost Tyneside singer, concertina player Reuben Shaw, then in his nineties, the Britannia Coconut Dancers from Bacup, and the Elliotts. Dave Eckersley, one of the stewards working the weekend, was very impressed and remembers,

> "I knew about the Elliotts as a family and about their songs. I had been at university when I had got hold of Jack's LP on the Leader label when it had first come out, and had been grabbed by his rendition of 'Rap 'er te Bank'. I very quickly found out when I tried to sing it out in the clubs that the song was so strongly linked with him and the family that I soon dropped it, but I had been marked by that performance. A strong impression on a young man of how the world really worked! Later on, I'd seen the family at the National Festival where I'd seen individual members do songs in the singarounds, and I had made cups of tea in the shared kitchen with the ever friendly and cheerful John Elliott. So I was looking forward to seeing them in Todmorden. Not surprisingly, in the Saturday singaround Pat, John and Pam, and young Bill who was along with his aunt and parents, did some great stuff. Pat in particular sang some great Irish songs and Pam also was in great voice that afternoon with a lovely version of the 'Pit Widow's Lament'."

Dave's description encapsulates so well the effect of the family on himself, so often echoed by so many people.

> "But it was the Sunday afternoon concert that I particularly remember. It was hot on the Saturday night at the ceilidh and the late night session at the Cricket Club was under attack from a swarm of midges despite a resolute defence by the staff behind the bar. So there was a gentle, slightly soporific feeling at the Sunday afternoon concert with lovely spots from Reuben Shaw and Brian Watson. That was until the Elliotts got up for their spot and arrived like a gale out of the North East that blew everybody's cobwebs out and made the entire company sit up and take notice. As they sang I suddenly got the reality of a 'living tradition' like a jolt of electricity. They came together on stage with Bill on guitar and cittern and settled into this 'presence'. At that moment on stage, the struggle of the working class and the injustices of the Miner's Strike were still present and as fresh as yesterday. By the time they finished with 'Miner's Life' I was hot and bothered, and as angry and as upset as I had been watching the police charge at Orgreave. Power of song or what?"

The description encapsulates so well an authenticity here lacking in many performers in the folk movement. Other people might not articulate the same analysis, but they are feeling the same thing.

# Paul Younger's Story

A decade earlier, as the Birtley Club celebrated its 25th anniversary, another man had come upon the family for the first time. It's interesting to see how such an established institution as Birtley Folk Club, with an average audience age then of probably the mid- forties, affected a young man in his early twenties. Paul Younger came to the club for the first time in 1986, twenty years after Jack's death. He was local, but had never heard of the Elliotts and didn't know any mining songs, despite being an accomplished musician. As with many before him, his first night there dramatically changed his views on many things, and endeared him to the family for life. It is worth looking a little more closely at Paul's story, a local working-class lad who has already been, at the age of forty-five, a professor of environmental engineering, and has recently been made a pro-vice chancellor at Newcastle University.

Paul's background, as with so many on Tyneside who gravitated towards folk music, was Irish Catholic working class. In his case, it was the

Hebburn shipyards that governed his upbringing. His was a musical family with no connection with the folk movement. As a teenager, he played music in several bands, graduated in Geology at Newcastle University, and then went to the States to do research. Whilst there, he was asked to sing something "really British", but didn't know what that meant, and so started mugging it up via records and books. On returning to Tyneside, he ran into Terri Freeman, organiser of the Davy Lamp Folk Club in Washington, who encouraged him to go along on a Saturday night. He did so, and there met Doreen and Bryan Henderson. During a chat at the interval, Doreen said, "Come to Birtley and meet my brothers." Such an invitation is not easily turned down, and after his first attendance he went there every week for many years, until his job started to prevent it. He became strong friends with Pete Elliott, a generation older than him, who was then technical manager in the same department at the University, in the next building to Paul. What brought them together as much as the music was the fact that they were both working-class lads in an academic culture. Even in the 1980s, apparently, old class barriers could still make working-class people feel uncomfortable, whatever their achievements, so Paul gravitated towards Pete. Pete was, despite his humble background, a very powerful force in his department, and as technical manager had academics running around in dread of him. Hence Paul and Pete had their "bait" together, every lunchtime, as "marras".

*"Come to Birtley and meet my brothers."*
**Doreen Henderson**

For Paul, going to the Birtley Club was almost like going to another part of the country. In the 1980s the Elliotts were still in healthy middle age, and just starting to look at retirement. Doreen became a surrogate grandmother to Paul's kids, and was the main reason for his family's eventual move to Birtley, where they still live. He was very impressed with the pit songs. It was a "voyage of discovery", as he'd never heard them before. Shipbuilding in the Hebburn area where he grew up had no songs. The Doonan family, famous folk musicians from Tyneside, also came from Hebburn, but had little interest in Tyneside stuff, playing 100 per cent Irish music over a century after the family had left Ireland. This Irish tradition was, in Paul's view, an immigrant culture, "Geordified in situ". There was also a Scots influence in the area, due to the shipbuilding firm Leslie bringing skilled people from Scotland when they set up the shipyard on Tyneside in the 19th century.

His passion for the Club is remarkable, and is demonstrated by the fact that he has still only been to two local clubs, Washington and Birtley. He has never been a "folkie", and has never been to a folk festival. He knew the Elliotts went to these if invited, but they didn't plug these visits at the club. The only connection he had with the wider folk world was the club swaps to the Stockton Club, where he first saw the Wilson family. He regards them as counterparts to the Elliotts, and notes the huge affection between the two families.

*"The Elliotts are in the folk movement, but not of it."*
**Paul Younger**

The Elliotts have heavily influenced Paul's views on folk music. He loves the singaround, which is "wonderfully democratic, as everybody gets their chance. At Birtley you get to sing." He says he was "spoilt rotten" by Birtley. It was a revelation to discover all this richness. As mainly an instrumentalist, playing mandolin and pipes, he found a virtue in unaccompanied singing for the first time, and is now "impatient with other kinds of singing". He is intensely busy with his career and family, which means he can now rarely get to the Club, but he has written an excellent article on North East folk music (2). Paul says the Elliotts are "in the folk movement, but not of it", meaning that they were not created by it, and is fond of recalling Jock Purdon's famous quote mentioned earlier in this book, "We didn't know we sang folk songs till Mr Lloyd came up and told us we did."

# The Club Regulars

The Elliotts' club in Birtley has seen thousands of singers in its 46-year history, some very famous, many much less so. Some went for a short spell in its heyday and have not been seen since. Others, as we have seen, found the club at various stages, enjoyed themselves for a time, and went other ways. There are still a handful of people, other than the family, who were there at the start and are still there. They include people we met in Chapter 2; songwriter Eddie Pickford, mentioned several times in the book, and 'Fra' Fraser, who were at the first night, and Don Stokoe, who arrived very shortly after that, all of them singing and playing still. A joy to behold, and some of their thoughts have been aired elsewhere in this book.

There are others who are, alas, no longer with us. Possibly the most important and influential was Jock Purdon, who died in 1998. Jock was an established writer of some powerful songs, mostly to do with pit life, strongly pro-Union, anti-bosses and anti-establishment. He had arrived from his native Scotland as a "Bevin Boy" during the war. Due to a shortage of miners during the war, some conscripts, instead of going into the forces, were drafted into the pits by a lottery, and were sent all over the country. The proposal had come from Minister of Labour Ernest Bevin, hence the name. Jock was a hard worker, and eventually became a deputy. Deputies were "gaffer's men", and were generally treated as such, even if they'd worked their time in the same pit. Even though he had a reputation for complete fairness, Jock was certainly not popular with the Elliott miners, and John still seethes at being docked a half day by him for racing gallowas down the pit. Ironically, Jock confessed in his songbook to having done the same himself before he was a deputy! That's what happens to people who get promoted, it seems, and perhaps explains the dislike of the men for deputies, even when they have worked their way up and earned their place by being good workers.

Jock had always written poems and songs since his early days in the pits. He used to go along to his local, the Plough near Pelaw Pit at South Pelaw outside Chester-le-Street, and contribute to the singing session there, just as Jack and Reece were doing a few miles away at Barley Mow. As he said himself in his songbook, "Ah had a fancy for singing something of my own, so ah put 'The Bevin Boys' Lament' together. Well, it went down very well, and that was me started off with the song writing." (3)

Jock's songs became noticeably more political later, after he retired from the pits. Don Stokoe's wife Sheila was impressed by the rebel in him, expressing such vicious sentiments when he was outwardly such a gentleman. Paul Younger says that Jock had a big influence on many people in the area, and there is no doubt that he was seen by most as part and parcel of the Birtley Club. He didn't attend it right at the start, but was there in the early stages when the Club moved to the Tuns, from at least the mid-'70s to shortly before he died. He was almost part of the furniture, sitting in the same seat to the right of the Elliotts, and to my knowledge always singing one of his own songs. His songs have been sung and seen by many as representing the political ethos of the coalfield. Don Stokoe remembers how proud Jock was when Don sang one of his songs at a competition and won.

An interesting aspect of pit politics was revealed recently when the new 'Cotia banner was made. It first appeared at the Durham Gala in 2004, and featured both Jack and Jock. As we saw in Chapter 4, there were many mutterings amongst the Union men about the idea of a deputy appearing on a lodge banner! But it is also interesting that the two figures represented also carried the cultural flag of the coalfield both in song and in performance.

Birtley forged strong allegiances. There were other regulars who were there every week until they died, none of them of old age. Eric Maxwell, one of the old Sunderland brigade from the '60s, Christine Smith, a local magistrate and lovely quiet singer, and Tommy Hodgin, who had long been afflicted with breathing problems yet was still delivering some really fine songs till very shortly before his death, all made their mark. Another stalwart was Alex MacKay, a prominent member of the South Shields folk crowd, and great singer of Irish songs. Although he has emigrated to Ireland, he makes regular visits to Tyneside, when he always makes the pilgrimage to the Birtley Club.

Regulars like Don Stokoe, who started in 1963, and Paul Younger, who started in 1986, never go to another club. They don't regard it as a folk club. It's just . . . well, Birtley. Whilst Birtley may not be everybody's cup of tea, for those who go it engenders a fierce and passionate loyalty. It is these people who, along with the Elliotts, make this a folk club in the original sense. It's not the flash concert stage with a big named guest every week, but it's the community singing, and having crack. Not a lot different from Saturday night in the Barley Mow or the Eel's Foot so long ago, described in Chapter 2, and the sort of thing eschewed by the general populace.

*Hi Canny Man ha your ha'penny oot*
*My father's in the spout,*
*And I canna get him out,*
*Hi Canny Man ha your ha'penny oot*

By 1991, most of the family were retired, and they decided that they would like to do more singing. So they set about making a cassette tape to use to promote themselves with folk clubs and festivals. This immediately provoked the inevitable fireworks in the family, as Bryan Henderson told them that they were becoming too commercial in their approach, and that he was resigning from The Elliotts of Birtley forthwith. As Pete says, "The thud of jaws dropping was almost audible." Doreen never seemed to be comfortable with matters after that, and there were some near disasters in family relationships before the tape finally got made. They could not agree on who should produce it, and the quality of the recording and subsequently the product was just not good enough for such a family with such a pedigree. It is also a pity that it used the same title as the magnificent Folkways LP of thirty years earlier, since the cassette that emerged was poor by comparison. It did not sell well, and most of the family have dismissed it from their minds. Further bad feeling emerged when the bookings it was supposed to generate failed to materialise.

However, it is characteristic of the Elliotts that despite some big rows, they come together for a good sing and for family occasions. So it was that the Birtley Folk Club 30th anniversary party held on 6th May 1992 was a huge success. The Doonan family band supplied the music for the dancing, and they did a set of their own, which was excellent. Pete Junior made a video of the event with his recently acquired camcorder, and observed in his own, somewhat dry way, "I've made over a dozen copies of it so far, for interested parties, and the demand hasn't slackened. It could possibly be as popular as *The Elliotts of Birtley* tape."

The early '90s saw the final death of the British coalfields, and during this period many splendid productive pits began disappearing. This often seemed literally true, as the demolition men moved in immediately the pit closed. Within weeks, all that was left was a pile of rubble, just as it had been with 'Cotia twenty-five years earlier. It was as if the Tory government, now under John Major, wanted not only to close loss-making mines, but to remove all signs of the culture that had grown around the industry over hundreds of years.

As in '84, the national focus of opposition was South Yorkshire, where Dave Douglass was still active. Some of the family sang at events connected with the '91 and '92 Yorkshire Miners' Galas, and the five of them sang at the 'Pitmen's Folk Night', organised by Dave Douglass, in Hatfield, a pit village near Doncaster. They were back home the next day to sing at Beamish Museum, the open-air museum near Stanley which commemorates the industrial and cultural history of North East England, and a notable employer of local folk musicians. A hectic, but enjoyable weekend. A year later, in 1993, the last three pits in Durham closed: Easington in May, Vane Tempest in June, and Monkwearmouth in November. Earlier that year, in June, the family had attended the Yorkshire Gala in Wakefield, followed by a folk night at Hatfield again. But within six months, a fortnight before Christmas, the pit there closed as well. "What a cracking pressy," said Pete with his usual sarcasm.

After that, nobody expected there to be a Yorkshire gala in 1994, but the NUM's sense of history made sure it went ahead, and there was yet another cracking night at the Hatfield pub. The family reunited again for the night's performance, and despite Bryan having resigned from the group the year before, both he and Doreen joined Pat and Pete for old times' sake.

# Recent Times

The rest of the '90s found the family continuing to do gigs, but with increasing health problems, particularly for Pete and Pat, these grew fewer in number. However, these two did manage to do some gigs on their own, even getting over to Ireland a couple of times, where exiled Geordies Jim Bainbridge and George Henderson looked after them and gave them gigs, Jim at the Courtyard in Schull, West Cork, and George at the Nenagh Singers' Circle in Co. Tipperary. Needless to say, they made a great impression, and on people used to seeing the very finest of performers. Folk clubs as understood in Britain hardly exist in Ireland, and the Nenagh Singers Circle was set up quite recently by like-minded people frustrated by the nature of 1990s pubs and their unsuitability for anything but very restricted singing. Pete and Pat loved it, and said it was like the old days at Birtley, providing a platform and a yardstick for solo singers who form the basis of the ongoing tradition. It's a fact that such groups are now thriving in the Irish midlands and this can only be good news for Irish traditional song. No coincidence that George Henderson was a regular at Birtley in the 1960s!

The Birtley Club carried on, still unique, still a place where you always had good crack and heard new songs. In 1998, the Ryton Folk Club, which was now thriving under Danny and Joyce McLeod, invited the Elliotts to do a whole evening during which they would talk about their lives and the songs as well as singing. It was a splendid evening, full of good feelings, with family rifts forgotten as they went through their repertoire, with banter and jokes galore.

Unfortunately, the Ryton night proved to be the last time they would be out as "The Six". Pete had been unwell for some time and was diagnosed with lung cancer, just like his father. He did at least get sixteen years' more life than Jack, but this was a big blow for the family. The funeral, in January 2000, was both a sad and uplifting affair. As with Jack, a humanist, Ray Wood, led the proceedings.

> "The value and meaning in life consists in living it and living it well. People who have been a strength and comfort to others and have devoted their time to useful work, in a cheerful way – and have derived fulfillment and satisfaction from such work – these are the people who create value and meaning in life. And Pete was such a person. As a teenager I saw the film *Death of a Miner*, which had a profound effect on my ideas and beliefs. Pete was a special person, articulate, intelligent with a positive feel for life and a spirit that appeared to be

inexhaustible. He was certainly a man of principle and integrity. A true socialist, not one of these New Labour neo-Tories we have in power now. Pete was strong-willed, independent and at times stubborn, and always astute. He was honest at all times and never minced his words. His wit could be quite cutting. But once he'd had his say that was the end of it; if the person at the end of his tongue didn't like it, hard lines. Pete didn't lose any sleep over it. But he was also very funny with a dry sense of humour and a wonderful turn of phrase. This, coupled with his intelligence, knowledge and debating skills, made him wonderful company. He was an excellent husband, father, brother and friend. He will be greatly missed."

Nowadays, our emotions are often manufactured and manipulated, as in the modern trend of getting a professional singer to lead the crowd at the Cup Final, or on celebrity TV "talent" shows. Real emotion can surprise us and create a unique experience. At his dad's request, Pete's son Paul sang 'What's the life of a man?'. Now Paul had never really sung, and with the emotion he was feeling, he was close to breaking down at several points. When other people joined in, everybody was weeping. What an utterly profound experience that was. Colin Ross had a similar experience to Paul when he played the crowd out at the end with 'Rap 'er te Bank' on the Northumbrian pipes, and everybody started to sing, one or two at first, then the whole lot of them, as they sang Pete out. It almost overwhelmed Colin.

But, so typically Elliott, what everybody remembers most vividly was the passion of the man combined with his own brand of humour. Pete's final epitaph got passed on to everybody who had been unable to get to the ceremony. The story has varied in its re-telling, so let us have the exact words, as read out by his brother John on the occasion.

"Before I come to a conclusion, I must mention Pete's last instructions. He asked for any limbs and organs to be donated to medical research, if required. However, he requested that his arsehole be sent to the Tory Party."

There was a memorable wake, followed by a memorable funeral tea at the Buffs, with a huge crowd of people from the folk world and the North East. The end of an era.

*'The Five' at the 40th*

> *"You can leave my arms and legs to medical science and you can leave my arsehole to the Conservative Party."* **Pete**

After Pete, the family continued to go out occasionally as a fivesome. The Doonans, the other great clan from the North East folk scene, mention one outstanding Elliott performance about this time. John Doonan had passed away in 2002, and the family put on a special night for their father at the Stoll Theatre in Newcastle. The Stoll is a magnificent Victorian masterpiece of theatre architecture, with boxes for the better-off clients of the music hall that had run there in its heyday. The place was full, and the Doonan family and friends were in full flow. Halfway through, they announced, "A special treat, we have with us tonight, in the Royal Box, the Royal family of Folk, the Elliotts of Birtley." What a great turn that was, full of feeling. The two families had been great friends, and here they were waking the Old Man of one family so soon after the wake of the Old Man of the other family. However, a lot of us watching this, and the Elliotts themselves, saw the funny side of this and couldn't help but think of Stadtler and Waldorf, the hecklers from the Muppet Show!

Over the next couple of years, Pat became increasingly disabled, and was unable to get to the Club which she had loved. Friends rallied round and took her to places she could get to, such as Ken Wilson's birthday weekend in January, but in the later part of 2003 she developed terminal cancer. She spent the last few months of her life at home, with Pete, Laura, and Paul who took leave from his job in London to be with his Mam. And with what dignity and lack of complaint she bore it, not succumbing to adversity nor allowing it to change her character. A constant stream of visitors was borne bravely by Pat and the kids alike. Sometimes it must have been a trial, but what they always got was a cheery smile and great crack. The earthy, wisecracking humour was there to the last, which was in January 2004. The funeral was similar to Pete's, still etched on people's memories to the extent that the two events seem to meld into one in the mind. It seems appropriate.

References for Chapter 5

1. Ian Watson, *Song and Democratic Culture in Britain*, Croom Helm, 1983, p.37
2. Paul Younger in David Archer, *Land of Singing Waters*, Spreddon Press, 1992
3. Jock Purdon, *Songs of the Durham Coalfield*, Pit Lamp Press, 1977

# Chapter 6
# Singing Traditions

It can be seen that the Elliotts were part of both their pit culture and also the Folk Revival, and some of their songs have been mentioned en route. However, it is time for a detailed analysis of their songs, how they came to the family, and how closely they relate to both the national English culture and the North East one. To do this, we should look at both of these cultures first. There is always much debate about the meaning of words like 'folk', 'oral', and 'traditional' in connection with songs; but let us look at the songs ordinary people have been singing over the last two hundred years by analysing the collections of such people as Cecil Sharp. The people who initially collected these songs were doing so for different reasons, came from a wide range of backgrounds, and varied in their knowledge, experience, and abilities.

There was no grand plan, no quality assurance other than the personal preferences and philosophy of the collector, which by its very selectivity could mask the bigger picture. They would reject Victorian parlour ballads, music hall songs, and anything they would consider vulgar. Sexual activity in lyrics would be recorded, but would not normally be published if it was too obvious or robust. Fortunately, the original transcripts of such songs are still available in the notes of the collections, and have seen the light of day in the more enlightened times of the Second Folk Revival. The attitudes of this group of early collectors became known to many of the singers, who therefore only gave them what they wanted to hear. Thus the collections were often unrepresentative of the singers' repertoires, although there were some examples that got through the "net", such as that of Henry Burstow in Sussex (1). Of course the broadsides, sold in the streets for a small sum, also reflect what songs attracted people to buy them. However, these are limited, and so for most of the time the collections, whilst only giving us part of the picture, are all we have.

## English Folk Songs

Before the 19th Century, there was little if any attempt to find what ordinary people sang, and collections were mainly full of the great ballads taken from manuscripts in stately homes and learned institutions, many of which eventually were set in aspic and are collectively known as the Child Ballads. A Child Ballad is one of the ballads published by Professor Francis James Child in the late 19th Century. He obtained thousands of manuscripts and broadside sheets from all over the country, mostly from landed gentry and institutional libraries, and decided that they all fell into one of the 305 stories depicted in his monumental collection, first published in the 1880s. The title of the collection was *The English and Scottish Popular Ballads*, which was misleading on two counts. The vast majority were Scottish, and they were never very popular, at least in the versions collected by Child, who paid little attention to what ordinary working people were actually singing.

Before the 1890s, only two collections claimed to have songs sung by working people, John Broadwood's *Old English Songs* of 1843 in a very restricted edition, and James Henry Dixon's *Ancient Poems, Ballads and Songs* published in 1846 (2). Although Dixon was from the North East, he obtained songs from all over England. Notable among songs he obtained from the North East were 'Blow the Winds I-Ho', which he obtained from a broadside and described as 'this Northumbrian ballad of great antiquity', as well as 'The Summer's Morning', better known to us as 'The White Cockade', which came to him from his brother at Seaton Carew and was written down 'as generally sung', and 'The Keech i' the Creel', which was apparently first printed by "a Northumbrian gentleman for private circulation … in 1845". Note that even in this small sample of songs from Dixon, not one is obtained directly from an ordinary working man, a feature which is characteristic of many 19th Century collectors who claimed this to be the case. All three of these songs would now be described as national rather than local, and although a lot of Dixon's songs were said to come from 'northern mining areas', there were no pit songs among them.

Dixon's findings were criticised by members of the Percy Society who had funded the project, and were republished with amendments along with Robert Bell's ballad collections later in the century (3). But it was not until the early 1890s that folk songs as we know them were published. Lucy Broadwood's *English County Songs*, Baring Gould's *Songs of the West*, and Frank Kidson's *Traditional Tunes* came out around the same time (4). The songs in these collections staggered many educated people by the quality of their tunes in particular, and stimulated several professional composers to incorporate the tunes into their compositions.

At the same time there was a move to look for more such songs, and to this end the Folk Song Society was founded in 1898. Fortunately, although collectors like Sharp, Hammond, and Gardiner were often more interested in the tunes than the words, they did for the most part record the latter, albeit sometimes somewhat superficially. This time they went to labourers' cottages and public houses to hear the singers themselves rather than get them second hand from the local "squarson" or other worthy. They brought in a great harvest of material which had never been printed before. There were splendid tunes and they had a certain language of their own.

However, unlike many of the Tyneside songs we will look at later, these songs did not relate to any particular area. A lot of the Somerset songs were found in Sussex and Oxfordshire, and rarely mentioned place names or people's surnames. William and Nancy were always parting tearfully, but we are almost never told where it's happening. Although the collectors went predominantly to the south and west of England, there was Grainger in Lincolnshire, Kidson continuing in Yorkshire, and others. What emerged was surprising in that although these two areas appeared to have a lot of local songs, they also shared a number of songs with the southern counties, which helped give rise to the notion of a corpus of national English folk songs.

It was little noticed at the time, but another great harvest of songs was being garnered by Greig and Duncan way up in Aberdeenshire, which even more surprisingly had songs in common with Somerset and Dorset. However, despite this new evidence to the contrary, the notion that these songs were English rather than British had by then stuck. The English scholars wanted a *Volkslied*, as in other parts of Europe, and now they had one. From now on, the term "folk song" will be used to mean the "Sharpian" type of song as collected by Sharp and the others.

This period, from about 1890 to 1920, is often called the First Folk Revival, which had a great impact on the middle classes and subsequently forced a lot of songs into schoolchildren through the educational system. However, by the time of the Second World War, these songs had largely died out under an avalanche of popular American records. Thankfully, after the War came to an end, another generation of people saw that these songs were still being sung by some older people in remoter parts of the country. Like Sharp and the others before them, they set out to retrieve these songs; only this time they were equipped with recording machines, mainly funded by the BBC. The best of this material was issued in America by Caedmon Records as a ten-volume set called *The Folksongs of Britain* (5). These recordings helped to lay the groundwork for the Second Folk Revival of the 1960s.

The great advantage of this, of course, was that we could now hear how the songs were customarily sung by amateur performers and traditional singers, and it was certainly not the "Owen Brannigan" style.

However, the collectors, led by Alan Lomax and Peter Kennedy, only travelled to areas where they knew they'd find songs, usually the remoter parts of Scotland, Ireland, and selected parts of southern England. The North East, and, it must be said, almost anywhere between Birmingham and the Scottish border, was again mostly ignored. There were three songs from Northumberland in the Caedmon series: Jimmy White with 'Canny Shepherd Laddies'; Jack Goodfellow with 'Jim the Carter Lad'; and Arthur Lennox with 'The Ram of Derby' (one local and two national songs).

Even after the Second Folk Revival got under way, there were many older singers, who up till then would have been considered old-fashioned by the community, who came into their own. The BBC project had revisited one Norfolk singer, Harry Cox, and discovered another, Sam Larner, who although quite different in style immediately came over as manifesting the traditional way of singing a song which many had thought lost with Sharp's singers. Then there was Jeannie Robertson, the traveller woman from North East Scotland, who sang everything from bawdy traditional songs to the great ballads. She not only had what they called the "coinneach", a cant word for "the secret of how to do it", but in my view also had a voice that was clearly different from, but of an artistic merit as high as that of any operatic diva you care to mention.

These and the others discovered in the '50s had a unique quality, which convinced people that a Folk Revival was possible. By the 1960s they were making recordings, mainly for Topic Records. As the Revival progressed, there were more source singers being revealed, people like Fred Jordan, Paddy Tunney and Walter Pardon. They included families such as the McPeakes from Belfast, the Coppers from Rottingdean in Sussex, and the Stewarts from Blairgowrie in Perthshire. In 1998, Topic Records published their *Voice of the People*, a 20 CD set with nearly 500 items representing the best of traditional singers and musicians, mostly from the previous fifty years (6). It is significant for this book that the County of Northumberland warranted almost a whole CD for its traditional tunes, but the whole of northern England had not a single song out of 500 items! The region was, apparently, lacking in either "folk" songs or "folk" singers. However, what it certainly has never lacked is songs and singers.

## The North East

In the 19th Century, when these songs came to light, it was obvious that the area bristled with wonderful song collections. The North East is richer in traditional music and local songs than any other part of

England. It has the unique Northumbrian pipes with its own brand of dance music, it has rapper, it has border ballads, the strongest broadside and chapbook activity outside the capital, and Tyneside music hall. It is known for shanties and keelmen songs and those magnificent creations of Ned Corven, Geordie Ridley, and J.P. Robson. It has travelled the world with 'Bobby Shaftoe', 'Cushie Butterfield' and 'Water of Tyne'. Its very dialect sings. Not only did Tyneside have these songs, but also people had written them down and published them, so that we have the record. The number of published collections is what distinguishes the North East, rather than the amount of material.

*"Its very dialect sings."*

Joseph Ritson, an eminent scholar from Stockton-on-Tees, was the first to at least try to find out what people were singing, and produced a series of anthologies entitled *Northern Garlands* in the last twenty years of the 18th Century (6). These still had many ancient ballads, albeit with a concentration on local ones, such as 'Rookhope Ride', but many of the more homely songs he did print rarely appeared again. However, he was the first to print three songs which are still favourite traditional songs today: 'Elsie Marley', about the landlady of the inn at Picktree, only a mile or two from Birtley, the iconic 'Follow the Horses', which was the first song about mining that we are aware of and has always been in the Elliotts' repertoire, and 'The Keel Row', which is almost as synonymous with the region as 'Bobby Shaftoe'.

Shortly after Ritson, John Bell, a Newcastle printer, surveyor, and obsessive collector of everything old, not only relied on contacts with the gentry to get rural songs, but also used his own personal contacts with the teeming life of the quayside to get together a splendid collection. His seminal *Rhymes of Northern Bards*, published in 1812, printed 'Bobby Shaftoe', 'Buy Broom Besoms', 'Dollia' and 'Water of Tyne' for the first time (8).

Given that mining was so important a part of life in the region, the number of pit songs included is surprisingly small. Popular though 'Bobby Shaftoe' and these other songs have been ever since, they are not pit songs, nor Elliott family songs. Bell did collect a few pit songs, though not very many, but he did include 'Byker Hill', 'Footy Agin the Wall' and 'The Collier's Pay Week'. Again, none of these are Elliotts' songs. David Harker has analysed Bell's collection of songs, as opposed to his *Rhymes*, in considerable detail, but the story is the same (9).

One song that was in Bell's collection but not in his 1812 publication was 'The Original Bob Cranky', a song written by John Shield about 1800 when Bell was collecting. Pitmen of the time, when "in toon" on a spree, were seen as boisterous, rowdy, swaggering and sometimes frightening to other people. The song essentially set up this figure as a stereotype, and three further songs were added by John Selkirk ('Bob Cranky's Complaint', 'Bob Cranky's 'Size Sunday', and 'Bob Cranky's Lamentation Neet'). The character also makes an appearance in Henry Robson's 'Collier's Pay Week'.

A similar mythical figure, a Lancashire weaver named 'John O'Greenfield', arose in the same period, and had no less than 16 songs written in subsequent years. The original has always been popular in the North West, including during the Second Folk Revival, whereas 'Bob Cranky' has very rarely been sung, the notable exception being the singer Brian Watson from Prudhoe.

Two late 19th Century song collections, *The Northumbrian Minstrelsy* and Stokoe and Reay's *Folk Songs of Northern England*, were as important as Bell's, and both were also very light on pit songs. *The Minstrelsy* was nearly thirty years in the making. It was put together by a committee of the Society of Antiquaries whose brief was to collect both songs and tunes from Northumberland and Durham. In the end, it was heavily reliant on previously published works, notably Bell on the song side. However, it introduced us to many fine songs, such as 'Blow the Wind Southerly', 'Captain Bover', 'Derwentwater's Farewell', 'I Drew My Ship', 'The Fair Flower of Northumberland' and 'The Oak and the Ash'. Stokoe and Reay's *Folk Songs of Northern England*, published in 1892, took almost all the songs from the 1882 *Northumbrian Minstrelsy* and added a significant number of other Tyneside and Northumbrian songs (10). Stokoe and Reay's book added songs which were, in the main, the much more robust Tyneside songs of great earthiness and vitality. Many of them were written during the period, and provided a contrast to the worthiness and antiquity of most of the original *Minstrelsy* songs. Here we have some real gems, such as 'Dance to Thi Daddy', 'John Peel', 'Skipper's Wedding', 'The Fiery Clock Face' and 'The Folks of Shields'.

At virtually the same time as Stokoe and Reay's book, the final edition of *Allen's Tyneside Songs* was published, which in terms of quantity surpassed the other collections, and some would say matched them in quality (11). The wealth of material in this collection from the streets and music halls, notably by J.P. Robson, Ned Corvan, Geordie Ridley and the most prolific of all, Joe Wilson, helped to define Tyneside song culture for all time. These artists performed during the first blossoming of music hall in the mid-19th Century, say 1840 to 1860, when both singers and songs were local in flavour. The Oxford Music Hall in Newcastle opened at the Wheatsheaf Inn in 1848 and was still going strong when the ex-miner George Ridley sang his own song 'Blaydon Races' there in 1862.

There was much worth singing about on Tyneside and the people revelled in their own culture. Much of this material is known to us from the hundreds of songs in Allen, with copious notes on the songwriters and quayside characters such as "Blind Willie Purvis", which paint a wonderful picture of life in "the toon" at the height of the Industrial Revolution, although there are still not many pit songs. Some say it was the Industrial Revolution itself that killed Tyneside music hall, in that the railway made it possible for the London impresarios and performers to travel north easily and make music hall national rather than regional. This was certainly the case in Newcastle by the 1890s.

However, there was a man still writing good local songs at this time. His name was Tommy Armstrong, and he came from Tanfield Lea near Stanley. Sometimes known as the "pitman poet", he was a latter-day music hall writer and performer who had really come too late for the genre. But he also wrote a lot of songs about pit life, strikes and disasters, which perhaps even in the North East were not of great interest outside the pit villages, something reflected in the fact that Allen had no Armstrong songs, and Catcheside-Warrington had only one. Barrass's *Pitman's Social Neet*, mentioned in connection with Reece Elliott's songs in Chapter 3, came too late for Allen, but would probably have been too "pitmatic" and serious for *Tyneside Songs*.

Of the four collections so far discussed, it is notable that Bell and Allen have more "street songs", i.e. the sort of songs that ordinary people liked (after all, Allen at least was interested in making money). The worthies who put together the *Minstrelsy* would have frowned on some of this material, but there was more to come. Catcheside-Warrington's *Tyneside Songs* was first published in 1912 by the Newcastle music shop J.G. Windows, and was still in print up to the 1990s (12). The books are not often mentioned in scholarly works, but the collection is outstanding in two respects. For most of the songs, it was the first time the music had been included (interestingly, it was provided by the same Samuel Reay who performed that role for *Folk Songs of Northern England*), and it included songs like 'Cushie Butterfield', 'The Lambton Worm' and 'The Blaydon Races', which have been identified with Tyneside around the world for 100 years.

But these four slim volumes of *Tyneside Songs* also contained those delights which Tynesiders have tended to keep to themselves. Many of these had been in Allen's, but now reached a wider audience. 'The Paanshop's Bleezin', 'Keep Your Feet Still Geordie Hinnie', 'Wor Nanny's a Mazor', and 'The Fire Doon on the Kee' were added to the list of songs which made the area utterly unique in England, the British Isles, and probably in the world. It was these books which many a North East family had in the piano stool in the years between the wars, and afterwards in the late '40s and early '50s, and which played a crucial role in keeping this culture alive during the first half of the 20th Century. No wonder Newcastle was so far ahead of other cities during the early part of the second Folk Revival, and no wonder it produced Louis Killen and The High Level Ranters, who would take this material and present it to a wider audience. But ... still no pit songs!

A remarkable piece of research by Ray Stephenson, originally for the first Roland Bibby lecture at Morpeth Gathering in 1999, has recently shed a little more light on these songs in the early 20th Century (13). By the time Charles Ernest Catcheside-Warrington started publishing his books, he was already an established entertainer and the most prolific of Tyneside recording stars, having started making cylinder recordings as early as 1893. Although a national entertainer based in London, where he recorded many standard music hall numbers such as 'My Old Dutch', he eventually settled back in Newcastle. Back home, he turned his attention to the vernacular songs of the area, but now he was recording on discs as well as cylinders. For example, in 1907 he recorded 'Geordie Haud the Bairn', 'Last Neet' and 'The Neebors Doon Belaw'. A lot of later recordings were stories and comic sketches, such as 'The Cullercoats Fishwife and the Census Man' and 'The Fishwife and the School Inspector', and in 1911 Warrington recorded Hawke's 'Man at the Battle of Waterloo', an example of quintessentially Geordie humour still performed by Louis Killen and others in folk clubs today. In the same year he made the first recordings of 'Cushie Butterfield' and 'The Paanshop's Bleezin'. Whilst it is not possible to say how popular these records were for all the dates, it is certainly the case that there were big sales recorded in the late 1920s, and so these recordings complemented the Catcheside-Warrington books in helping to keep these songs alive during the dead period between the two World Wars. Another artist, J.C. Scatter, recorded 'Howden for Jarrow', 'The Row Upon the Stairs' and 'Blaydon Races' in 1909, whilst Harry Nelson made a few recordings right at the end of his career. These included 'Hi Canny Man, Hoy a Ha'penny Out', an Elliott favourite, and 'Oh Hey Ye Seen Wor Jimmie', another song still popular in Tyneside folk clubs.

There was a lull in the recording of Tyneside songs between 1914 and 1927, but there came renewed interest in the 1930s, with Warrington making a brief comeback in the late '20s. His last recordings took place in

London in 1931, mostly repeats of previous songs, but also including Tommy Armstrong's 'Wor Nanny's a Mazor'. It was also in the late '20s that W.G. Whittaker published his *North Countrie Songs*, which had traditional North East songs, many collected by him, and arranged for choirs (14). These became very popular in schools throughout the country, and helped establish such songs as 'Bobby Shaftoe' and 'Billy Boy' nationally. A Jesmond singing teacher, Ernest J. Potts, recorded some of these, notably 'Sair Fyel'd Hinny' and 'Dollia' in 1927. Potts was a mentor to Owen Brannigan, who became famous for this style of singing through his records made after the Second World War.

As was shown a little earlier, there was a whole corpus of splendid national folk songs, largely based on those collected in the South West of England, but nobody had come up to the North East a-collecting. There are those who say that if they had, they would have found the same songs as they found in the south. One exception was the later collector, James Madison Carpenter, an American academic who toured England and Scotland by motor-car in the late 1920s. As with other collectors before him, he had his own agenda. His reasons for coming to the North East were not to get versions of English songs, nor Tyneside songs, nor pit songs. He wanted ritual sword dances, and sea songs, which eventually came from a few ex-sailors and sea captains who lived in Trafalgar Square in Sunderland. And he did get his sword dance – from Earsdon, which came to be recognised in the Second Revival as a classic example of this traditional dance.

So, a strong culture of Tyneside songs developed during the 19th Century, and a quite separate body of national songs was retrieved during the 20th Century. It was the late 1950s before anybody started to ask what traditional songs were being sung in the North East. People knew about 'Cushie' and 'Bobby Shaftoe', but they were almost national property, like 'Widdecombe Fair'. So, although Johnny Handle and Louis Killen got together at the jazz club, they were singing mostly American songs; when they started their folk club at the Sink in 1958 they pulled out all the British traditional songs they knew. (The meeting of Louis and Johnny and the start of the Bridge Folk Club has already been described in Chapter 2.) Jack and Pete Elliott, who walked though the door on the first night, had their family songs, but they too were performing a lot of blues, and what we would now call American folk songs.

Indeed, for many people at that time the term "folk song" meant cowboy songs, largely because of the influence of records and films. It's a bit difficult to realise this last point so many years on, but with all that's been written about folk song and folk music since the 1960s it's important to stress this point. It also explains why folk had to have a Revival to reclaim a separate identity! The other singer in the early days of the Newcastle club was John Reavy, who sang mainly Irish songs, and it was Reavey who had a copy of Lloyd's *Come All Ye Bold Miners*. He showed it to Louis, who showed it to Johnny. Johnny, in particular, was knocked out by this, and took it as his bible from then on. Both he and Louis were keen to find out about all kinds of local songs, and Jack Elliott, the pitman from Birtley, although twenty-odd years older than these lads, joined in this effort with gusto. The North East Folk Revival had started!

# The Elliott Family Songs

The Folkways LP was an excellent representation of the Elliott repertoire, and in the notes MacColl classifies the songs thus: "three traditional (Child) ballads, six music hall songs, five classic folk songs, nineteen children's street songs, five local songs, nine children's 'song games', and seven mining songs." Some of these were unique to the family or the local community, whereas others were more widely spread throughout the tradition. Some occurred perhaps just in the North East coalfield, some perhaps in the rest of the world. Note also that there were few mining songs, and the ones they had were cheerful. No disasters here, because, as we have already seen, the miners' way of coping with the dangers of the pit was continually to joke about them. Of course, they knew the perils, but brooding was not the way. Or, to quote Ian Watson, "The Elliotts have worked and suffered – and know why they sing."

The ever articulate MacColl, writing in his autobiography *Journeyman*, talks about "crack, the conversation of men who can make words ring like hammer blows on a face of anthracite; who, when they talk, enrich the bloodstream of the national vocabulary with transfusions of pitmatic – the bold, bitter, ribald, beautiful talk of miners."(15) The second side of the record begins with an excerpt from the diary of Jack Elliott's grandfather, including some interesting pieces of satirical poetry, and telling of nineteenth-century hardship. Responding to this stimulus, the family recall local and family events in a pattern of historical continuity from the days of transportation and imported cheap labour through to the experiences and hardship of their own lifetime: unemployment in the Depression, the young wife's fear of pit accidents and the child's horror at witnessing the indignity of dead miners, wrapped in sacking, being trundled home in an open hand-cart. "But then," say Jack and Em, "we could always sing at the weekend." (16)

# *'But then, we could always sing at the weekend.'*

One of the most interesting features of family performances was the sets, consisting of fragments or short songs they would string together, songs which they had always known since childhood. Some were funny fragments, often local parodies or music hall snatches, but most were children's songs, including game songs. When they were younger, the parents would join in with the kids' games, Jack coming out to the fields with his band and Em turning the skipping rope. My experience of these songs was much more limited, and certainly didn't involve *my* parents, who only showed when it was time to come in. It was also, as I remember, mostly the girls who did the singing, because most of the rhymes were to do with skipping, and I didn't sing any of them after I was about ten. The Elliotts, on the other hand, carried on singing them when they were grown up, both at home and on the increasing number of bookings they got as the Revival advanced. On their 1998 night at Ryton, mentioned in Chapter 5, the highlight of the night was all six of them, in their sixties or seventies at that time, doing a ten-minute spot in which they took it in turn to do a selection of these songs. A really touching moment. And it was done without a break, because this night was unique in the family's history; for the first time ever they had actually practised! However, one thing they didn't get right; they only managed to get as far as 1964, so had to come back and finish the story another night!

*My father died a month ago, and left me all his riches*
*A feather bed and a wooden leg, and a pair of leather britches*
*A coffee jug without a spout, a cup without a handle*
*A baccy box without a lid, and half a farthing candle.*

I have identified no fewer than 69 children's songs in their repertoire, of which 22 are game songs. Of these, about half are reasonably common, four are very rare, with only one or two other occurrences elsewhere, and three I have not managed to find any other versions of. The rest of these short songs are often described as "street songs". Very few of these appear to be widely known, most being unknown outside the Durham coalfield. I also asked several people from the area, mostly women in their late fifties, from both rural and inner city areas, whether they remember any of these songs, and was surprised to draw something of a blank. Once more, the pit community appears to be separate from the rest of the area.

An interesting book which has recently come to my attention throws more light on this aspect of the family's children's songs. Frank Rutherford, who has been mentioned previously in this book and who had been known to Johnny and Louis when he was librarian at the Literary and Philosophical Society in Newcastle, was an avid collector of and authority on traditional songs in the North East (17). By the mid-'60s he was librarian at the Institute of Education at the University of Durham, and had been collecting local children's songs for some time. The result was his book *All the Way to Pennywell*, subtitled *Children's Rhymes of the North East* (18). This book is a gem and extremely informative. It contains 296 rhymes, each one of which has the source, identified as 'Woman, 58, Birtley, 1962' or 'Girl, Annitsford, 1966', together with any known history, tune, and references to other published versions. The Elliott family come in for special mention, as three generations of the family provide no fewer than 51 of the rhymes, and according to Doreen (who had not seen or heard of the book until very recently) knew another 30-odd of them. This book contains only a selection of his collection.

The full songs the Elliotts sang before the Revival are fewer in number, about twenty in fact, but of great variety, as indicated in MacColl's list. About half are local, i.e. they had not been found outside Durham and Tyneside prior to the Revival. 'The Collier's Rant' and 'Bonnie Pit Laddie' were in print in the late 18th Century, of unknown composer, probably coming to Ritson from the South East Northumberland coalfield, and have seemingly passed down by oral tradition to the family during that time (though it is possible that Jack got them from Lloyd's *Come All Ye Bold Miners* in the late 1950s when he and Johnny Handle were devouring songs from that book). 'Stanley Market' was written about 1900 by Tommy Armstrong, just a few miles from Barley Mow.

Their other local songs were, as far as is known, only sung by the Elliotts. 'Celebrated Working Man' was an American import, but Jack did a conversion job on it – "Geordification" and "Pitmatification" are two of the words he used to identify this process! 'Billy to Bob', 'Geordie's Penker', 'Twenty Pound Dog' and 'The Unlucky Duck' are all comic songs of unknown origin outside the family, as are 'Doon the Wagonway' and 'Little Chance', which is analysed in detail below.

The other full songs, though small in number, are a fascinatingly varied range of different types of song. Three of them were "Child Ballads" (discussed earlier in this chapter). The classic Child ballad is usually of epic rather than homely proportions, and often tragic or even lethal for one or more of its characters. But one or two are more "domestic" in nature, including Number 274, 'Our Goodman', a tale of a wife deceiving a rather dim husband by pretending that she isn't in bed with a man. The Dubliners' 1960s hit 'Seven Nights Drunk' is the best-known version, but the Elliotts' 'The Blind Fool' is just as good. 'We Went Along a Bit Further' is a bit like a precursor of all the jokes starting "There was an Englishman, an Irishman, and a Scotsman ...", and is customised to County Durham, maybe by the Elliotts, or by somebody they got it from. The family's third Child ballad, 'Henry my Son', is discussed in detail below. The remaining songs sung by the family before the Revival are 'Johnny Bugger' ('Johnny Bucca'), 'My Old Man ('Chamallie'), 'The Sucking Pig', 'Was It In the Kitchen?', 'Still I Love Him', and 'The Barley Mow'. The tunes and words for all their full songs are given in the Songbook in the Appendices, together with brief notes. However, a couple of these deserve a little more attention.

## 'Little Chance' ('Busty Fields')

From the earliest days of the Revival 'Little Chance' has been associated with the Elliott family and in particular with Jack Elliott. Busty Fields received its name from the Busty seam of coal that makes up the Great Northern coalfield, mined from Harraton Colliery. The song is about a pit pony (a "gallowa"), and is unique to the North East coalfield. It has been immensely popular during the Revival, mostly due to Jack Elliott's version being recorded and sung widely by him, the other Elliotts, and Bob Davenport. A version had been collected by Bert Lloyd, from Charles Bevill from Fir Tree Drift in the west of the coalfield, and published in the first edition of *Come All Ye Bold Miners*. However, the lack of tune and its rather poor text compared with the Elliott version meant that hardly anybody had noticed it, although a version from Bert Draycott did crop up in Fishburn, in the middle of the county. Whilst this version was not so full or rich in imagery as Jack's version, it came together with some fascinating information on Christmas and New Year pit ceremonies which Jack himself was later to embellish with further information from the West Cornsay colliery. Bevill's first verse is the same as the Elliott version, but the other two verses are unrelated. During the 1960s, another three versions were collected by Maxine Baker, an undergraduate from the School of Dialect Studies at Leeds University (19), and in the 1970s four more by Beamish Museum. In 1980, Pete Elliott produced a further three versions, one nonsense song and two fragments, which he published in an excellent monograph, *Little Chance for Little Chance*, unfortunately no longer available (20).

In attempting to find out how the song spread, three versions occupy a particularly important role. Jack's song has three verses about pit work, mostly about how rough the work is. There are phrases used in everyday chat in the pit, still talked about by the family, such as the man who could never find his pick, or the man who comes home so exhausted that he cannot make it up the stairs and just falls asleep on the mat. Verse four is the only one about the gallowa pony, virtually identical to the Bevill version, and the last verse is a funny one about the mother-in-law getting drowned at the seaside.

The earliest version is that sung by Mr J. Hutchinson of Bowburn, a pit village a few miles to the south-east of Durham city, but learnt by him "down Lambton D pit in 1915". As that pit is only three or four miles from Harraton pit, we should compare this with Jack's version. Hutchinson's is entirely about the pit pony, but without the humour, the chorus, or the mother-in-law verse, with only one or two phrases in common, and the gallowa Little Chance is actually killed. It ends with the somewhat callous observation by the boss that he'd rather have lost the pit laddie, because he's cheaper than the pony!

The only non-Durham version is by another Hutchinson, a Billy Hutchinson from Bedlington, a pit village near Ashington in Northumberland. He has four verses, all comical, no connection with the pits, no mention of a pony, but he uses the same tune as Jack, with the "titty fal lah" lines and a final verse which is virtually a compound of two of Jack's verses. No Little Chance here, but the gallowa appears at the last minute! Most people use the term "music hall" to characterise the funny verses in this song, although Pete Elliott in his monograph preferred the term "pure pit-pub", where you could add and delete verses at will. As with so many things, Pete was on the ball. The tagline "titty fal lah etc" was added by Jack, and probably came from a fragment of one of Em's songs.

Based on the twelve versions that have come to light, the following scenario could be suggested. The song was written as a serious song in praise of gallowas in general and one in particular, and was being sung in the Fencehouses area by 1915. By the mid-'20s, a somewhat lighter version was being sung in the Consett area in at least one, probably two pits. By the '30s it was with Jack Elliott from Barley Mow, as a much more developed pit song, a better tune, with a chorus, not much about the pony, and an extra funny verse to boot. By 1951, a different version, much shorter and badly remembered, was in the Tow Law area, and a similar one in Fishburn. The '60s revealed two full versions, one a seeming music hall version in Northumberland, and Jack's version without the funny last verse in Spennymoor at the other end of the coalfield. There seems to be no relationship between versions and location, but a lot of *ad hoc* adaptation to local pits and miners, and different attempts to make it jollier.

# 'Henry My Son'

Their version of 'Lord Randal', probably the most widely spread of the Child Ballads amongst ordinary people, has been in the family for as long as any of them can remember. Child gave his Ballad Number 12 the title of 'Lord Randal' as being based on a real event involving the Earl of Chester in the 13th Century, but it goes under various titles throughout Europe. The story is that a young man comes back from hunting and is questioned by his mother about the events of the day. He has been in the woods or fields, and is ill on account of something he has eaten, which is poisoned. It's most commonly fish or eels, and the poisoner is his sweetheart or his sister. The mother then asks who he will leave his wealth to, and what he wants to happen to the poisoner. Some of the more than 500 versions of the ballad that are known are sinister, threatening stories with grand, imposing tunes, such as the one MacColl sang. But, like

*Jack and Em at the seaside*

a lot of other Child Ballads, many of the versions are degraded, or jokey, or used as kids' game songs. A subset titled 'Henry my Son' are in this class, in which the young man has usually been in the fields and been poisoned by his sister. Most of these have been collected in the 20th Century, following Child's publication. In the early days of the Folk Revival, the popular version in the clubs was 'Ge-reen and Yeller', a jokey version usually sung with a Cockney accent, but there have been many others.

The Elliotts' version is similar in tune to those from several parts of England, notably those of George Dunn from the West Midlands, Mrs Holden from Worcestershire, and Sheila Hughes, the daughter of the famous Dorset gypsy singer "Queen" Caroline Hughes. The Elliotts' words and tune for the chorus seem unique to them, as do the use of snails to poison Henry, and that the poisoners were gypsies. (It is tempting to make a link between the "gypsies" line and the gypsy history in the family, as Doreen's grandmother's mother was of gypsy stock, and had the name of Ann Lee-Ramn. The family mention this link a lot, but it is a long way back in the family pedigree.) The inheritance/retribution part of the tale is missing from their version. The song was mostly sung by the women (Em and Doreen), though on the LP there is a wonderful coming together of the family, and the tale of how Em Elliott had to return to the source of the song, Mrs Renee Green, to settle differences between family members as to the text and sequence of the verses. Mrs Green, as Renee Pearson, had been a school friend of Doreen's at the Boody concerts, which is where she had first learnt the song.

In writing this book, it has often struck me as odd that Jack did not do any Tommy Armstrong songs except for 'Stanley Market'. After all, Stanley is only about nine miles from Birtley, and Armstrong, the pitman poet from Tanfield Lea, travelled widely in the coalfield. The Elliotts and others have laughed this off in typical fashion by saying "the buses didn't run that way". Well, I think this is more a comment on the insularity of pit villages than the quality of public transport in North West Durham (Author's note: they could have got the 775 or 776 which I used to travel to work in the 1970s!). Another gem was Doreen's comment, "Nine miles? That's holidays!"

Armstrong came from the wrong area for the Elliotts. Tom Gilfellon, a member of the original High Level Ranters, and another famous son of Stanley, who revived interest in Armstrong in the late '60s with recordings and a book (21), suggests, "You've got to realise the importance of the A1 in this area. West we all relate to Newcastle, and talk like Tynesiders, but if you're on the other side, you're a Mackem – the two groups just didn't talk to one another." "Mackem" is a derogatory name the Tynesiders have for Wearsiders, i.e. people from Sunderland. It's to do with the way the latter pronounce "make them", and is used particularly by Newcastle United supporters, who are so rabidly "anti-mackem" that when the football results come on the telly on a Saturday afternoon, they look for the Sunderland result first to make sure they've lost before they look for their own result! Tom's use of the term here makes his point, but Birtley people talk differently from either Newcastle or Sunderland; very definitely Durham.

More seriously though, Gilfellon went on to remark that Armstrong's songs weren't even being sung in Stanley in the 1960s when he was researching. Armstrong was a notable performer, which is why people went to see him, but perhaps they didn't think of singing the songs themselves. In fact, the only person he came across was his own mother, who sang 'Wor Nanny's a Mazor'. This chimes in with Johnny Handle's experiences of looking for songs in the area, and it looks as though Armstrong suffered the same loss of interest in his work after his death as did Alexander Barrass from nearby Consett. Fortunately for Tom Gilfellon and the rest of us, the poet's son published a small book of his father's songs in the 1920s (22).

However, it turns out that Jack Elliott had purchased several copies of Armstrong's book and was distributing them to interested people, which makes me even more surprised that he didn't do more of Armstrong's songs. Although he did learn 'The Ghost that Haunted Bunty' later, perhaps because Bunty was his nickname in the pit, 'Wor Nanny's a Mazor' and 'The Row Between the Cages' surely were right up his street. Definitely his kind of song. It's also notable that the Armstrong song Jack cottoned on to was the cheery, optimistic view of life in a big, bustling pit town at the height of its prosperity, a 'Penny Lane' of its day.

## *"The buses didn't run that way." "Nine miles? That's holidays!"*

So that was the Elliotts' repertoire in 1961; but, as was said earlier, the pioneers of the Folk Revival in the North East had still to find their own culture. They quickly came to realise that they had to look beyond Catcheside-Warrington, and set about actively looking for local songs and, in the case of the Elliotts, pit songs and local songs in particular. Among the local songs they came across quickly were 'The Clog Dancer' from Johnson Ellwood, miner and champion clog dancer who lived about a mile from Brown's Buildings, 'The Harrin's Heid' from Bob Davenport's family, 'The Blackleg Miner' from Louis Killen, and 'Buy Broom Besoms'. Some songs learnt from the early '60s have become as strongly linked with the family as their longer-known songs. For example, a song perhaps more linked to Jack than to the family was 'The Banks of the Dee' or 'The Old Miner', a Durham song from *Come All Ye Bold Miners* already being sung by Louis. Jack, who was about the age of the man in the song, and already well past his best working days, naturally made it very much his song. In typical Elliott fashion the family inherited it and made it their own,

To use a mining metaphor, the Elliotts found in their search for pit songs that the seams were not very deep, and often ran out quickly. There were songs in books, but there were few miners singing songs about pits. Indeed, some of the best songs about the pits that came to light were written about this time. Johnny Handle grew weary of trying to find songs from pitmen, but with his knowledge of the pits and creative talents soon started writing them, starting with 'Farewell to the Monty'. The two most notable songs Jack got in this period became Elliott songs, and were written by an unknown pitman from Hetton-le-Hole, a mining village between Sunderland and Durham. 'Jowl Jowl and Listen', and 'Rap 'er te Bank' came to Jack via the headmaster of Birtley school, Walter Toyn, and it's the quality of Jack's rendition of the songs as much as the words which has made the second of these in particular such an anthem of the coalfield ever since.

Walter Toyn was an interesting man, who had researched North East vernacular song as a personal interest for many years. In a rare interview in the John North column of the *Northern Echo* in January 1968, in connection with the collection of tapes for Jack's LP, Walter summed up his lifelong interest in folk music.

> "Through folk music the people of the past come through to present times. You know what they thought and how they felt. This was the medium for expressing themselves. They give the true picture of life as it was then in their music. Listen to the folk songs of the time and you get the real picture of press gang victims suffering appalling food and murderous discipline before being thrown back on the streets maimed and useless to beg for a living."

New songs, Walter admits, are increasingly difficult to find, even on Tyneside, which he reckons to be the most prolific centre in England. The bottom of the barrel has been well and truly scraped. But he still manages to stumble across rare discoveries in his lectures and travels. Take those two remarkable miming songs, 'Jowl and Listen' and 'Rap 'Er Te Bank', which he now teaches to his own pupils in music lessons and which are included in collector-scholar A.L. Lloyd's *Folk Song in England*, just out this week. He passed those songs to his folk singing friend, the late Jack Elliott, whose fame spread far beyond his native Birtley.

Walter has seen men at Annfield Plain, Sacriston and many parts of Durham and Northumberland sitting with tears in their eyes listening to the words that recall their own boyhood days when Dad took them down the pit at the tender age of 11 or 13. Many have offered to buy his taped recordings of those songs. For him, the singer is really symbolising through the image of the cage hauled up the shaft the end of a dying miner. The song is sad but true, a precious record of a vanishing way of life, which is why he includes such songs in school music lessons.

> "I feel children ought to have a knowledge of the lives, feelings and emotions of their forefathers. With so many pits closing down it's more important than ever that this heritage of song should be preserved. The negro mirrored his life in the blues. So, too, the miner down the years has preserved in song a portrait of life as it was, as he knew it and felt about it and suffered for it."

Before giving the afternoon music class an intriguing glimpse of another world behind the words and music of 'Rap 'Er Te Bank', Walter added: "The joyful thing is that children love these songs. They sense the local atmosphere, the grit and coal dust between the lines. Pits may close but these songs must never be allowed to die. And if some sociologist 100 years from now tries to tune in to the North East of yesterday his study will not be complete without a recording of the singing miner himself, the late Jack Elliott, founder of the Birtley Folk Club."

At least one other song, 'The Unlucky Duck', came to Jack via Walter Toyn, and we know when he got it because he wrote the words out on 5th September 1965. It was originally a poem, and Jack put it to the tune of 'Merrily danced the Quaker's Wife'.

Jack was also very impressed with Ed Pickford's mining songs, and sang his 'Pound A Week Rise', whose words we saw earlier. Amongst Pete and Pat's papers are the words of 'Ee Aa Cud Hew', another of Ed's songs. Ed comments only that he didn't know whether Jack sang it, but recalls a Blackpool Taverner assuring him that Jack had written the song. "No," says Ed, "I wrote it." "No," says the man, "Jack Elliott wrote it. You're too young." Since the man had heard Jack sing it, it means that he was still pursuing new songs right up until the time he died. And when you consider the quality of the song, is it any wonder?

*The words of 'Jowl Jowl' in Jack's handwriting, learnt from Walter Toyn, seen teaching mining songs to his class.*

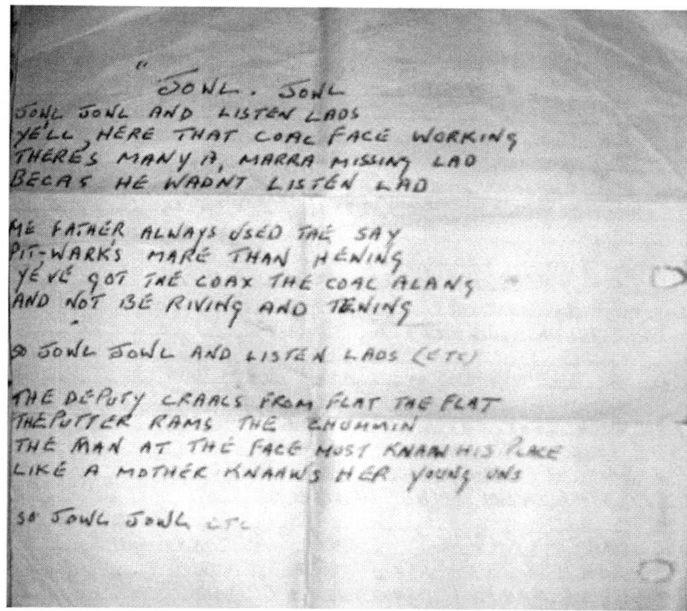

JOWL. JOWL

JOWL JOWL AND LISTEN LADS
YE'LL HERE THAT COAL FACE WORKING
THERE'S MANY A, MARRA MISSING LAD
BECAS HE WADN'T LISTEN LAD

ME FATHER ALWAYS USED THE SAY
PIT-WARK'S MARE THAN HEWING
YE'VE GOT THE COAX THE COAL ALANG
AND NOT BE RIVING AND TEWING

SO JOWL JOWL AND LISTEN LADS (ETC)

THE DEPUTY CRAALS FROM FLAT THE FLAT
THE PUTTER RAMS THE CHUMMIN
THE MAN AT THE FACE MUST KNAW HIS PLACE
LIKE A MOTHER KNAAWS HER YOUNG UNS

SO JOWL JOWL ETC

*When Ah was young and in me prime*
*Ee aye Ah cud hew*
*Ah was hewin' aal the time*
*Noo me hewin' days are throo, throo*
*Noo me hewin' days are throo.*

*Ah've lain down flat and shovelled coal*
*Ee aye Ah cud hew*
*Me eyes did smart in the dust filled hole*
*Noo me hewin' days are throo, throo*
*Noo me hewin' days are throo.*

*Ah've worked with marras and they were men*
*Ee aye Ah cud hew*
*They were men and sons of men*
*Noo me hewin' days are throo, throo*
*Noo me hewin' days are throo.*

*Ah knaa that work was made by men*
*Ee aye Ah cud hew*
*But wee made dust Ah'll nivver ken*
*Noo me hewin' days are throo, throo*
*Noo me hewin' days are throo.*

*It's soon that pit nee mair Ah'll see*
*Ee aye Ah cud hew*
*But Ah'll carry it round inside of me*
*Noo me hewin' days are throo, throo*
*Noo me hewin' days are throo.*

(words from the *Ed Pickford Songbook*)

It was in 1964 that Jack had a conversation with Johnny Handle on the subject of his lungs. He'd been short of breath for many years, and hadn't been diagnosed with anything specific, but was almost certainly suffering from pneumoconiosis, the "miner's disease". Johnny was moved by Jack's account of how the conditions down the mine brought this on, and it inspired him to write the song 'Dust'.

All members of the family were partial to local songs from Tyneside and County Durham. But they also learnt folk songs from elsewhere, in common with thousands of other folk song enthusiasts all over the

*Dust from Johnny Handle's Songbook*

country. Jack in particular sang a number of Scots songs such as Jeannie Robertson's 'My Son Edward' (he and Em often went to Scotland for their holidays). Pete and Pat on the other hand sang a number of Irish songs. 'Nine Miles from Gundegai', 'Lassie wi' the Yellow Coatie', 'The Sun and the Moon', 'The Collier Laddie' and 'Fourpence a Day' are particularly linked with individual family members. Two other songs from the Revival in particular became family songs, 'Wild Mountain Thyme' and 'Miner's Life'. Not only did they all sing all the words of these, but they became "finishers" on gigs, or the songs they would sing if they just got up for one or two at some gathering. 'Wild Mountain Thyme' came from another great folk family, the McPeakes from Belfast. The Elliotts became very friendly with the McPeakes, the two families having a great deal in common. The other was 'Miner's Life', an American song with Welsh origins that they embraced with rapture. It has to be said that the Elliotts embraced the Folk Revival lock, stock, and barrel, and were feted wherever they went, both giving and receiving.

After Jack died in 1966, a more concerted effort was made to retrieve traditional songs from the area. When the FED (North East Federation of Folk Clubs) started, they bought a second-hand tape recorder from the BBC, a Uher portable machine which was then the state of the art, and sent people such as Johnny Handle, Tony Wilson, Phil Ranson and Pete Elliott off to find music and songs amongst ordinary people. The other agency working in parallel was the recently established Beamish Museum, which was extremely fortunate in having John Gall work for them. He ensured that resources were made available for recording singers and musicians particularly from County Durham. Whilst the Beamish tapes are held on one site, with public access, this was not the case with the FED tapes, which by and large finished up amongst those who had recorded them.

However, more recent wisdom has resulted in the FARNE project (Folk Archive Resource North East, a collaboration between Folkworks and Gateshead Council), where these recordings, together with a huge number of manuscripts and other artifacts relating to traditional music and song are available to everybody with a few clicks of a mouse (23). As the website is held up as a definitive representation of the area's folk music and customs, it is interesting to look at what sound recordings of traditional song it holds. Of 96 such items, no fewer than 62 are by one or more of the Elliotts, with another 28 from Bert Draycott of Fishburn, County Durham, a pit deputy whose contributions are almost all to do with the pits. This is a salutary reminder of the fact that folk song in the North East is at its strongest in the urban industrial districts rather than the rural areas. It's no surprise that the only other artist with more items on the site is Billy Pigg, the supreme Northumbrian piper. Where are the ballads, the romantic songs from the shepherds of the Rede? Was nobody singing J.P. Robson's songs, or Robert Nunn's, or Geordie Ridley's (except for 'Blaydon Races')? It seems that without the pit songs of the Durham coalfield, there were no singers of songs anybody had bothered to record! (Johnny now says that "they just didn't get round to it".) It seems, indeed, that coalfield songs were a surprise not just to the folklorists like MacColl and Lloyd, but to the people of the North East themselves.

It was the revelation of the existence of North East pit songs, which helped generate the notion of industrial folk songs in general, as is revealed in Lloyd's 1967 treatise *Folk Song in England* (24). The book has a whole chapter on the topic, whereas his much earlier book, *The Singing Englishman*, had not mentioned the subject at all (25). When in 1978 he compiled the second edition of *Come All Ye Bold Miners*, the great expansion of the text was based almost exclusively on the North East coalfield, much of it from the Elliotts (26). The 1962 landmark album *The Iron Muse*, a compilation of "industrial folk songs" produced by Lloyd and released by Topic Records, contained 26 tracks, of which 16 were from the North East and sung by North Easterners (27). A great pity to my mind is that there isn't an Elliott on it. When it did arrive, the English industrial folk song appeared to be from one of only two industrial camps, the coal industry and the cotton-weaving industry. There were Durham mining songs or Lancashire mill songs, with other industries hardly getting a look-in. As Bert commented, as if in explanation, these were long-established industries before the Industrial Revolution. But the songs on *The Iron Muse* are mostly railing against the iniquities brought about by the Industrial Revolution, especially the cruelties of the owners of heavy industry.

And yet, as Paul Younger remarked when he discovered the Elliotts and their pit songs, "There are no songs in the Hebburn shipyard community", and Graeme Miles looked everywhere on Teesside for songs about steelworks without success. He ascribes this to a transient workforce. "There were choirs, because there were a lot of Welsh workers," says Graeme. But I think we now know that even miners were often migratory, and certainly similar influxes of Irish and Scots didn't prevent a robust singing tradition at the height of industrialisation in the mid-19th Century. Paul Younger's family and the Doonans have both shown how pockets of their culture existed alongside but separate from the Tyneside traditions. There was one beneficial outcome of this, though. When Graeme started visiting the Tyneside area, and particularly the Three Tuns at Birtley, he was "stunned by going up there", a factor which no doubt influenced the subject-matter of some of his songs, and probably also the other great Teesside songwriters like Vin Garbutt and Pete Betts.

## Reece's Songs

Reece sang a great deal in the pub with his brother Jack. But unlike Jack and Em's set-up, his own family apparently did not sing at home. However, he had his own separate songs, and again he didn't distinguish between folk songs and other songs he sang. He had a number of pit songs, notably four from Barrass's *Pitman's Social Neet*, namely

*Reece's nephew John with his wife Pam*

'A'am a Poor Aad Shifter Noo', 'The Hewer' and 'The Driver and The Putter'. Two other local pit songs he had were 'The Travelling Candy Man' and the wonderfully comic 'The Volunteer Putter'. Later in life, he sang Jock Purdon's 'Farewell to 'Cotia', which I believe to be the only one of Jock's songs the Elliotts sang regularly, though Doreen remembers singing 'Blackleg Mining Man' at a concert "down in Yorkshire". Of course, the subject matter was very close to the Elliotts' heart, so Jack put the tune to it, and Reece sang it.

Others of Reece's songs were the pop songs of his childhood, such as 'Little Pal' and 'I Loved You Better Than You Knew', a song written by the American Johnny Carroll in 1893 and popularised by the country singer Bradley Kincaid. The same was true for Harry Wincott's 1909 song, 'The Little Shirt me Mother Made For Me'. Then there were what we'd probably call music hall songs, such as 'A Very Funny Thing Occurred' and 'When Hackenschmidt Wrestled wi' Me'. There were also kids' songs like 'There Was a Man up a Tree', 'The Guiser's Song' (which he sang in a mummer's play in his youth), and the funny piece 'Always Look After Thee'sel' which originated in Yorkshire.

# Jack's Stories and his 'Other Songs'

Jack Elliott may have been viewed by some outside the area as a custodian of a tradition, and indeed he was. But like many other traditional singers and musicians from all over the British Isles, he had a much wider range of musical interests than some folk scholars would like to think. Whereas some academics and collectors of an older generation might label some songs as good because they had some intangible "folk" quality, and look askance at a song whose author was known, for instance, many of their "sources" were equally at home with an American country song, or a bawdy parody of a traditional song, as with one of their "own songs". They saw the differences, but did not classify a song as "good" or "bad" as a folk scholar might. A good song was something they enjoyed singing, whether trivial, noble, serious, or comic. The Edwardian collectors, led by Cecil Sharp, were only after a certain kind of song, and would reject music hall, bawdy songs, or drawing-room melodramatic Victorian songs. The few traditional singers still left in their natural environment after the Second World War, such as the Copper family, Phil Tanner from the Gower, George Dunn from Quarry Bank near Birmingham, and the wealth of singers from Eel's Foot and the Blaxhall Ship in Suffolk, all had a healthy mix of a wide range of song types. So it was with Jack and Reece Elliott.

Fortunately, during his short period of fame for the five years before his death in 1966, Jack made many recordings, and nearly always the recorder wanted only his standard repertoire of family songs. But it is notable that on amateur live recordings, such as at Birtley Folk Club, he would often do one of his stories or monologues. These were all comic, and probably represent the best of "pitmatic". There are biblical parodies such as 'The Preacher and the Atheist' and 'The Parable of the Lost Shekels', and there are the more homely comic stories like 'Porridge' and 'The Pound of Cod'. Lots of the stories concern the details of life underground, at work, a further example of the way miners coped with the dangers and misery of the job.

Some of his longer recording sessions were made for Beamish Museum, and unlike some of his other sessions, he must have been asked to just sing what he liked. Em was with him on these sessions, but it is mostly Jack we hear. The songs were mostly accompanied on guitar or mandolin, and there is even 'My Son David', the immortal Jeannie Robertson version of the Child Ballad 'Edward'! However, that song is not typical of the list, which must be one of the most catholic any traditional singer has ever presented. Some are fine folk songs that some of us had never heard him doing before, like 'The Barrin' of the Door', 'Adam Buckham', 'I Once Loved a Lass', 'Stormy Old Weather', and 'The Wild Rover'. But there are lots of sets of tunes, and lots of American songs like 'Waitin for the Train' (Around a Western Watertank), 'I'm in the Jailhouse Now' (Jimmie Rodgers), and 'The Old Pine Tree'. Here is the full list of songs sung by Jack on the Beamish tapes, which he didn't record elsewhere:

'The Barrin of the Door'
'Far Across the Sea Laddie'
'Banks of the Dee'
'Old Woman's Ass'
'Where ye Gannin Em'
'I Married A Wife (Single Again)'
'Adam Buckham'
'Hey Hey So Wanton'
'Birmingham Jail'
'Paddy McGinty's Goat'
'I Once Loved a Lass'
'My Love She's But a Lassie' (sung with guitar)
'The Wind Blew the Bonnie Lassie's Pladdie Away'
'A Soldier and a Sailor'
'An Old Man He is Old'
'Waitin' for the Train'
'I Don't Care What You Used to Be'
'Riggs of Barley' (Corn Riggs)
'Stormy Old Weather'
'Dark as a Dungeon'
'How Many Times Have You Heard Someone Say?'
'Carry me Back to the Mountains'
'Striklin Toon'
'The Empty Saddle' ('Bonny George Campbell')
'I Wish I Was a Maid Again'
'Cushie Butterfield'
'Last Night I Had a Sweet Dream'
'When the Harvest Moon is Shining'
'I'm in the Jailhouse Now'
'The Old Pine Tree'
'Same the Whole World Over'
'I Saw the Forty Twa'
'When the Sun Goes Down Again'
'Wild Rover'
'The Wagoner'
'Come Back To Me' (old pop song)
'My Son David' (Jeannie Robertson's version of Edward)
'Hear Them Bells' American religious song
'Died for Love', unaccompanied
'Four Little Boys'
'My Lad Says Cuddle In'

The Beamish tapes have a whole series of tune sets, played by Jack variously on guitar, mandolin, banjo, melodeon, and "mouthie" (mouth organ). The following list of the ones that are recognisable gives the flavour.

'Marie's Weddin'' / 'Muckin of Geordie's Byre';
'Blow the Wind Southerly' / 'Minstrel Boy' / 'Rowan Tree';
'Bonnie Lassie' / 'Keel Row';
'Scotland the Brave';
'Oh Susannah';
'Flowers of Edinburgh';
'Bluebell Polka';
'Peggy O'Neill' / 'Scottish Soldier';
'Early One Morning Just As the Sun Was Rising'.

What is not clear about this "extended repertoire" is which songs and tunes he learnt before the Revival and which afterwards. Jimmy Rodgers and the other American songs he would have been singing for a long time. 'Stormy Old Weather', however, may well have come from Bob Roberts, Norfolk fisherman and singer, and 'My Son David' would almost certainly be from Jeannie Robertson, the undisputed queen of Scots traveller singers.

From this extensive repertoire it's obvious that Jack left a fine legacy to his family, as well as the strongest possible desire to find more songs. As we have seen, his children were well up to the challenge.

*Jack with Doreen and Pete, about 1930*

## References for Chapter 6


1. Henry Burstow, *Reminiscences of Horsham*, 1911. Available on http://www.folk-network.com/miscellany/burstow/burstow_songs.html
2. John Broadwood, *Old English Songs*, Balls & Co., 1843; James H. Dixon, *Ancient Poems, Ballads and Songs of the peasantry of England*, C. Griffin and Co., 1846
3. Robert Bell, *Early Songs and Ballads*, George Bell & Sons, 1889
4. Lucy Broadwood and J.A. Fuller Maitland, *English County Songs*, Cramer, 1893; Sabine Baring Gould & H. Fleetwood Sheppard, *Songs and Ballads of the West*, Patey & Willis, c.1891–2; Frank Kidson, *Traditional Tunes*, Chas. Taphouse & Sons, 1891
5. *The Folksongs of Britain*, series of ten LPs of original recordings of traditional singers, ed. Peter Kennedy and Alan Lomax, Caedmon Records, New York, 1961
6. *The Voice of the People*, a series of 20 CDs of original recordings of source singers, ed. Reg Hall, Topic Records, 1998
7. Joseph Ritson, *Northern Garlands*, E & G Goldsmid, 1784–93.
8. John Bell, *Rhymes of Northern Bards*, John Bell, 1812, reprinted Frank Graham, 1971
9. David Harker, *Songs from the manuscript collection of John Bell*, Surtees Society, 1985
10. John Stokoe and Samuel Reay, *Songs and Ballads of Northern England*, Walter Scott Ltd, 1892, reprinted Frank Graham, 1974; J. Collingwood Bruce and John Stokoe, *Northumbrian Minstrelsy*, Society of Antiquaries, 1882, reprinted Folklore Associates, 1965
11. Thomas Allan, *Tyneside Songs*, Thomas and George Allan, revised edition 1893, reprinted Frank Graham, 1972
12. C.E. Catcheside-Warrington, *Tyneside Songs*, J.G. Windows, 1912
13. Ray Stephenson, *A Slice of Geordie Heritage (A potted history of vernacular gramophone and phonograph recordings made by Tyneside, Northumbrian, and Durham artistes 1893–1943)*, private printing, NE62 5YA
14. W.G. Whittaker, *North Countrie Songs*, Curwen, 1921
15. Ewan MacColl, *Journeyman*, Sidgwick and Jackson, 1990
16. Ian Watson, *Song and Democratic Culture in Britain*, Croom Helm, 1983
17. Rutherford, Frank, *The Collecting and Publishing of Northumbrian Folk-Song*, Northumberland Press Limited, 1964
18. Rutherford, Frank, *All the Way to Pennywell*, University of Durham Institute of Education, 1971
19. Maxine Baker, BA Thesis, 1965, Leeds School of Dialect and Folk Studies, Brotherton Library, University of Leeds
20. Pete Elliott, *Little Chance for Little Chance*, private printing 1980
21. Tom Gilfellon, *Tommy Armstrong Sings*, Frank Graham, 1971
22. W.H. Armstrong, *Song Book*, Noel Wilson, 1930, reprinted 1953
23. FARNE website, www.asaplive.com/FARNE/Home.cfm
24. A.L. Lloyd, *Folk Song in England*, Lawrence & Wishart, 1967, Chapter 6
25. A.L. Lloyd, *The Singing Englishman*, Workers' Music Association, 1944.
26. A.L. Lloyd, *Come All Ye Bold Miners*, Lawrence & Wishart, 1st edition 1952; 2nd edition, 1978
27. *The Iron Muse*, Topic Records, 1966, now on CD, TSCD465

# Chapter 7 "Some Conclusions"

I started this project because I thought the family were important to the Folk Revival and that their story ought to be told. But I always thought there was more to them than the music, as indicated in the prologue. So I think it's important to look at that, but I'd like first to assess their importance to the Folk Revival.

Encouragement, crack and good fun, when added to this family's presence, were an irresistible combination. What attracted people to the club was the same thing that brought people to Brown's Buildings, the personalities of the family, above all Jack's charisma as a man, a singer, and a raconteur, the family's cohesiveness in spite of fierce arguments about important issues, and their great sense of humour. We've seen how, when they started the club, they did it differently from others. Not in a contrived, staged way, but in a natural way. The kitchen needed bigger premises, so it moved out to the Welfare Hall, then the pubs, but there was no need to change the format. The rest of the Brown's Buildings people, like Eddie Pickford, went with them.

Other, like-minded people came flocking, not only because of the Elliotts but also because they got a chance to sing there, a '60s precursor of the "open mike" we see today. Jack's short run of national prominence as a source singer added to the heady atmosphere, and coincided with the height of the Folk Revival when all the clubs were hugely popular. The word 'authenticity' has been used a lot in the book, because they brought a "touch of the real thing" when middle class younger people who had just come upon the songs for the first time set up so many other clubs. They could get songs from books, but when Jack Elliott sang a song, it stayed sung. There was a sense of something valuable coming down the years from a simpler time, which he and the family personified.

People often say that the family "represented their community", and indeed this point has been raised in this book. But I wonder if that is the case? They may be seen by some as representing their community, but they certainly didn't set out to do that, and as has been pointed out at several places in this book, I don't think they were typical of their community or any other. If in the past there had been many families like this, well that reinforces the belief that perhaps those times, though meaner, harder, and poorer, were in some ways better than what we've got now. But it's a long time since Birtley was the isolated pit village which would have fostered this spirit, and though miners have certainly been a community in themselves wherever they are, by the nature of the work and their inheritance, nevertheless I think their fellow pitmen and their families have seen the Elliotts as something very unusual, and their singing as "not for them".

A great deal has also been made of them somehow representing 'industrial song', particularly by the scholars who certainly got a lot of mining songs from them. However, I've tried to emphasise how the family repertoire before the revival did not contain much of this. It's been said more than once in this book that pitmen use humour to cope with the horrors of the job. By not singing many songs about disasters, it makes it all the more meaningful when they do say or sing something a bit deeper. One example that comes to mind is Pete Elliott singing 'Senghenydd'. This is a song about the 439 miners who lost their lives in the Universal Colliery, Senghennydd, in South Wales, on 14th October 1913. The emotion he brought to this makes it a lot more than just a song, and it's all the more effective as Pete, unlike his brothers, never worked down the pit. So passionate was he about the pit community that he in many ways behaved like a pitman and there are some who say he wishes he'd been one despite his rejection of the work at an early stage in his life. Dave Douglass thought he was a deputy!

Jack had the sort of attitude and personality that was widespread amongst traditional singers-he was a "character" in his own community, was very aware, and very intelligent. Peter Kennedy, one of the most prolific of the post war song collectors, observed that most of his traditional singers recorded by in the 1950s were, 'local 'rebels', refusing to conform to local religious or political pressures. They were traditionalists but at the same time were often outrageously progressive. They never accepted without question what they were told or what they had read until they had either experienced something for themselves or knew it to match their own personal conviction. So what touched you was their utter sincerity, and when they sang their songs you knew without question that they understood and felt what they were singing about.' (1). Does this not sound just a bit like our man Jack?

As the Revival gathered pace in the 1960s, most of the audience were middle class, well educated, and some of them fully fledged academics, who talked a language that many of the people they so admired did not really follow. Most of these source singers would be polite to their investigators, keeping their counsel about their thoughts on some of the high-flown erudition. But what was really rewarding was to watch the instant spark between these singers who were meeting each other for the first time. What a relief-they could relax! This is what happened when Jack Elliott met the likes of Scan Tester, the Sussex Anglo-concertina player, and Francis Shergold, the musician with Bampton Morris in Oxfordshire. All of these men were custodians of their own traditions, but were not precious about it. So, given half a chance, they'd be in the bar playing tunes, many of which were not folk tunes. After all, since their lives had been dominated by American music, and the dance bands of the '30s. Here was their chance! They weren't snobbish, but enjoyed playing all kinds of music. (We saw something of Jack's extensive repertoire in Chapter 6.)

*The young family at 'The Huts'*

The Elliotts' repertoire, as we have seen, is an interesting mixture of folk songs and other songs, some of which can be categorised, others which present difficulties in this regard. It may therefore be interesting to look briefly at this issue in a wider context. The question of what is a folk song is such a vexed one these days that some people avoid using the term, preferring the word 'traditional'. Somebody who has always had such views is that great Tyneside singer Bob Davenport. "I was never that keen on folk music." Bob is famous for singing sets of songs which might include folk songs, pub songs, and blues thrown in together, and which when accompanied by a band like The Rakes, or the Marsden Rattlers from his native North East, creates the most relaxed feeling of authenticity. This approach to music was much in evidence in Bob's hands at the Fox in the '60s and the Empress of Russia in the '80s, both in London, but alas not so common elsewhere. He says (Bob Davenport), "I always thought of myself as a traditional singer. I still do." (2) He goes on to explain what might at first seem a cryptic remark. "When I was a boy on Tyneside in 1947, I bought a record, 'Nobody Knows You When You're Down And Out', by Bessie Smith. Years later, in 1967, I was performing at the first Smithsonian Institute Festival in Washington DC and, by chance, met the woman who was accompanying Bessie Smith the day she made that recording. That's why I sing, and why I still sing that song. Traditional music from all over the world, whether it's a Negro protest song from New Orleans of something from the north of England, has a kind of connection. It's solid, I suppose you could say."

It is exactly the sort of attitude Jack and the rest of the family have had to singing, whether in the kitchen or on the stage, and it is interesting to note that another singer who has the same attitude is Jim Bainbridge, again from Tyneside. Of course, what is 'traditional' is as difficult to define as what is 'folk', but Bob's repertoire and that of the Elliotts are certainly a good start. It is also now clear that the singers of the Edwardian period, as well has having 'folk' songs, also had music hall songs, vulgar ditties, Victorian 'parlour songs', Gilbert and Sullivan, and other stuff. For them, folk songs were just one type of song in their repertoire. It has something more to do with how a song is sung, i.e. the style of delivery, on the occasion, and on the personality of the singer As Peter Kennedy remarked, even as far back as the '50s, the radio programme As I Roved Out was not so much dependent on the songs as the emerging personalities of the singers, whose conversations were taped as well as their singing.

However, what interests me, and others no doubt, is what people actually sang when they got together, i.e. in the pub on a Saturday night, let us say during the early 20th Century, and then we might get some answers. There seems to be no record of this from the Edwardian era, i.e. before recording emerged in a significant way. We have the example of the Eel's Foot in Norfolk in 1938 mentioned in Chapter 6, and Bob Copper in his books has given us an insight into Rottingdean on the Sussex coast during the same period (3). In these two cases, there was a heavy emphasis on 'Sharpian' folk songs, but I believe that these must have been exceptional. I think this because of the almost total ignorance about folk songs in my parents' generation, when we young people picked up these songs in the early '60s. They had been born in the first decade of the 20th Century, and I remember what they sang when they got together with "the crowd" as their friends were called. It was "songs from the shows", George Formby, and American pop songs. I can't remember any folk songs. And it wasn't as if they'd consciously replaced their parents' folk song repertoire. Their ignorance of folk songs implied their absence from their parents' upbringing or memory, the 'lost generation' that went to the trenches of the First World War, at a time when Sharp was hoovering up these songs in Somerset. Of course, this could well illustrate simply the difference between rural and urban. My parents and all their "crowd" were from Manchester. Norfolk and Sussex were obviously a better representation of rural areas.

It should not be imagined that the Elliotts are a group of saintly people whose sole purpose in life has been to keep this song culture going. They are in many respects a rough bunch. Their language is earthy, sometimes coarse. The splits in the family have been many, and an open secret with the North East folk fraternity. It is notable that the "four" have 15 children between them, and only one, Bill Elliott, has shown any interest in folk music. The divisions in the family have sometimes made it difficult to assemble material for this book. There was a great reluctance after Jack

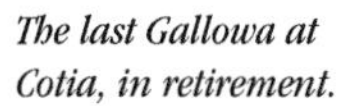

*The last Gallowa at Cotia, in retirement.*

died for the family to go out as a group, and it was not until the early '90s that they started looking for family gigs. And yet, as Barrie Temple says, "People go in different directions in various walks of life but this music pulls them back together." This is something that was exemplified by the booking of the 'six' at Ryton Folk Club described earlier. And the fact remains that nobody could get an audience reaction like they do for 'Miner's Life'.

How did the Elliotts compare with the other families that have become well known during the Folk Revival? The most notable of these are the Coppers from Rottingdean in Sussex, the Stewarts of Blairgowrie in Perthshire, and the McPeakes of Belfast. The Coppers' repertoire is entirely what I call 'folk songs', as defined by Sharp and the other Edwardian collectors, overwhelmingly rural in nature, day-to-day in nature rather than having the sweep of the big ballads. The Stewarts similarly had 'folk songs' from the rural Scottish North East, laced with travellers' songs in the cant, and many of the 'big ballads'. The McPeakes, although from a big city, again had a very old, rural repertoire.

The Elliotts joined this 'elite' by virtue of doing the same thing for industrial songs as the others were doing for rural songs, and yet somehow they seemed to me somewhat detached from 'folk song'. As somebody not from the North East, but certainly from the 'industrial north', I've probably in the past been a bit defensive and uncertain as to how "folky" we are. However, they were certainly regarded as in the same 'league' by Ewan MacColl & Peggy Seeger when planning their new book in the early '70s. "Their book was to cover all points between Banffshire and Dorset, bolstered by scholarly notes detailing the provenance and history of each song, and estimated to run to over 600 pages. The repertoires of Sam Larner of Norfolk, the Elliotts of Birtley, the Stewarts of Blairgowrie, Ben Bright and the Black Country chain-maker George Dunn would be integral to the project" (4). Jack's LP, was not only the first one to be issued on Bill leader's 'Leader' series, where he featured eminent source singers, but was linked with the great Sam Larner by being reviewed jointly in English Dance and Song along with his LP *Now is the Time for Fishing*. (At that time, many leading authorities saw Sam as the best living example of a singer in the traditional English style).

The great 'folk families' are of course recognised as bearers of continuity in traditional song, and with the Elliotts we have Roz and Bill continuing to sing folk songs. A comparison of the other families reveals some interesting differences. The Coppers are keeping it going with the 'Young Coppers', now in their forties, which gives them at least four generations of singers. Similarly the McPeakes have recently come back to the music after a spell in the mid '80s, when Francie III ran the music school his father had started. Recently, his son (yet another Francie) has persuaded the family to come together again as a performing unit. So, that's four generations, as with the Coppers.

On Tyneside there is the Doonan family where John Doonan's sons Kevin and Michael, both musicians, play with his granddaughters Frances and Sarah, who are spectacular traditional dancers. When I was chatting to the family at Kevin's house, and asked about the origins of their songs and music, and their relationship with the Elliotts, Kevin said: "The one you really need to talk to is mi dad. So, if we all hold hands round the table......" The Doonans are the latter day Elliotts. The kitchen's a bit different, a lot posher now, but they started at the same level, most definitely working class.

In contrast to these continuing families, there are other families who are not carrying the tradition forward. Sheila Stewart regards herself as the last of the line, none of the next generation having taken up the songs. If we look a little further, we find other patterns. The Ian Campbell folk group, famous in the 1960s, were started by Ian and his sister Lorna. Their parents sang and were obliged to move from Aberdeenshire to Birmingham, where their culture was maintained by their children, and whilst it is no doubt pleasing that their grandsons became profesional musicians, it was not with folk music, but with the hugely popular reggae-based group UB40

But, whilst Campbell family have left folk music, other families have come into it in the Second Revival. The Wilson family, from Billingham, had no particularly strong singing background, but have become very successful, with six out of seven members of the family singing in harmony. Now that they have grown-up kids, one or two of them are showing signs of carrying on this legacy within the tradition.

And then of course there's the most famous folk family of them all, the Watersons of Hull. Although Mike, Norma, and Lal with cousin John Harrison were singing folk songs as a harmony group around about 1960, and are part of the warp and weft of the Folk Revival, they did not get their songs from the family. They are well known, in fact, for having dug up many traditional songs for themselves in the days before records and books became widely available, (as did the Elliotts in their early search for mining songs). However, Mike Waterson relays Bert Lloyd's comment about them that they'd learnt the process the traditional way; by their childhood singing together at home, and with the granny who brought them up, although it would be hymns, and popular songs of the day. That's like the Elliotts again, isn't it, the kitchen, the boody concerts, the back lane street songs.

*Tony Benn, a regular visitor to the Big Meeting, at Harraton Welfare with Len, John, and Bill*

With regard to their music, I think that the Elliotts have shown us how working class people in poor circumstances can achieve great things despite lack of money and opportunity. Two other examples come to mind as a comparison; the ballet dancing miners' son *Billy Elliot* (no relation, only one T) and *The Pitmen Painters*, the group of Ashington miners who produced astonishingly good paintings of everyday life in a pit community in the 1930s. The playwright Lee Hall, of working class Newcastle background, created Billy for the 1999 film, and has recently written a play on the painters. He says he wanted "above all to remind people of what the working class is capable of - that given the right circumstances ordinary people can achieve extraordinary things." Thus Billy who became a successful ballet dancer, and the Pitmen Poets achieved things beyond the comprehension of their colleagues, family, and friends, and I think the Elliotts have achieved something similar.

The difference is that this family excelled at maintaining and promoting the community's culture, so whilst the reaction to the fictional Billy and the real painters was explicable as the art form was "highbrow", in the case of the Elliotts, it was really their own culture that was being shunned. The community would also largely shun the family's politics and their atheism. Working people do not get much of a choice in the life they lead, but the Elliotts did have a choice, and they took the harder, but infinitely more worthwhile route of sticking to what they believed in. As

Bob Davenport observed: "If you knew Jack Elliott he gave you a yard-stick to test what was real in life simply by being himself at a time when people were being encouraged by TV, newspapers, preachers and folklorists, to be anything but themselves. Jack's music reflected the man."

The Birtley Folk Club was and is an integral part of the family, so it's fair to ask how it and other clubs are faring in the first decade of the 21st Century. Folk music is still being enjoyed by many people, but in a different way from the past. A lot see it not as something to participate in, but as just another form of entertainment, and they attend the big concerts at home or away at festivals rather than the clubs. That fine Tyneside folk singer Anni Fentiman with a reputation on both sides of the Atlantic, recalls how she recently found herself at the back of a large concert at a folk festival, with Eliza Carthy on the stage. Eliza was singing songs like 'The Pace Egging Song' and 'The Good Old Way', and Anni naturally started joining in the choruses as she has always done. Not only was she the only one doing this, but she also got critical stares from some members of the audience. This audience had come to listen to a piece of art, and did not see it as any different from, say, a piano recital in that respect. The place these people are not going to is the folk club. And, disappointingly, neither are many of the younger performers starting on a career in folk music. Small wonder then, that the current folk club scene is not healthy.

I examined this problem in a recent article I wrote on the demise of the folk clubs nationally (5)

'Although much reduced in number, the clubs of today still present a wide variety of mode, some with the big room, stage, PA, and a top guest every week, some still singarounds with hardly ever a guest, and many good ones which alternate between modes. In my area, there are four or five clubs which cover this range, and are thriving. In Yorkshire, Pete Coe, who has tried everything there is to try in folk music in his time, recently reported that his club had house-full signs for the first two nights of the season. I could quote any number of clubs that are doing the right thing, but whatever the model of club, the problem they have in common is demographics.

So, accepting that the clubs might carry on keeping my generation happy for another decade, is there any reason why they should be carried on by the younger generation? Well, there's a need for something outside the festival and the workshop scene, I think. Whilst a lot of folk music has adapted to the big venue, like the Albert Hall, Cambridge Folk Festival, or Sage Hall 1, and we've had very successful 'folk rock' bands in the past, a lot of the music is intrinsically for a small crowd. After all, it's how it was created.

*Pete in benign mode*

For those who cherish the communal aspect of the music, the folk club has given such opportunity in the past and could in the future. There are clubs where British traditional music is deliberately mixed with other genres, and maybe that will attract people who might take it up. But if they do, then like we did, they will want to do more and more of it, play it, and start gravitating to another place with kindred spirits. Perhaps there'll be a rebirth as they realise that whether it's called a folk club or something else, it has some merit.'

The clubs have served their purposes admirably. They have gone from being all that there was, to having a major support role, to being an archaeological remnant of where and how songs should be sung. You need somewhere to just get together and do something. Being an audience listening to a superstar being paid for it will never be enough for some people. There will always be a need to do it yourself, so I believe that something like the folk clubs will eventually return. The form it takes must be decided by the younger generation, who might let the existing clubs collapse before starting something else up under a different label.

*Doreen & Bryan*

And Birtley Folk Club? In contrast to the new 'Young Turks', the average age at Birtley is well over sixty and rising. But what is keeping them going? It certainly isn't the place. For 35 years it's been at "The Buffs", a place which was never great, but is now terminally depressing, dilapidated, empty, a purpose built social club run by the RAOB, which has seen better days. It has a huge bar and concert room, shabby and grim, with hardly anybody ever there, the beer is awful, and the bar staff surly to the point of rudeness. (There's a story about Tom Lewis, the shanty singer, who likes to get dressed up and psyche himself up in advance of a booking, who turned up early, i.e. about eight o'clock. Nobody in the clubroom, two men in the bar, so Tom and his wife go in there, to be told by the barmaid "Nae women in the bar." There were two people in there, she was a woman, and this was 1998. True story, it gives you the feel of the place! Pete Elliott walked into the clubroom at 8.40 pm to find Tom sitting there all teed up. "Wae, ye'z are here sharp" At 8.40!)

One reason that keeps the people going is that they have crack, even on the quietest of nights. I was at the club on the last Wednesday in March 2008, when there was no guest, and a total of eleven people in the room. Even by modern day Birtley standards, this was a low turnout, to the extent that Doreen remarked, just prior to the start, "Why don't we go round to ours?" Going "widdershins" round the room, (anticlockwise, the way the singing has always gone), those who sang were Doreen and Bryan, two Jims, Yorkshire Anne, myself, Joyce Dickinson, and Don Stokoe. Three people, Sue, Sheila Stokoe and Brian didn't sing. Three of the assembly were there in the very early days at the Welfare Hall in 1962, Doreen, Bryan and Don. It was, despite the awful beer, the sheer emptiness of the rest of this very large rundown social club, a very enjoyable evening, as it always is. We all did two songs, and then the timing was difficult for Bryan in the Chair. The sheer amount of crack had meant that he hadn't enough time to get everybody in for a third song. What would he do? The tension fair crackled through the air, as we waited for a sign. "Aa knaa", says Bryan, "we'll draw the raffle". Now I remember a time when Birtley folk club used to raffle thirty bob, which was almost certainly illegal, but we are in modern times. The prize was a bottle of Argentinean Red Wine. As chance would have it, I won, the first time I've won a raffle since the old king died, I might add. So, by the time that was done, the Chair decided, and this is the sort of inspiration that only emerges in the tightest of corners, that the raffle winner would do another song, and that would be it. Well, there was one happy bunny who emerged from the RAOB Birtley that Wednesday night. And the Argentinian proved to be not too fierce

Most guest nights still have a respectable crowd. It's not the early '70s of course, but what club is? There's an awful lot of chat between songs, much of it highly entertaining, and if it wasn't for this, I think they would pack it in. There is no doubt that it is a social meeting place for this group of older people, but the humour is superb (one of the secrets of old age is that you can laugh at life instead of trying to compete all the time). And let's not forget that the standard of both songs and singing continue to be excellent. You still hear songs there you've never heard before.

So, there's the reasons for them carrying on with the club. I think it'll go on as long as Doreen and Bryan are still alive and kicking, and then it will finish. It will finish because there is nobody appropriate to carry it on, and because, for the young, folk clubs are not the place to sing these songs. However, if there is a bit more life left in the club, they will be doing it in a bit more comfort. As of June 2008, there is another venue! They have moved to the nearby Catholic Club, which is smart, warm, and has great beer and pleasant bar staff. It's an interesting manifestation of the loss of suitable venues for folk clubs when the most famous atheists in folk music have to move to this venue, and some people are having to divert their gaze from the crucifix on the wall! I forecast a new lease of life for Birtley folk club, and have every confidence it will make its 50th anniversary.

Although they became very famous in "folk circles" they never let it go to their heads. Two recent examples illustrate this. Pat celebrated her 70th birthday, in a wheelchair, not long before she died. She was staggered by the turnout, with people coming from all over the country. She genuinely had no idea of the regard and love for her. When I gave a talk at Whitby Folk Week in 2007, and asked Doreen and Bryan down to contribute, she was worried in case nobody turned up! They are so unspoiled by their large exposure to the media. (Doreen only mentioned the Mining Review film about her to me very recently.)

And, even more recently, the two of them did a gig at the Wilsons' club in Wolviston. They were staggered to be asked: "What? A gig? Us? Just us? The whole night? Are you sure?" They got a packed room, sang till nearly midnight with three encores, and were told at the end that they "were coming back again". The two of them got back home early, but were so overwhelmed with the reception that they couldn't sleep. And, I think we may be in for a treat. After that night they'll be making another CD, this time with "a lot of the really old American songs we know". This is Jack's legacy indeed!

### References for Chapter 7

1. Peter Kennedy, *Folksongs of Britain and Ireland*, Cassell, 1975.
2. Review of Bob Davenport's CD *The Common Stone* in *Camden New Journal*, Thursday 14th October, 2004. (www.camdennewjournal.co.uk/2004%20archive/141004/f141004_3.htm
3. Bob Copper, *A Song for Every Season*, Heinemann, 1971; *Songs and Southern Breezes*, Heinemann, 1973; *Early to Rise*, Book Club Associates, 1976.
4. Ben Harker, *Class Act: The Cultural and political life of Ewan MacColl*, Pluto Press, 2007, p.225.
5. Pete Wood, 'Are the folk clubs doomed, and does it matter?', *Living Tradition* magazine, Issue No. 72 , 2007.

# Epilogue

The prologue set a goal: to explain what the family have to offer us about traditional human values in the 21st Century, something harder to define than their singing. The seven chapters since then have, I hope, helped answer this.

The thing that stood out about Jack was his dignity, a feature shared by Em. Whatever the hardship and poverty they had known in their lives, however silly or even juvenile some of the jokes were, whatever ailments were afflicting them, they stood above it all. When things were tough or serious, they had a moral authority to withstand it, which they passed on to their children, underpinned by their socialism and their atheism. And the hard times didn't stop after the war. Pete, Doreen, John, Len, and their partners, had a tough time bringing up kids in the 1950s. It wasn't in fact till quite recent times that the Elliotts were able to enjoy a comfortable life. They make those who lead such a cushy life these days and still complain feel small indeed. And they have shown, and continue to show, generosity and kindness in abundance.

*A mid-60s splinter group, Pete, Jack and young Pete*

Although in the past life had been mean, hard and poor, often with a brute struggle to get by, there was a community spirit, shared memories and values. You left your door open, not just because you'd nowt to pinch, but because life was more open, you knew your neighbours were all pretty much in the same boat. Some would dismiss these thoughts as mere sentimentality, but I think sentiment does no harm because it makes us realise that whilst our material lives are incomparably better than they were, we've lost something less tangible than digital whatsits, mp3s, and satnav.

Jack and his family have the power to remind us constantly of this through their singing and their common humanity. This sense of community has always been both the platform and the stage for folk song, and folk song has always provided an outlet in vernacular culture for issues and 'complaints' by those who, by their class, were otherwise excluded from voicing their concerns in the outlets of the day-the press and Parliament. In this respect the Elliotts were at the top of their culture and continued a legacy of expression dating back hundreds of years

In a world that has shown great changes in peoples' attitudes, with increasing levels of superficiality and trivia in everyday life, the Elliotts have always remained true to their class and their beliefs and never let their fame deflect them from these. Fashions in folk music, like everything else, have come and gone, but whether sitting round the kitchen table or in august company away from home, they have remained themselves. Their music, their atheism, and their politics made them unique amongst their fellow pitfolk, and their convictions made them unique in the folk scene. These convictions, about what is right, what is wrong, and what is important, remind us that the 'voice' behind these songs deals with issues that have affected people's lives, issues that they have died for. Just as they had the courage to stand out on their own for what they believed in, so they would turn this into action in the face of injustice, either with others or if need be on their own.

The Elliotts are the real, authentic voice of the people, and I for one am grateful that they have been a part of this Folk Revival for the last half century. Let us finish by quoting again part of Sid Chaplin's comments:

*"As a human being Jack was big and generous, brimming over. Em burnt with a zeal that could never be damped. She was Jack's helpmate. They brought a family up. They remembered their roots. They sang in their lives, and I shall never forget them."*

# Elliott family tree

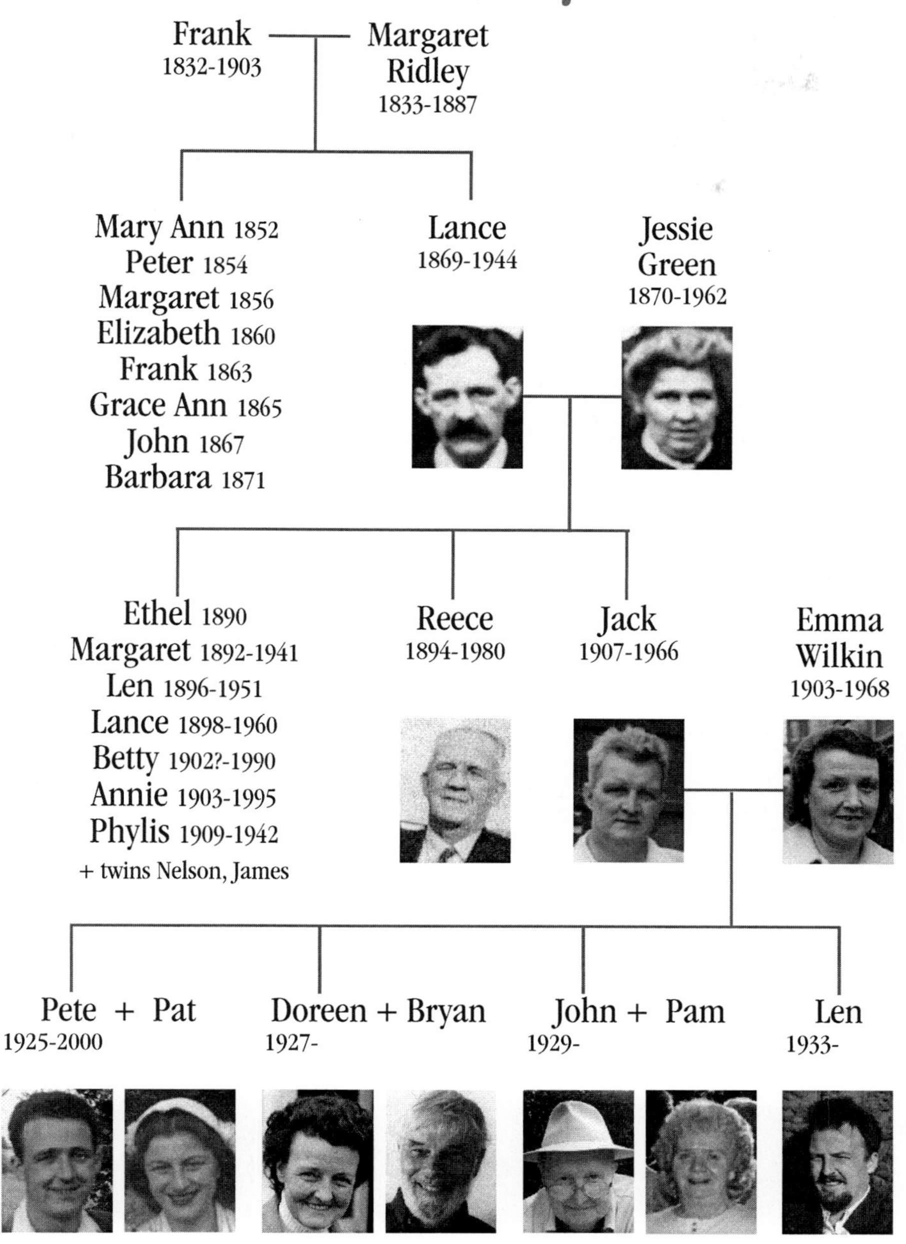

# Introduction to the songs

As outlined in Chapter 6, the main family songs, i.e. the ones they sang before the '60s Folk Revival got going, consist of 20 'full songs' and many short songs. Some of the latter are to be found scattered throughout the text in this book. What follows here are the 20 full songs.

Local pit songs particularly associated with Jack and the family:

1. The Banks of the Dee
2. Billy to Bob
3. The Bonnie Pit Laddie
4. Celebrated Working Man
5. The Collier' Rant
6. Geordie' Penker
7. Jowl, Jowl and Listen
8. Little Chance (Busty Fields)
9. Rap 'Er Te Bank

Other Local Songs:

10. Stanley Market
11. The Twenty Pound Dog
12. The Unlucky Duck

Other Songs:

13. The Blind Fool
14. Henry My Son
15. Miner's Life (is like a Sailor's)
16. My Old Man (Chamallie)
17. Old Johnny Bugger
18. The Sucking Pig
19. Was It In the Kitchen?
20. We Went Along a Bit Further

# Appendix 1: Songs

## 1 The Banks of the Dee

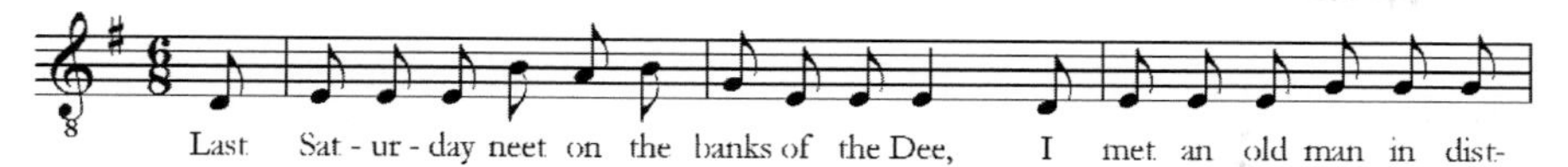

*Chorus*
*I am an old miner, aged fifty and six,*
*If I could get lots, I would raffle my picks,*
*I'd raffle them, sell them, I'd give them away,*
*I can't get employment, for my hair it's turned grey.*

*Last Wednesday neet to the reckoning I went*
*To the colliery office I went straight forenenst*
*I'd gettin my pay, I was walking away*
*When they give us my notice, 'cause me hair it's turned grey.*

*When I was a young chap, I was just like the rest*
*Each day in the pit I'd do my very best*
*When I had a loose place, I'd be fillin' all day*
*Now at fifty and six, my hair it's turned grey.*

*Now all ye young fellers it's ye that's to blame*
*If you get good places, you'd do just the same*
*If you were in a loose flat, you'd be fillin' all day*
*But at fifty and six, your hair it's turned grey.*

This song was sent to Bert Lloyd by Mr J. White, a miner of Houghton-le-Spring, in 1951, who says that it had been sung in the Durham coalfield "for many years". As well as commenting on the lot of an ageing miner, it tells us something of the cruel wage system in the old days. If the miners earned too much, the owners simply dropped the rate for the job. Bert Lloyd included it in the first edition of Come All Ye Bold Miners, where it was spotted by Johnny Handle and Louis Killen, who passed it on to Jack. The song is more reflective than many of Jack's songs, and it must have been particularly poignant for him to sing about a man of 56 being past it, as he would be approaching that age when he learnt it. The song rapidly became a great favourite. There is a bit of a question mark about the title. According to one scholar, Dee is another word for the River Wear, but Pete Elliott suggested it may be a punning reference to the surface of the 'D' pit. Johnny Handle suggests that it may have come down with the Scots miners in the 19th Century, who would have been familiar with several rivers of that name in their native country.

# 2 Billy to Bob

*"We'll all gan a-shootin'," says Billy to Bob*
*"We'll all gan a-shootin'," says Billy to Bob*
*"We'll all gan a-shootin'," says Jack mi lad*
*"We'll all gan a-shootin'," says every-one.*

*"What'll we shoot?" says Billy to Bob, etc.*
*"We'll shoot a cock-sparrow," etc.*
*"What'll we dae wi it?"*
*"We'll sell it for a tanner,"*
*"What'll we dae wi' the money?"*
*"We'll buy a pot of whiskey,"*

*"What if we get drunk?"*
*"How'll we get hyem?"*
*"We'll gan in the train,"*
*"How'll we pay him?"*
*"We'll pay him wi' a poker,"*

This is said to be the industrial parody of the 'Cutty Wren', a song of great antiquity seen by Bert Lloyd as an integral part of the Peasants' Revolt of the 13th Century and used in St Stephens' Day ceremonies in several parts of the British Isles till well into the 20th Century. The wren was seen as the king of the birds, and the 'cutty wren' was a mythical huge wren, which was hunted on Boxing Day. In this version, which may well be unique to the Elliott family, the bird is the humble cock sparrow. Of the many versions of 'The Cutty Wren' found in Britain, Ireland, and America, only one other version, from Yorkshire, is related in text to the Elliotts' version.

# 3 The Bonny Pit Laddie

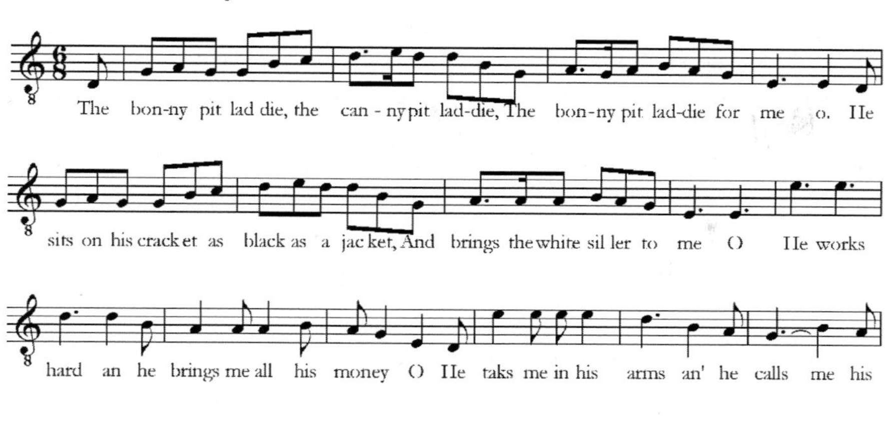

*The bonny pit laddie, the canny pit laddie,*
*The bonny pit laddie for me, O.*
*He sits on his cracket as black as a jacket*
*An' brings the white siller to me, O.*
*He works hard, he brings me all his money, O,*
*He takes me in his arms, an' he calls me his binny, O.*

*The bonny pit laddie, the canny pit laddie,*
*The bonny pit laddie for me, O.*
*He sits on his bunkers and yacks at the bunkers,*
*An' just brings the coppers to me, O.*

*Now, he comes hyem an' tells me all his troubles, O,*
*He's had a fight wi' the gaffer about his lazy marras, O.*

*The bonny pit laddie, the canny pit laddie,*
*The bonny pit laddie for me, O.*
*Now he's had his yo kens an' keeps all his tokens*
*An' brings the white siller to me, O.*
*Now he's all reet with all the men and gaffers, O,*
*An he comes hyem an' he calls me his binny, O.*

A classic North East song which is found in all the major collections from Peacock onwards. Jack collected this version in the 1950s from a Mrs Short of Fatfield, near to the 'Cotia pit, who died in 1960 aged 85. This text is the one Pat sang, and is longer and seemingly more relevant to 20th Century pits than the one in the 19th Century collections.

Dawney described it as "the finest and most lyrical of variants so far recorded". The song was usually sung by Pat or Pam.

# 4 Celebrated Working Man ('In the bar-room')

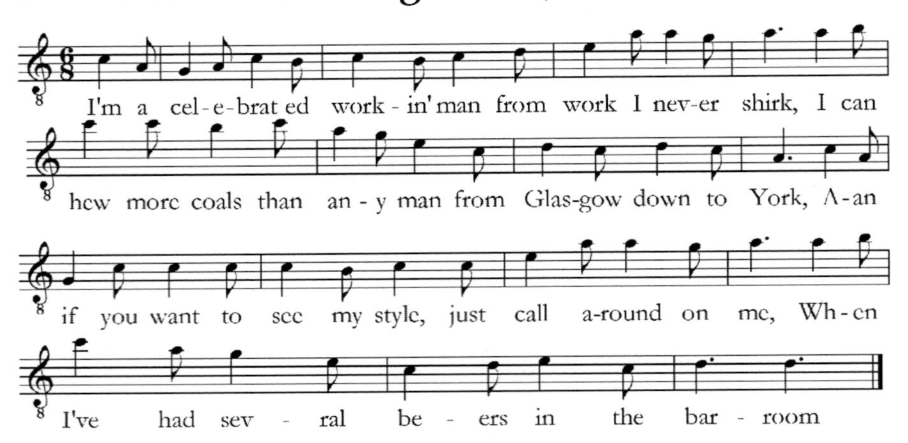


*I'm a celebrated working man, from work I never shirk,*
*I can hew more coals than any man from Glasgow down to York,*
*An' if you want to see my style, just call around on me,*
*When I've had several beers in the bar room.*

*Chorus*
*In the bar room, in the bar room, that's where we congregate,*
*To drill the holes and fill the coals and shovel back the slate.*
*And for to do a job of work, Oh I am never late;*
*That's provided that we do it in the bar room.*
*At puttin' I'm a dandy, I hope you will agree,*
*And gannin' alang the gannin' board I mak the teum 'uns flee.*
*Your Kelly sweeps and back-ower torns they never bother me,*
*When I'm sittin' on the limmers in the bar room.*

*I can judge a shot of powder to a sixteenth of a grain,*
*I can fill me sixteen tubs though the water falls like rain.*
*And if you'd like to see me in a perpendicular vein,*
*It's when I'm settin timmer in the bar room.*
*And now my song is ended, perhaps we'll have another,*
*Now don't you fire any shots in here or we will surely smother,*
*The landlord here would sooner draw beer than go to all the bother*
*To put up the ventilators in the bar room.*

As Pete Elliott memorably remarked on one occasion, "There's mair coals hewed on a Satdy neet than in a week's shift." A man bragging in the pub is not unique to miners, but the Durham men had a way with a song, and on this occasion used an import from America. Ed Foley wrote the original in 1892 at Mount Carmel, Pennsylvania, in the heart of the US anthracite mines. (There are two Durhams and a Northumberland County in Pennsylvania). The Elliotts' version was learned in 1916 from 'Yankee' Jim Roberts, a Geordie who had returned from Louisville, Kentucky to settle in Birtley, where he was active in the Miners' Union, and "worked marras" with Uncle Reece. It has subsequently become 'Geordified' and despite its foreign origin has always seemed four-square in the Elliotts' tradition. It now has a markedly different text from the version in Korson's Minstrels of the Mine Patch (1938), but the tune is apparently similar.

# 5 The Collier's Rant ('Follow the Horses')

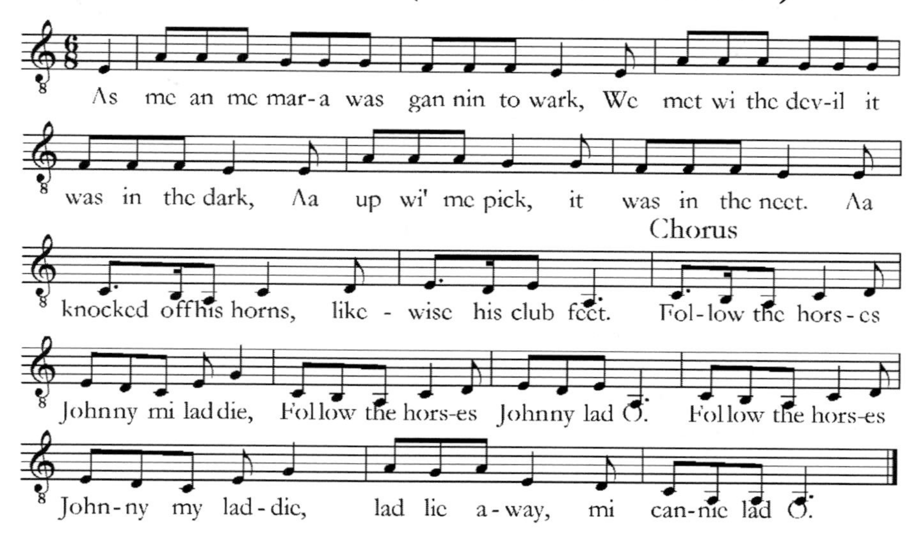


*As me an' me marra was loadin' the tram,*
*The leet it went oot an' me marra went wrang.*
*Ye wad ha' laughed at such a fine gam;*
*Old Nick took me marra but Aa got the tram.*

*O marra, O marra, oh, what does tha think?*
*Aa've broken me bottle an' spilt aal me drink.*
*Aa've lost aal me tools amang the big styens.*
*Draw me to the shaft, it's time to gan hyem.*

*O marra, O marra, oh, where hes tha been?*
*Drivin' the drift from the low seam.*
*Drivin' the drift from the low seam.*
*Haad up the lowe, lad, de'il stap oot thy een!*

*Noo, there is me horse an' here is the tram.*
*Two tins full o' grease will make her to gan.*
*There is me marra stretched oot on the groond.*
*Ye can tear up his shirt, for his minin's aal done.*

This has been seen by many as the defining song of the North East coalfield since its publication in Joseph Ritson's Northumbrian Garland in 1793, with the tune published by Topcliffe in 1815. Both John Bell and Thomas Allen included it in their seminal collections, and its infectious rhythm, tune, chorus, and sentiments seem to have helped define the North East pit culture during the present Folk Revival. It is said to have been sung "by massed choirs of miners on vesting day in 1947 to mark the nationalisation of the pits", but some see this story as apocryphal. Several of the Elliotts have sung this, but their texts vary a bit!

# 6 Geordie's Penker

*Our Geordie's lost his penker,*
*Our Geordie's lost his penker,*
*Our Geordie's lost his penker,*
*Doon the double raw.*

*It rolled into the cundy, etc.*
*So I went and got the claithes-prop, etc.*
*And I rammed it up the cundy, etc.*
*But still it wouldn't fetch it, etc.*
*So I went and got the terrier, etc.*
*And I tied it to the claithes-prop, etc.*
*And I rammed it up the cundy, etc.*
*But still it wouldn't fetch it, etc.*
*So I went and got gun-pooder, etc.*
*And I rammed it up the cundy, etc.*
*I set fire to the pooder, etc.*
*There's nowt left o' the cundy, etc.*
*I've blawn down double-raw, etc.*
*But wor Geordie's foond his penker, etc*

*It was in his bliddy pocket,*
*It was in his bliddy pocket,*
*It was in his bliddy pocket,*
*An he's blawn doon double raw.*

Another great favourite in the North East, this song came to the Elliotts via Len's father-in-law, Joe Barker. Mr and Mrs J Ford of South Shields have another version, and call the marble a "plonker", rather than the Elliotts' "penker", showing a remarkable variation of dialect in places only a few miles apart. In Lancashire we called them "murps" – maybe the humble marble has more synonyms than most. A couple of songs on the same theme have been recorded, one from Bob Cann in Devon, and the other from Hawick. It rather looks like the Bob Cann version is his Anglicised version of the Elliotts' song, an interesting example of how the Folk Revival brought about at least one transmission between source singers. It seems that the Elliotts added the last two verses about getting the "penker" back. Eternal optimists, you see!

# 7 Jowl, Jowl and Listen

*Me feyther aalways used te say,*
*That pit work's more than hewin',*
*Ye've got to coax the coal along,*
*An' not be rivin' an' tewin'. So,*

*The depitty craals fre flat te flat,*
*The putter rams the tyum 'uns,*
*And the man at the face must knaa his place*
*Like a mother knaas her young 'uns.*

*CHORUS:*
*Jowl, jowl an' listen, lad,*
*You'll hear that coal-face workin'.*
*There's many a marra missin', lad,*
*Because he wadn't listen, lad.*

'Jowl, Jowl and Listen' and 'Rap 'Er Te Bank' both originate with a pitman from Hetton-le-Hole in East Durham. His nephew, a schoolteacher called Henry Nattress of Low Fell, obtained them and passed them to the Birtley headmaster Walter Toyn, who was interested in dialect poems and songs, though he never went to the Birtley Club. It was Frank Rutherford, the local North East folklorist, who mentioned them to Jack. When Jack went to see Toyn at the school, Frank describes Jack as "falling on them with delight". This all happened in 1962, the year the folk club started, when both Jack and Pete were actively seeking new songs, particularly pit songs. The older miners stressed the importance of "pit sense", i.e. being able to read what the pit was going to do next, particularly the roof! Reece was highly regarded for his pit sense.

# 8 Little Chance ("Busty Fields")

*Ye're gannin' ower Busty fields te gan doon the pit,*
*Ye get your lamp oot, ye gan in bye an' there ye sit at the kist,*
*The deputy says thi' place is holed, thou'll ha' te gan straight on,*
*Aa says te him, "What's the matter wi' me aan?", he says "She canna gan on".*
*Aa filled fifteen oot of a jud, titty fa la, titty fa lay,*
*Eh by hell she was good, titty fa la, titty fa lay,*
*Aa came oot te get a shaft, when the timmer it gie a crack,*
*When a stone fell on mi back, titty fa la, titty fa lay,*
*Tra la lala la la, ower the waal's oot!*

*Noo, ye're sure te ken me brother Bill, for he's se full o' wit.*
*He got a job o' puttin' up at 'Cotia pit.*
*Now when Bill comes hyem fre wark, he's like a droonded rat;*
*Instead o' gannin upstairs te bed, he lies upon the mat.*
*Noo, he puts a thoosand or more, titty fa la, titty fa lay,*
*They pay him by the score, titty fa la, titty fa lay.*
*He fills his tubs se quick, withoot any delay,*
*But he can never find his pick, titty fa la, titty fa lay.*
*Tra la lala la la, ower the waal's oot!*

*Noo, Jack an' Bill, two marras, were in a public*
*hoose.*
*They talk aboot the cavils, lad, it wadn't frighten*
*a moose.*
*Jack says te Bill, "By Gox, she's hard!*
*The tops is like bell-metal but the bottoms is not*
*se bad.*
*Aa only got ten the day, titty fa la, titty fa lay.*
*Aa only got ten the day, titty fa la, titty fa lay.*
*Aa'd have getten another fower, Aa wes wishin*
*the shift wes ower,*
*When the putter got off the way," titty fa la, titty*
*fa lay.*
*Tra la lala la la, ower the waal's oot!*

*Noo, me name is Jackie Robinson, me name Aa*
*do advance.*
*Aa drive a little gallowa, they caal him Little*
*Chance.*
*Two greasy feet, likewise a kittly back,*
*An' gannin' alang the gannin'-board he makes*
*the teum 'uns knack.*
*Aa wes comin aroond the torn, titty fa la, titty fa*
*lay.*
*Chancy wadn't haad on, titty fa la, titty fa lay.*
*The tubs they gave a click, Aa got off the way at*
*the switch.*
*Ye bugger, aa smashed the deputy's kist, titty fa*
*la, titty fa lay.*
*Tra la lala la la, ower the waal's oot!*

*Noo, me an' me wife, me mother-in-law, we*
*went te the silvery sea.*
*The mother-in-law gat into a boat, a sailor she*
*wad be.*
*She hadn't gone passin' twenty yards when all of*
*a sudden there's a shoot,*
*Me mother-in-law falls into the sea, an' there*
*she's splashin' aboot.*
*She shoots "Help aa canna swim," titty fa la titty*
*fa lay.*
*Aa says, "Noo's thi time to try," titty fa la titty fa*
*lay.*
*Mi wife she says, "Ye hoond, tha's not ganna*
*watch her drooned,"*
*Aa says, "No aa'll shut mi eyes," titty fal la titty*
*fa lay.*
*Tra la lala la la, ower the waal's oot!*

A song unique to the Durham coalfield, it has been immensely popular during the Revival, mostly due to Jack Elliott's version being recorded and sung widely by him, the other Elliotts, and Bob Davenport. The song was originally a quite serious song about the usefulness of gallowa ponies down the pit, dating back to at least 1915, but was not seen in print till the first edition of Come All Ye Bold Miners. Bert Lloyd had recorded it in 1951 from Charles Bevill, a shot firer at Fir Tree Drift near Tow Law. Whilst this version was not so full or rich in imagery as Jack's version, it came together with some fascinating information on Christmas and New Year pit ceremonies which Jack himself was later to embellish with further information from West Cornsay colliery. The song has received a great deal of scholarly interest, notably by Maxine Baker, who collected five versions in the 1960s, and Pete Elliott, who wrote a monograph on the song in 1980, in which he adds several more versions and analyses their relationships. All save one came from County Durham, and they ranged from the original to a version from Billy Hutchinson from Bedlington, which only mentions the pony at the end of the last verse, and is an entirely comic song, whereas Jack's version has rather more on the pony. This is the song that prompted Pete Elliott to reject a music hall origin, saying that "pit pub" songs were those where you could add and delete verses at will, and were certainly comic in character.

# 9 Rap 'Er Te Bank

*Mi feyther used te call the torn,*
*When the lang shift it was ower,*
*As gannin' oot bye, ye'd hear him cry,*
*D'ye knaa it's after fower?*

*Chorus*
*Rap 'er te bank mi canny lad,*
*Wind 'er away, keep tornin',*
*The back shift men are gannin' yem,*
*They'll be back in the mornin'.*

*And when that aaful day arrived,*
*The last shift for me fethyer*
*A faal o' stones an' brokken bones*
*But still above the clatter, he cried ...*

*Rap 'er te bank, mi canny lad*
*Wind 'er in slow that's clivor,*
*This poor owd lad is taken bad,*
*He'll be back here, never.*

Although this song is recognised by many in the North East and beyond as one of the Elliotts' "anthems", it is not an original family song. Like 'Jowl, Jowl and Listen', it came to Jack from Walter Toyn, the Birtley headmaster. (See notes to that song.) The song is still amongst the most popular songs in the North East, a tribute to both the writer and Jack's way with a song.

# 10 Stanley Market

*If you're bad and off your meat,*
*And would like to be put reet*
*Take a walk some Friday neet*
*Up at Stanley Market.*
*All kinds of doctors there you'll see*
*They're all as busy as can be*
*It's who to tell the biggest lee,*
*When telling ower what they can dee*
*To hear them all, they are that clever*
*They can make new lungs and liver*
*In fact they'll make you live forever*
*Up at Stanley Market.*

*Fol de ral de raldy dee*
*Fol de ral de daldy dee*
*Fold de ral de raldy day.*
*There they stand and gape and shoot*
*And when the crowd gets round aboot*
*They'll tell you they can cure the goot*
*Up at Stanley Market.*
*They preach away and never smiles*
*It's really grand to see their styles*
*They can tell a man they can cure the piles*
*Tumours, ulcered throats or biles,*
*There they'll stand from six till ten*
*And tell of the good they've done for men,*
*They think the pitmen doesn't ken*
*That gans to Stanley Market.*

*Now when you get mixed up with the throng*
*You'll find it hard to travel along*
*And you'll hear some stranger singing a song*
*Up at Stanley Market.*
*There's a chap wi' second-hand claithes*
*And boots and shoes, he's full o' praise,*
*But take no notice of what he says*
*He only wants your bits of pays.*
*There's sausage, ducks and saveloys*
*An here's a stall wi nowt but toys*
*To please the little girls and boys*
*Up at Stanley Market.*

*There's bullets and spice and pies and wigs*
*Taty choppers, brakes and gigs*
*And you'll often see a chap wi' pigs*
*Up at Stanley Market.*
*There's black-puddings nearly white*
*They're made to suit your appetite*
*One will serve from six till eight*
*They suit a chap that's rather tight.*
*In rain or snow you needn't fret*
*There's umbrellas for you to get*
*To keep you dry among the wet*
*Up at Stanley Market.*

*There you'll see a grand machine*
*It shines like silver, nice and clean*
*It tries the nerves of fat and lean*
*Up at Stanley Market.*
*There's legs of pork from Rotterdam*
*Bacon, beef and home-fed ham*
*Blackcurrant and strawberry jam*
*And any amount of veal and lamb.*
*You can get a tip but do not tae' it*
*If you diven't know how the horse is bred*
*There's pots to stand below the bed*
*Up at Stanley Market.*

A song from Tommy Armstrong, the "pitman's poet", as this wiry character of a man from Tanfield Lea was known. Many of his songs have flourished in the Folk Revival. This one is a joyful description of the busiest day of the week in a pit town, and sounds to me like the 'Penny Lane' of its day. Jack was at his very best singing this to MacColl and Seeger in 1961. It's interesting that the Elliotts did not sing any more of Armstrong's songs, considering how close he was. Perhaps it's an illustration of the insularity of the separate mining communities.

# 11 The Twenty Pound Dog ("Champion")

*My name it is Michael McCarthy, I come from a place of renown*
*I had a bet with old Timothy O'Flaherty, that my bulldog would wallop the town.*
*Now he told me of one Terence Murphy, who lived a way out in the bog,*
*An' who kept a black and tan terrier that would murder me twenty pound dog.*

*Now I laid out me bold twenty-pounder, he looked just as good as a king,*
*How he eyed that black and tan terrier, as they both sached right round the ring.*
*Now they fought for an hour and a quarter, it was a way out in the bog,*
*The terrier he took all the laurels, and a corpse lay me twenty pound dog.*

*Now I swore I'd have satisfaction, so I off with me coat and me hat,*
*I made a race for the whole Murphy faction, from Big Terence down to Little Pat.*
*Then I made a race for the terrier, and I kicked him way out in the bog*
*And all the way home I swore vengeance, sweet vengeance for me twenty pound dog.*

This song, of seemingly Irish origin, about a prize-fighting dog, has not been found elsewhere, and has become very popular in the North East.

# 12 The Unlucky Duck

*The spuggy chirping on the tiles,*
*He never suffers from the piles*
*Because there never was one yet,*
*That got his backside sopping wet*
*That got his backside sopping wet.*

*The little duck that never smiles,*
*Has ne such luck – he gets the piles*
*Why when he's walking round and round,*
*His backside's bobbing on the ground*
*His backside's bobbing on the ground.*

*How would you feel if your arse*
*Was trailing on the sopping grass?*
*And when he floats on water blue,*
*The nagging pain strikes through*
*The nagging pain strikes through.*

*Everytime he dips his heed*
*To get his neb down tiv a weed*
*He cocks his backside up on high,*
*To try to get the bugger dry.*
*To try to get the bugger dry.*

*So if you hear a duck go quack,*
*Divn't huff and turn your back*
*Divn't shout ye great daft thing,*
*Or sing ye flat-arsed bugger sing*
*Or sing ye flat-arsed bugger sing.*

*Do you think the bugger would,*
*Even if the bugger could*
*The duck gans quack but don't forget,*
*His backside's always sopping wet*
*His backside's always sopping wet.*

'The Spuggy' was always a favourite amongst Elliott fans. This was another poem collected by local headmaster Walter Toyn, and put to the tune of 'The Quaker's Wife' by Jack himself.

# 13 The Blind Fool

*As I was walking home one night, drunk as a*
*man should be,*
*I went into the stable, another man's horse I see;*
*I says, "Wife, dearie, Wife, whatever's this I see,*
*Another man's horse I see, where my old horse*
*should be?"*
*She say, "You blind fool, you silly fool, can't you*
*plainly see?*
*It's only a milkin' cow my mother gave to me."*
*Miles I have travelled, a hundred miles or more,*
*But a bridle on a milkin' cow I've never seen*
*before.*

*As I was walking home one night, drunk as a*
*man could be,*
*I went into the hallway, another man's hat I see;*
*I says, "Wife, dearie, Wife, whatever's this I see,*
*Another man's hat, not my old hat, where my*
*old hat should be?"*
*She said, "You blind fool, silly fool, can't you*
*plainly see?*
*It's only a chamber-pot my mother gave to me."*
*Miles I have travelled, ten thousand miles or*
*more,*
*But a hat-band on a chamber-pot I've never*
*seen before.*

*Another man's pants I see,*
*Only a pair of bloomers ... braces on a pair of bloomers ...*

*Another man's face I see,*
*Only sister's baby boy I've got in bed with me ... whiskers on a baby's face*

*Another man's thing I see,*
*Only a rolling pin my mother gave to me ... balls upon a rolling pin*
*I never saw before.*

Immensely popular during the Folk Revival, largely due to the Dubliners' version, this is found in a large number of variants all over the British Isles and America. It's also a Child Ballad, number 274.

# 14 Henry My Son

*Where have you been all day, Henry, my son?*
*Where have you been all day, my beloved one?*
*Fields, dear mother, fields, dear mother,*

*CHORUS*
*Oh, make my bed, for there's pains in my head,*
*And I want to go to sleep.*

*Who took you there, my son, Henry my son?*
*Who took you there, my son, my beloved one?*
*Gypsies, dear mother, gypsies, dear mother.*

*What did you eat all day, Henry my son?*
*What did you eat all day, my beloved one?*
*Snails, dear mother, snails, dear mother.*

*Where did you find the snails, Henry my son?*
*Where did you find the snails, my beloved one?*
*Churchyard, dear mother, churchyard, dear mother.*

*What did you have to drink, Henry my son?*
*What did you have to drink, my beloved one?*
*Water from the flowers, water from the flowers.*

A version of 'Lord Randal', one of the most widespread of the Child Ballads in the oral tradition, this has been in the family for as long as any of them can remember. As MacColl points out in the notes to the Folkways LP, there are at least three features of the Elliotts' version which are unique: the gypsies doing the poisoning, snails being the source, and the absence of a legacy or retribution as the reason. The song was mostly sung by the women (Em and Doreen), though on the LP there is a wonderful coming together of the family. There's also the tale of how Em Elliott had to return to the source of the song, Mrs Renee Green, to settle differences between family members as to the text and sequence of the verses. Mrs Green, as Renee Pearson, had been Doreen's school friend at the Boody concerts, where Doreen had first learnt the song.

# 15 Old Johnny Bugger

*Old Johnnie Bugger he lived by himself,*
*As long as he had perfect health,*
*He took unto himself a wife*
*To look after him for the rest of his life.*

*Chorus*
*Singing, I do believe, I will believe,*
*Old Johnnie Bugger was a gay old Bugger*
*And a gay old Bugger was he.*

*The doctor ordered her to bed,*
*He called Johnnie in and he says to him:*
*"You've got to rub your wife's left leg with gin."*

*Old Johnnie Bugger thought it was a sin,*
*To rub his wife's left leg with the gin,*
*He poured the gin right down his throttle,*
*Rubbed his wife's left leg with the bottle.*

*The Lord made the bees, the bees made the honey,*
*The Lord made man and man made money,*
*The Lord made Hitler and Hitler made sin,*
*The Lord'll have to make a hole to put the bugger in.*

This song seems very familiar to those who hear it for the first time, and they assume it to be common. In fact, there are very few other versions of the song. It started life as a minstrel song called 'Old Johnny Bigger' with the politically incorrect chorus "Old Johnny Bigger was a gay old nigger". It later changed to "Booker" and was a favourite among soldiers in both the First and Second World Wars. Jack Elliott was perhaps best known for purveying the song to the folk scene. Brian Dawson has one from Lincolnshire called 'Johnny Poker'. The Elliotts always sang "bugger".

# 16 Miner's Life (is like a Sailor's)

*You've been docked and docked again, boys,*
*You've been loading two for one.*
*What have you to show for working,*
*Since your mining days begun?*
*Worn-out boots and worn-out miners,*
*And your children looking pale*
*Keep your hand upon your wages,*
*And your eye upon the scale.*

*In conclusion bear in memory,*
*Keep this password in your mind:*
*God provides for every worker*
*When in union they combine.*
*Stand like men, and stand together,*
*Victory for you'll prevail,*
*Keep your hand upon your wages,*
*And your eyes upon the scale.*

It's not clear how long the Elliotts have been singing this song. (Though Reece recorded it, as with other songs sung by several of the family, their words vary.) However for the last ten or twenty years they have certainly finished with it, or if they're asked to do one song somewhere, this is the one they choose. Most notably in recent times, when the new 'Cotia banner party stop to do a turn for the "nobs" on the Durham Royal County Hotel balcony, Doreen Elliott stands out in front and leads us in this, and stops the show, with Tony Benn leading the tremendous applause. It's originally Welsh, but has always been more popular in the States.

# 17 My Old Man (Chamallie)

*What wilt thou have for supper my old man*
*What wilt thou have for supper, come cuddle me*
*my lamb*
*What wilt thou have for supper my old man*
*Thou's the best old man that's alive, that's alive,*
*that's alive;*
*Thou's the best old man that's alive, that's alive.*
*(spoken) Eggs ye bitch.*

*What wilt thou have them boiled in my old man*
*etc.*
*(spoken) Chamallie ye old bitch.*

*Chamallie'll poison ye my old man etc.*
*(spoken) I'll dee all the sooner ye old bitch.*

*Where will thou be buried my old man etc.*
*(spoken) Under the hearth styen ye old bitch.*

*That's ower hot a place my old man etc.*
*(spoken) Thou'll get a hotter place ye bitch.*

A song dating back to the 17th Century, but apart from this version it is common only in the West Country and in the United States. The fullest version was collected by George Gardiner in Cornwall, and explains that the old man calls his wife a bitch because she has been unfaithful. The version sung by Jack and subsequently by John and Pam comes from the manuscripts of John Bell around the turn of the 19th Century, although it was not published in his Rhymes of Northern Bards. Jack and the collector Frank Rutherford adapted it by modifying the incomplete final verse.

# 18 Sucking Pig

*Oh it's loud and it's long as a temple bar*
*With a ton of bristle on it*
*And when its tail was stretched out strite*
*It was larger than the comet.*

*Chorus*
*Oh perhaps you will think it's not all true,*
*But I don't care a fig,*
*For what I say I know is true,*
*About this sucking pig.*

*Seven thousand men got set to work,*
*Arm'd with knives and choppers*
*It took them all about seven years*
*To cut off one of his trotters.*

*They sent the bones up to the mill*
*To grind them into flour*
*They filled about seven thousand bags,*
*In less than half an hour.*

This short song again seems unique to the Elliotts. Having recorded it for MacColl and Seeger, the family do not appear to have sung it again on record, although Frank Rutherford recalls it as having been one of Jack's favourites. As Jack got the song from a workmate who had been in India with the British Army, MacColl describes the song as a "barrack-room remake of the Derby Ram".

# 19 Was It In the Kitchen?

*Was it in the kitchen, the parlour or the hall,*
*Or was it in the backyard, right up against the wall?*
*It wasn't in the kitchen the parlour or the hall,*
*But it was in the backyard, right up against the wall.*
*Listen all you maidens, take this as a tip from me*
*Never let a pitlad get an inch above your knee*
*Let him tie your garter, or squeeze you as he likes,*
*But never let him wave his Union Jack beneath your apron.*

A popular folk song in many parts of the country; MacColl comments that this version is likely to come from the barrack-room version 'Never Let a Soldier an Inch Above Your Knee'. Its most common title is 'Underneath Her Apron'.

# 20 We Went Along a Bit Farther ('Three Jovial Welshmen')

*We went along a bit farther and nothing could be found,*
*We came across Durham Gaol and that we left behind;*
*The Englishman said it was Durham Gaol, The Scotchman he said "Nay,"*
*Pat said it was a lodging house and we had no money to pay.*

*CHORUS*
*So look at that now, So look at that now,*
*Titti fa la fala falay, Titti fala falay.*
*We went along a bit farther and nothing could be found,*
*We came across a hedgehog, and that we left behind;*
*The Englishman said it was a hedgehog, The Scotchman he said "Nay,"*
*Pat said it was a pin-cushion with the pins stuck in the wrong way.*

*We went along a bit farther and nothing could be found,*
*We came across a cow-plat and that we left behind;*
*The Englishman said it was a cow-plat, The Scotchman he said "Nay,"*
*Pat said it was a tea-cake with the currents all blown away.*

This is a widespread, popular folk song, commonly called 'Three Jovial Welshmen', with a bit of a regional twist.

# Appendix 2

## Sounds gone from the streets

### Doreen Elliott

As I lay in my bed about 66 years ago, waiting to get up for school, I knew it was Monday because of the "thump, thump" rhythmic possing of women already at the weekly wash. Washing days were the hardest workday of the week. All the water had to be heated in pans on the fire. The poss tub had to be emptied of rainwater from under the downcomer in the yard. It was kept filled with water to prevent the wood from shrinking through drying out and so leaking. The poss tub was then "booled" into the kitchen. The mats would have been lifted and "dadded" or dashed against the wall and hung over the dividing walls in the yard.

I remember my mam saying, "By, Millie's only got two penn'orth of water in the tub." Millie lived three doors down, but by the noise the possing made, you could tell how much water was in the tub. Well, my mam could. She knew if the lads were kneeling when they used the pee pot upstairs. After the clothes were "possed" they were scrubbed, so you had a sort of slish-slosh noise, and this was going on all over the street, probably all over the county, as Monday was the universal washing day.

When the clothes were finally rinsed, starched and "blued", they were hung out in lines stretched across the back lanes and in gardens and then, "Think it'll stay dry Emmie?" or "Has the postman been yet?" The usual gossip and chatter between the women as they hung the clothes out, wrapping their pinnies over their arms as they had five minutes gossip, feeling the cold after the hot, steaming kitchens. No such thing as "ten o'clocks" or coffee mornings. Life was run to a tight schedule and anyway, coffee was too expensive.

While there was an abundance of hot, soapy water, the outside toilets and floors were scrubbed. This was when you heard the women singing. Daisy next door would sing 'Dancing with my Shadow', Millie would give out with 'We Meet Tonight, Just for the Last Time', and me mam 'There's Nothing Left for Me of Days That Used To Be'. When you heard the singing, you knew that the worst of the washing was done , "broken its back" me mam would say. On washdays the yards were swilled. Again the swish of the broom against the bricks of the path. Monday was a quiet day in the street for callers and tradesmen, as everyone knew it was washing day, and delivery men knew they wouldn't be popular trying to negotiate flapping wet sheets. But the muffin man would come walking with his big basket covered with a muslin cloth, shouting his wares in his checked apron.

Pitmen who were on first shift would come home between 11.00 and 11.30 a.m., and at least twenty of them, clattering in their pitboots (and in their muck, before pit baths) chatted and whistled down the lane to the Monday dinner of "caad warmed up". I'd better explain what "caad warmed up" was. It's all the vegetables left over from the Sunday's dinner, fried. I liked mine with a crispy batter, cold beef or mutton, sliced beetroot or pickles. A popular meal, followed by cold rice puddings, which me dad said was an aphrodisiac. Between 4.00 and 4.30 the back lane fairly came alive as all the school kids came home. There were about 60 kids in the street give or take a couple, from 34 houses, and we all played out, so you'd hear your friends standing at the gate shouting for you, or they'd come shouting your name at the door. You'd ask them in to wait for you if your mother was in a good mood, or they waited outside and then out to play a game we could have started a week or two previously. Some games were never-ending.

We had Harry Cann from Birtley, who was our fisherman, and then Diddler Green who had been crippled by polio, was set up as a fishman by his doting parents, and as he lived at Pelaw Grange just over the road, we supported him. Mind, we didn't know where he kept his fish or who made his fish cakes, as they only had two bedrooms, a kitchen and a sitting room like us. It was rumoured that the outside toilet made a handy fridge! They shouted out the price of the fish and its quality. Diddler Green went out of business when his horse was so thirsty one summer's day, he drove it to the green which had a pond and the poor thing galloped to the water before the cart could be taken off and it drowned as Diddler couldn't swim. So back came Harry Cann.

The man with the most distinctive voice was Mr Moon, also from Birtley, who didn't have a horse and cart but a little blue van, and he pressed his horn to let you know he was in the back lane, and he only shouted one word, which was 'oil', and the oil was paraffin. As he pulled away you could hear the clang of the metal measures, pints and gills (a gill was a half-pint) against the drum of paraffin. He also sold steel wool and scrubbing brushes etc. He only came once a week and did a good trade as most people had bedside lamps powered by paraffin. Even when we got electricity, paraffin lights were still put in the outside toilets to try to keep the pipes from freezing. See, this progress to flush toilets had its drawbacks. You didn't get frozen pipes with a dry midden; frozen bums but not frozen pipes!

My mam always lit her little oil lamp by her bedside as she read by it

but the lamp was on for when my dad was on night shift and come home about 2 a.m. She needed the light to go and let him in without disturbing us with the bright electric light.

Tosh Lee, also from Birtley, was the local fruiterer and he came on a Saturday, but as most pitmen were keen gardeners and grew most of their own vegetables, there wasn't much call for veg. I say Tosh only came on a Saturday as I do remember so vividly the day my youngest brother was born, through the Friday night, and telling Tosh about it next day and being presented with a bag of monkey nuts, or peanuts (the proper name) and sharing them out with me two brothers. We didn't buy much from Tosh as fruit was a luxury, but my mam would sometimes buy a pomegranate and give us half each and a pin to pick out the seeds. We'd sit on the kerb for hours. Sometimes as a special treat for me dad, she'd buy a Calabash pear. Doesn't that sound grand – Calabash? I must tell you this. When I mentioned pit men being keen gardeners, the best and cheapest fertiliser was horse muck and as nearly all the tradesmen had horses, there was always a rush with bucket and shovel for the horses' droppings. Well, one day, two gardeners got to the pile at the some time and started rowing about who it belonged to. "It's nearest my door," said one. "Aye, well that might be so," said the other, "but it's a Store (the Co-op) horse and thoo's not a member, so it's mine."

Tosh Lee would also "shift you" when you moved house. I loved that; getting a ride in his cart as he had a tarpaulin cover on it and you could smell the fruit and veg. And if you were lucky, you'd get a few small, blue tissue paper squares from the fruit – a luxury in the lavatory after squares of the Daily Herald. I never could understand what Tosh Lee was shouting. It sounded like "Apple a pound pears" but I could be wrong.

Everybody knew when they heard a bicycle bell that it was either Eldorado ice cream or Walls (Stop Me and Buy One), They both had three-wheeler bikes with a box on the front and two doors on the top. When these were opened, out came an ice-cold mist, in went his hand and out came delicious frozen lollies. The best and fruitiest lollies came from Tommy Walls' bike. His was a blue tricycle and Dorado's was white. They sold mainly frozen ice cream in distinctive blue and white wrappers. It was beautiful, but dearer than the frozen fruit lollies of Walls.We used to sing:

*Eldorado, Tommy Walls*
*Went to see the waterfalls*
*Tom fell in, and couldn't swim*
*Eldorado, Tommy Walls.*

You could also buy these two delicacies at all picture houses. I do

*Em at the front door of Number 7, Brown's Buildings*

remember an Eldorado costing 2 pence and a tub 6 pence. You only got one of them when your boyfriend was trying to impress you. You got a tiny little wooden spoon to eat it with. We used to ask the ice cream man for a piece of hot ice, which he gave us from inside his freezer box. And it really did burn you so you spent your time throwing it from one hand to the other as somebody always knew somebody who didn't keep it on the move and they lost three fingers.

Talking of keeping things moving, carbide lamps were used by pitmen down the pits, I think mainly in drifts but I'm not sure about that. If you found a piece of carbide and put it in the palm of your hand and spat on it, it frothed and got hotter and you had to keep it moving. It gave off a strong, pungent smell after spitting on it.

It was 100% pit tenants in the street, although the street was divided between pitmen and overmen and deputies and the distinction was that the actual workers, such as hewers, fillers and cutters, putters and shot-firers, had two bedrooms, no bathrooms and outside lavvies and were built of stone, while the deputies and overmen had three bedrooms (even if they couldn't fill them), inside flush lavvies, and a bathroom with hot water filled from the set pot. And they were brick built. Pitmen weren't equal even to the quality of the 'free' coal the pitmen were allowed. It was delivered by horse and cart. The driver's name was Kit Barker. That name will be familiar to my family as my brother married a girl with the surname of Barker and as her given name was the same as mine, he called her Kit to distinguish us. She remained Kit until she died. Getting back to the coals, the bosses got roundies, chinleys or deputies' nuts – good quality coal, while we sometimes got coal shale and duff, which was like powder. Mind, the worst thing was when there was stone (sometimes called Devil's Purse) mixed in with the coal and it exploded, literally, out of the fire into hot fragments onto the mats, chairs and sometimes the poor cat, who always had the best seat in house.

Kit Barker didn't make a sound as he tipped the coal in the back lane but we knew the distinctive sound of the huge iron wheels, which were the size of the sides of the cart. Both cart and wheels were made at the pit. When we turned into the back lane our hearts would drop like stones if a load of coals had been dropped at our door, as we knew we had to hoy them through a little hatch into the coal house, always remembering to put the boards in at the door end. What a job! Especially if it had rained and the coals were a ton weight. We always ended up like miniature pitmen – we even had the pulleys in! "Having the pulleys in" was having coal dust round your eyelash area, which took some shifting. Me dad used to use butter, best of course, rubbed into his lashes to remove the dust. I remember one day a cousin of mine hoying a woman's coal in for her and a load was a ton, you know. When he'd finished she gave him two custard cream biscuits for his bother. Now the going rate was a threepenny dodger or a threepence piece, or a tanner, so he was vexed. Bang went his treat to the pictures so he hoyed them all out again. After the sound of shovels being scraped along the ground, out would come the brooms and pails of water to swill the back lane where the coals had been dropped..

The local Co-op sent their butcher's cart out twice a week, Tuesdays and Fridays. Our butcher was Freddie Carr from Birtley. He didn't have a bell or a whistle, he just shouted "Butcher!" Of course, not being self-employed like the fishman or oilman, he didn't have to have a sales pitch and of course he had the added advantage of the 'divvy' system to help sell his meat. The dividend worked like this. When you enrolled to become a member of the local Co-op you got a number. Me mam's was 1295 and every time you made a purchase, you gave your store number and the amount was credited to you. At the end of the quarter you got maybe a shilling or even two shilling in the pound refund. The meat cart was a beautifully built little cart, all blue and white, with a muslin curtain which fell down over the back of the cart to keep the flies off, but it wasn't the flies I was bothered about, it was the dogs. It was like a rodeo, all yapping and barking, trying to get at the meat and the poor horse getting agitated at all these dogs round his feet. Freddie Carr was shouting at the dogs, and trying to calm his horse at the same time. Very noisy!

Talking of posh carts, the best one was Rington's Tea, all black and gold and the horses looked like thoroughbreds, all sleek and proud-looking with polished brasses. They didn't shout anything as they had regular customers, but the drivers delivered the tea in a big basket held over their arm and they sometimes had special offers on like tins of biscuits or tea caddies or teapots. Very civilised was Rington's Tea. The first time I went to a car boot sale, I was immediately transported back to the day the rag man came in the back lane, with his distinctive call of "Any rags or bones?", ringing his big hand bell. Despite the popular belief that you just gave the rag man your old rags, you could buy off his cart like a mobile jumble sale. Many times women would be seen scratting, looking for a pair of black trousers, skirt or jacket to finish off the border of a clippy or hooky mat they were making. "Please, mam, have you any old rags so I can get a balloon or a celluloid windmill?" Even a piece of black man's cacky, which we loved. It wasn't until years later that we found out it was locust pods dried, quite sweet and longlasting. The term "black man's cacky" we wouldn't use now, not wishing to offend, but the term was used with the innocence of childhood. If we were lucky, mam would find something for us to give and let us choose what we got, but only if she didn't need scoury stone. The scoury stone was used to decorate steps, concrete floors and windowsills by rubbing the stone onto damp surfaces and it dried white and into whatever pattern the housewife chose. During all the transactions I've mentioned, at any of the carts, the banter and laughter would be loud and enjoyable, even flirtatious at times, all harmless fun and part of life in the street.

I have left until last the most endearing, thought-provoking and joyful noises of all – the noise of us children of the street at our games. The noise was constant, particularly during school holidays and at weekends, when the street resounded with the sounds of competitive games: "Out", "It's a sixer", "Goal", "Sod off, it wasn't", "Right then, gi's me boll", "Alright, ye con bat again", "By, yer big bobby, it hardly touched yer", "Ower the waal's oot". We played Hot Rice, my favourite game, Jack Shine the Moggie, and the shouting, "Give a holler, holler, holler", where you had to find the opposition by following their voices. This was played at night, before eight o'clock, as the street was nearly empty of children, for the mothers had called them in by then. We played Rounders and Platters, a game played with tins. We got the tins by lifting the little iron grid at the back of the midden and "howking" the tins out with a brush. Depending on how many tins we had, they were stacked up. There were two teams: one side knocked them down with a ball and the other side had to build them up again without being caught. These games were played by both boys and girls. Girls did have their own games, houses and shops. Dolls were in short supply so a brick would be wrapped in a piece of cloth and a face put on with a dod of coal. No doll was ever more loved than my brick baby. We had lots of singing games: 'Poor Mary Sat a-Weeping', 'On the Mountain'; 'B.I.N.G.O'; 'Oh, the Big Ship Sails Through the Illy Ally Oh'; 'Charlie Can I Be Over the Water'; 'The Farmer Wants a Wife'.

There were skipping games which also had rhymes. I've seen my mother play these games with us on summer nights, linking arms behind our backs, becoming horses, cadging a ride from anybody who had a bike, riding inside a tyre, lending your best friend one of your skates. All the while, the air was filled with the noises from the houses; gossip, laughter, whistling, street singers, bairns crying, men cobbling shoes, dadding pit clothes and mats, scraping pit boots, sharpening knives on the step, pigs squealing, hens clucking, all making for a warm sense of belonging and security.

# Index